Sunset

Entertaining
FOR ALL SEASONS

By the Editors of Sunset Books
and Sunset Magazine

LANE PUBLISHING CO. • MENLO PARK, CALIFORNIA

**Produced and Designed by
The Compage Company**
*in cooperation with
the Editors of Sunset*

Editor
Kenneth R. Burke

Text and Photo Styling
James McNair

Associate Editor
Jessie Wood

Special Projects Editor
Beverley DeWitt

Graphic Design
Williams and Ziller Design

Photography
Michael Lamotte

Food Styling
Amy Nathan

Illustrations
Ellen Blonder

Special Consultant
Jerry Anne DiVecchio
Home Economics Editor
Sunset Magazine

Acknowledgments
Brown's, San Mateo, California
Lin Cotton, Mill Valley, California
Ken and Christine High, San Francisco
Ronald James, San Francisco
Forrest Jones, San Francisco
Sue Fisher King, San Francisco
Tiffany and Company, San Francisco

Michael Toohey, Photography Assistant
Kathy Hadley, Food Styling Assistant

Cover: Spice Cake dripped with thick Caramel Icing is part of a "buffet that can grow," described on pages 54–57. For easy entertaining, the cake can be made and frozen well in advance, then thawed and iced the day before your party. Photography by Tom Wyatt. Cover design by Williams and Ziller Design. Photo styling by Sara Slavin. Food styling by Susan Massey Weil.

Editor, Sunset Books: Elizabeth L. Hogan

Third printing February 1989

America enjoys year-round bounty that is unexcelled in the history of good dining. Each season brings its own fresh produce and fruits: tender young grasslike spears of asparagus and the first strawberries in spring, mountains of tasty summer squash and juicy ripe melons, colorful pumpkins and crisp apples in autumn and the crunchy root crops and creamy pears of winter.

And we have the ever-changing harvest of the sea, poultry and meats of every description, and a vast array of dairy foods. Our transportation system speeds fresh seasonal offerings to all parts of the country, allowing us to enjoy them at the peak of freshness. Coupled with domestic and imported seasonings, this abundance of fresh foods makes cooking and entertaining vastly more creative and enjoyable than at any time in the past.

Cooking with seasonal bounty not only ensures the best tasting meals, but makes for economy. When foods are plentiful, prices are lowest. What better time to entertain guests or family? Thus the parties in this book are organized by season, to help you take advantage of the freshness of America's harvests.

In keeping with the seasonal spirit, our recipes emphasize fresh ingredients whenever possible, with dried or frozen products recommended as alternatives. With most of the menus we also list several alternatives for those times when you or your guests are counting calories as well as when you need to watch the budget.

Seasonal entertaining is more than just good food. Take advantage of the natural materials readily available for decorating the party setting and table: flowering spring branches; summer garden blossoms and decorative vegetables; autumn leaves and dried grasses; or winter greens, berries, and interesting bare twigs.

Success is ensured when you plan an event that you know you would enjoy. Your own pleasure is contagious. A key to being a confident host or hostess is self-expression. Select a theme, menu, place, and style that appeal to you and simply share what you create with others.

In this book we offer a wide range of entertainments that have been staged to the last detail and are tested successes. You'll find something for every time of day—early morning breakfast to late night dining. In size the menus range from special times for you and only one guest to gatherings for 50 to 100 people. Most of the events are informal, but a few are more elaborate for the festive times in your life. The parties run the gamut from formal dining to lazy picnicking.

All recipes have been thoroughly tested in *Sunset* kitchens so that you can cook with confidence. With each menu you'll find a timetable for easy cooking that lists the order in which things should be accomplished—from more than a month ahead to what happens in the kitchen during the party.

Entertaining ease comes from working ahead. The table and other decorations can often be readied at least the day before. Many of the dishes can be made well in advance, to minimize last-minute effort. You give a party because you want to visit with your guests, not be trapped in the kitchen while everyone else is having a great time. The menus in this book allow you to enjoy the company of your guests, with a few minutes' time out here and there to finish up in the kitchen. Of course, you can also prepare everything immediately before the party.

There are times when you'll want to have help, whether you act as your own caterer and hire cooking and serving assistance or choose professionals to carry out your party plans. The guidelines on pages 150 to 152 tell you how to go about it all.

We give specific menus for each party, but encourage you to adapt them freely to your own life-style as well as to the tastes of your guests or family. Combine elements from several menus, add old favorites, or substitute something new to create a self-styled party.

In addition to the ideas for party settings shown in the photographs, the information beginning on page 142 explains the details: table coverings, napkins, dishes, utensils, glassware, flowers, and other decorations.

Keep in mind that the key to entertaining, whatever the season, is creating a feeling of relaxed hospitality. Make the event fun for yourself as well as your guests. Pretensions and old-fashioned rules are out. Inventiveness, congeniality, and fun are always in.

SPRING

Sweet strawberries, tender asparagus, succulent lamb, and tables set with pastel linens and pots of flowering bulbs welcome spring along with your guests.

Spring Garden Supper
  Menu and Plans **6–7**
  Recipes **82**
Tabletop Sushi
  Menu and Plans **8–11**
  Recipes **83–84**
Birdwatcher's Breakfast
  Menu and Plans **12–13**
  Recipes **85–86**
Salad-Sandwich Buffet
  Menu and Plans **14–17**
  Recipes **87–88**
After the Egg Hunt
  Menu and Plans **18–21**
  Recipes **89–92**
Late Night Romance
  Menu and Plans **22–23**
  Recipes **93**
Entertaining with French Flair
  Menu and Plans **24–25**
  Recipes **94–97**

SUMMER

Luscious melons, armloads of fresh herbs and vegetables, meats smoking over aromatic woods, and an outdoor table say it's time for summer entertaining.

Showy Salad in an Edible Bowl
  Menu and Plans **26–27**
  Recipes **98**
Picnicking Made Easy
  Menu and Plans **28–29**
  Recipes **99**
An Afternoon of Cheese and Wine
  Menu and Plans **30–31**
  Recipes **100–101**
Potluck Fisherman's Stew
  Menu and Plans **32–33**
  Recipes **102**
Dinner Under the Stars
  Menu and Plans **34–37**
  Recipes **103–105**
A Red, White, and Blue Lunch
  Menu and Plans **38–39**
  Recipes **106–107**
A Cool Lunch for a Summer Day
  Menu and Plans **40–41**
  Recipes **108**

ENTERTAINING FOR ALL SEASONS

AUTUMN

Crisp apples, butter-rich squash, roasted fowl, hanging braids of garlic, and tables laden with colorful leaves and Indian corn add magic to the autumn party.

Welcome Autumn with a Garlic Festival
    Menu and Plans **42–43**
    Recipes **109–110**

Simply Delicious Dinner
    Menu and Plans **44–45**
    Recipes **111**

An Autumn Brunch
    Menu and Plans **46–47**
    Recipes **112**

Big Burger Before the Big Game
    Menu and Plans **48–49**
    Recipes **113–114**

Dinner at Eight
    Menu and Plans **50–53**
    Recipes **115–117**

A Big Buffet that Can Grow
    Menu and Plans **54–57**
    Recipes **118–120**

Western Harvest Thanksgiving
    Menu and Plans **58–61**
    Recipes **121–124**

WINTER

Crunchy chestnuts and root vegetables, spicy seasonings, sinfully rich chocolates, and tables set cozily by the fireside make winter guests feel at home.

Big Breakfast Bonanza
    Menu and Plans **62–63**
    Recipes **125**

Winter Warmup
    Menu and Plans **64–65**
    Recipes **126–127**

Come for Chocolate and Coffee
    Menu and Plans **66–67**
    Recipes **128**

Holiday Fiesta
    Menu and Plans **68–71**
    Recipes **129–132**

Fireside Dinner
    Menu and Plans **72–73**
    Recipes **133**

Chinese New Year Celebration
    Menu and Plans **74–77**
    Recipes **134–137**

Winter Salad Supper
    Menu and Plans **78–80**
    Recipes **138–140**

PLANNING FOR EASY ENTERTAINING

The special mood of each season is carried through with attractive table settings, festive party decorations, unique appetizers, and innovative garnishes to make your meals sparkle.

Planning Guide **142**

Planning Large Parties: When You Do Your Own Catering **150**

When It's Time to Call a Caterer **152**

Easy Openers for All Seasons **153**

Making the Meal Look Special **153**

Special Woods for Flavorful Barbecuing **155**

Colorful Party Flags **156**

Wine Chart **158**

Notes and Recipes **160**

Index **162**

Metric Chart **168**

SPRING
GARDEN SUPPER
For 4

Fresh Tiny Peas in the Pod
Fruity Chenin Blanc

Young Vegetable Platter
with Sliced Ham and Green Sauce
Croissants with Sweet Butter
Chilled Dry Zinfandel Rosé

Lemon Ice
Coffee

Recipes on Page 82.

SPRING GARDEN SUPPER

When the warm spring sun brings young vegetables to their tender best, plan a late afternoon-early evening supper to show them off.

Consider setting the table in the garden, with torches, wind-protected candles, or kerosene or electric lanterns for evening lighting. Decorate the table with vegetables or a few blossoms cut from the flower garden.

Open a bottle of fruity white wine to accompany sweet tiny peas eaten fresh from the pod for the beginning of the evening's relaxed entertainment. Move along to a chilled dry Zinfandel rosé or white Zinfandel to complement the platter of mixed garden vegetables served with sliced meat and tarragon sauce.

Tart lemon ice could be served in hollowed-out lemon shells left over from juicing. Fill ahead and place in the freezer until a few minutes before serving.

SHOPPING LIST

From the garden or market
32 to 40 tender young pea pods
3 or 4 medium-size leeks
1 pound slender asparagus
½ pound edible-pod or sugar snap peas, or green beans
1 medium-size green cabbage, preferably Savoy
Watercress (½ cup leaves)
Fresh tarragon (1 tablespoon)

From the market
12 lemons (for juice)
Fresh or frozen croissants
Sweet butter
1 egg
¾ to 1 pound thinly sliced cooked ham or plain or smoked turkey, chicken, or pheasant
1 bottle Chenin Blanc or other fruity white wine
1 bottle dry Zinfandel rosé or white Zinfandel

Staples
Dry tarragon (½ teaspoon) if fresh is not available
Dijon mustard (2 teaspoons)
Salad oil (1 cup)
Sugar (2½ cups, plus enough for coffee if desired)
Coffee
Cream or milk for coffee

Opposite: Wicker baskets and white pottery dishes show off Young Vegetable Platter with Sliced Ham and tarragon-flavored Green Sauce.

Left: Hollowed-out lemons make zesty serving bowls for Lemon Ice garnished with African violet and citrus blossoms.

ALTERNATIVES

—Substitute cornbread or another favorite for croissants.
—Use large whole green onions instead of leeks.

Calorie counters
—Omit bread and butter.
—Substitute sliced turkey, chicken, or pheasant for ham.
—Serve mineral water or iced tea instead of wine.
—Offer fresh strawberries instead of lemon ice.

Budget watchers
—Serve a dry white wine throughout the meal instead of the two suggested.
—Use turkey or chicken instead of ham.
—Serve a less expensive bread, such as cornbread.

EASY TIMETABLE

Up to a month ahead
—Make sugar syrup and lemon ice.

One day ahead
—Make and chill green sauce.
—Chill wine.
—Rinse peas.
—Cook and chill vegetables for platter.
—Squeeze lemon juice for ice.
—Freeze lemon ice and place in freezer.

Just before the party
—Arrange vegetable and meat platter.
—Open wine.

During the party
—Make coffee.

TABLETOP SUSHI

An informal supper for 6

Hot Miso Soup

Sushi Selections
(Tray of assorted toppings
including crab, halibut, salmon,
caviar, prawns, and vegetables)

Sushi Rice   Seaweed Wrappers

Condiments:
Wasabi Paste, Pickled Ginger,
Fresh or Pickled Radish,
Toasted Sesame Seed,
Sesame and Soy Sauces

Hot or Chilled Sake or Japanese Beer

Sliced Kiwi and Pineapple

Green Tea

Recipes on Pages 83–84.

Any fears of staging a sushi party, based on the showy presentations of Japanese restaurant chefs, should quickly vanish if you think of serving sushi as simply putting out sandwich fixings that guests can assemble to their own tastes. In Japan and in American Japanese homes, sushi is enjoyed as sandwiches are by most of us—finger foods that make a great appetizer or snack and, when served in quantity, a light meal or perfect picnic fare.

Of all the styles of sushi, hand-rolled (temaki) is the easiest to prepare and serve. It consists of the typical slightly sweet-sour vinegared rice and a choice of vegetable and fish toppings; all are assembled at the table and rolled, one portion at a time, in a crisp seaweed (nori) wrapper. Toppings include both cooked and raw fish to suit timid or more adventurous palates. Sliced avocado adds an American touch to the more traditional Japanese basics.

Tabletop sushi is all ready before your guests sit down to their bowls of hot miso soup (quickly stirred together from a mix). At each place you'll need a small bowl or dish for soy sauce; a plate on which you have arranged a small cone of hot Japanese horseradish (wasabi) to add to the sushi or the dipping sauce, thinly sliced pickled ginger, and finely shredded fresh or sliced pickled white radish (daikon) for nibbling as a palate refresher between sushi concoctions; small glasses for sipping sake or large beer glasses; an Oriental teacup; and chopsticks or, if you feel you must, forks. Napkins folded fanstyle (see page 147) and the center tray of beautifully arranged sushi toppings are all the table decorations needed.

Show guests how to assemble temaki sushi by laying a piece of seaweed in the palm of your hand. Spoon a small quantity of sushi rice into the center; sparsely top with one or a combination of items from the sushi tray, adding wasabi or sesame sauce and seed to taste. Overlap opposite sides of the seaweed square to loosely enclose the fillings; then dip, bite by bite, in soy sauce, spiced to taste with some of the wasabi.

The sliced kiwi and fresh pineapple dessert can be prearranged in individual dishes kept at room temperature until serving time, or presented on a large platter and spooned up at the table.

To create the proper party mood, consider hanging paper Oriental lanterns and placing a few flowering quince or other seasonal branches at strategic places in the entertaining area. Of course, you could go all the way and seat kimono-clad guests on cushions around a low Japanese-style table placed about one foot above the floor. Rest a card table, with its legs folded, on milk crates or cement blocks. Unless you have a beautiful tabletop, choose a simple cloth and top it with woven straw placemats or lay a thin rolling Japanese straw mat across the table.

Opposite: Traditional Japanese Sushi selections and a few American additions attractively arranged on a lacquer tray serve as an edible centerpiece.

Right: Selected toppings are combined with sushi rice to be rolled inside a toasted seaweed wrapper. Condiments include pickled ginger, Japanese horseradish, and shredded white radish.

SHOPPING LIST

—Most of the items you'll need can be found in a well-stocked supermarket that carries Oriental foods; however, you may need to visit an Oriental market for nori, wasabi, pickled ginger and pickled radish, and the soup stock mix. Health food stores often carry most of these items, too.

Oriental market

Miso soup mix (or broth) for 6
Roasted or unroasted nori (1½ ounces)
Wasabi powder (3 tablespoons)
Oriental sesame oil (1½ teaspoons)
Soy sauce (about ½ cup)
Pickled ginger
Pickled radish (optional)
Seasoned rice vinegar for sushi (⅔ cup)

Other markets

2 medium-size carrots
1 pound spinach
2 small ripe avocados
1 English cucumber
1 bag (3½ oz.) fresh enoki mushrooms
3 lemons
2 or 3 kiwis
1 small ripe pineapple
½ pound cooked and shelled crab
½ pound cooked and shelled medium-size prawns (or small whole shrimp)
½ pound boned and skinned yellowfin tuna, sea bass, halibut, or snapper
¼ pound thinly sliced smoked salmon
¼ cup (2 oz.) salmon caviar
3 cups short-grain rice
Sake or Japanese beer
Green tea

Staples

Distilled or white wine vinegar (⅔ cup) plus sugar (8 teaspoons) if seasoned rice vinegar is not used
Mayonnaise (1 cup)
Sesame seed (¼ cup)
Honey (4 teaspoons)

ALTERNATIVES

—Substitute any flavorful but simple hot broth or stock for the miso soup.

—Finely shredded cabbage or lettuce can be used in place of fresh daikon; thinly sliced regular mushrooms can be substituted for hard-to-find enoki.

—Select any local fish specialties or favorite vegetables for toppings.

Calorie counters

—This is a fairly low calorie meal to start with. To save further, add more vegetables and offer less salmon and avocado.

—Serve only tea and sparkling water as beverages.

Budget watchers

—Serve more vegetable toppings and less fish; eliminate prawns, smoked salmon, and caviar.

—Omit sliced kiwis.

EASY TIMETABLE

One day ahead

—Make sushi rice.

—Toast sesame seed.

—Make sesame sauce.

—Chill sake or beer.

Day of the party

—Roast seaweed and cut into squares.

—Prepare toppings and arrange on tray.

—Mix wasabi paste.

—Make soup from mix.

—Shred daikon.

—Slice fruit for dessert.

During the party

—Make tea.

Opposite: Lemon-garnished Miso Soup accompanies sushi. A garnish of yellow ginkgo nuts adds an exotic touch.

Right: A platter of fresh pineapple and kiwi garnished with mint sprigs makes a colorful and refreshing ending to the meal.

BIRDWATCHER'S BREAKFAST
An early morning party for 6

Orange and Grapefruit Segments
Soft-cooked Eggs
Beehive Bread
Wildflower Honey   Sweet Butter
Coffee or Tea

Recipes on Pages 85–86.

BIRDWATCHER'S BREAKFAST

This early-bird breakfast is guaranteed to delight anyone who enjoys watching a spring morning burst into life. If the weather is good, take breakfast and guests near a birdbath, to watch our feathered friends enjoy their morning showers. Or set up a table indoors or out with binoculars for keeping an eye out for these heralds of spring. If you have caged birds, place them near the breakfast table. If the weather is bad, your guests may enjoy lingering over their coffee as they look through books about birds that visit your area.

Since spring is traditionally a time for thoughts about birds and bees, the fanciful and delicious beehive bread that doubles as a handsome centerpiece seems appropriate. Serve it warm or, for a picnic, cool with sweet butter and chunks of comb honey. Choose either the slightly sweet egg dough or the wheat-flecked version. If you prefer, turn the bread upside down to become a basket and serve the eggs from it (a great idea for Easter eggs as well). At any time you can enjoy either of these bread doughs shaped into loaves or rolls.

For easy entertaining, of course, you'll want to bake the bread ahead of time and reheat it while you cook the eggs to your preference. Peel the citrus the night before and slice or cut into segments.

SHOPPING LIST

2 medium-size grapefruits
3 large oranges
1 lemon (for grated peel)
Eggs (6 to soft-cook, plus 6 for golden beehive or 1 for wheat bread)
Sweet butter (½ cup [¼ lb.] for golden beehive or ¼ cup [⅛ lb.] for wheat bread, plus ½ cup [¼ lb.] for spreading on either bread)
Active dry yeast (1 package for golden beehive; 2 packages for wheat bread)
½ cup wheat germ (for wheat bread)
Comb honey

Staples
Sugar (½ cup for golden beehive bread, plus enough for tea or coffee if desired)
All-purpose flour (6 cups for golden beehive; 4 cups for wheat bread)
Whole-wheat flour (2 cups for wheat bread)
Milk (⅓ cup plus 1 tablespoon for golden beehive; 1 tablespoon only for wheat bread)
Salt (½ to 1 teaspoon, plus salt for eggs)
Pepper for eggs
Coffee or tea
Cream or milk for coffee or tea

Opposite: Early morning breakfast treats include (clockwise from top) Beehive Bread, Wildflower Honey, Orange and Grapefruit Segments, Soft-cooked Eggs, and Sweet Butter.

Left: Alternatively, the beehive can be inverted and used as a basket, completed with a twig handle.

EASY TIMETABLE

Up to a week ahead
—Bake beehive bread and freeze.

The night before
—Remove bread from freezer to thaw.
—Prepare citrus segments.
—Set table or pack picnic supplies.

Day of the party
—Reheat bread.
—Make coffee or tea.
—Cook eggs.

SALAD-SANDWICH BUFFET

A do-it-yourself lunch for 8

Curried Chicken Salad

Tuna Salad

Marinated Mushroom Salad

Celery Root Salad

Ratatouille Salad

Thinly Sliced Ham
and Swiss Cheese

Mayonnaise   Mustard

Butter or Leaf Lettuce

Buttered Baguettes

Chablis or Iced Tea

Homemade Fresh Banana Gelato

Recipes on Pages 87–88.

SALAD-SANDWICH BUFFET

Options at this leisurely party are as varied as the wares of a delicatessen. You provide made-ahead flavorful salad-style sandwich fillings and guests put them between, on, or alongside crusty buttered baquettes. They're on their own to construct open-faced or closed sandwiches, with or without lettuce, sliced ham, or cheese, or to sample the varied fillings as salads accompanied by bread.

Set up the buffet indoors or out according to the weather. The meal adapts well to entertaining in the living room, dining room, or kitchen, as well as on the deck, patio, or lawn.

Gelato parlors seem to be popping up everywhere. This rich Italian-style ice cream is a perfect ending to the party.

What makes Italian ice creams different from their American-style counterparts? Americans measure ice cream quality by richness and smoothness. Italians, on the other hand, go for flavor intensity. This is achieved by using a much leaner base resulting in texture that is a bit less silken, but the flavor packs a wallop. In our recipe, you'll really taste fresh bananas that are combined with a simple custard cooked carefully on direct heat.

Use the basic gelato recipe and experiment with adding nut butters, melted chocolate, strong coffee, or other flavorings instead of the banana purée.

Opposite: White lilac and pink nerine add spring fragrance and color to an all-white setting featuring (clockwise from top) Curried Chicken Salad, Ratatouille, Marinated Mushrooms, Sliced Ham and Cheese, and Buttered Baguettes.

Right: A bit of lemon zest adds color to Fresh Banana Gelato.

SHOPPING LIST

Lemons (about 4 for juice and peel)
1 bunch celery
2 green onions
3 onions (2 small; 1 medium-size)
1 small apple
1 head garlic
1¼ pounds small mushrooms
1¼ pounds (about 2 medium-size) celery root
1 small (about ¾ lb.) eggplant
1 medium-size zucchini
1 medium-size green pepper
3 medium-size bananas
4 small heads butter or leaf lettuce
Fresh basil leaves (1 tablespoon), optional
Fresh parsley (¾ cup chopped)
3½-lb. chicken or 2 whole breasts (1 lb. each)
Thinly sliced cooked ham (about ¾ pound)
Sliced Swiss cheese (about 16 slices)
About 2 ounces Parmesan cheese (to make ⅓ cup grated)
½ cup (¼ lb.) butter
3 cups milk
6 eggs
Sliced almonds (3 tablespoons)
Major Grey's chutney (2 tablespoons)
Tomato-based chili sauce (1 cup)
1 can (14½ oz.) pear-shaped tomatoes
1 can (4½ oz.) whole pitted ripe olives
2 cans (about 7 oz. each) solid light tuna in oil
1 small jar Italian pickled peppers (peperoncini)
Baguettes (1 to 2 pounds)
Chablis or tea

Staples

Mayonnaise (¾ cup, plus bowl for buffet)
Olive oil (1 cup)
White wine vinegar (3 tablespoons)
Garlic salt (½ teaspoon)
Curry powder (1 teaspoon)
Cayenne (⅛ teaspoon)
Prepared mustard (½ teaspoon, plus bowl for buffet)
Prepared horseradish (2 teaspoons)
Dry basil (2 teaspoons)
Salt
Sugar (about 1 cup)
Whole black pepper (½ teaspoon)
Coriander seed (½ teaspoon)
Mustard seed (½ teaspoon)
Caraway seed (1 teaspoon)
Vanilla bean (½) or extract (1 teaspoon)

ALTERNATIVES

—Turnips (about 4 medium-size) can be substituted for celery root.
—Regular loaves of French bread or French rolls can fill in for the long skinny baguettes.
—Romaine, red leaf, or iceberg lettuce may be substituted for butter lettuce. (You'll need about 2 heads.)

Calorie counters
—Use tuna packed in water instead of oil.
—Omit ham and cheese.
—Cut down on bread.

Budget watchers
—Omit sliced ham and cheese.

EASY TIMETABLE

Up to a week ahead
—Make and freeze gelato.

One day ahead
—Prepare salads.
—Slice ham and cheese and arrange on tray.
—Chill wine.

Day of the party
—Make iced tea.
—Arrange salad platters.
—Split and butter baguettes.

Tuna Salad and Celery Root Salad round out the Salad-Sandwich Buffet. Guests concoct their own variations.

AFTER THE EGG HUNT
Easter dinner for 8

*Steamed Mussels Provençal
with Baguettes and Butter*

Gamay Beaujolais Blanc

Roast Lamb in Crust
New Potatoes Rosemary
Pistachio-buttered Asparagus
Petite Sirah

*Spinach Salad with Shallots
and Crumbled Cheese*

Seasonal Fruits in Cooky Baskets
Coffee

Recipes on Pages 89–92.

AFTER THE EGG HUNT

Eastertime brings a bounty of fresh produce and herbs, ripening berries, succulent fruits of the sea, and tender spring lamb for an afternoon or evening of feasting.

Fill the house with sweet-smelling paper-whites, grape hyacinth, tulips, daffodils, and other blossoms of spring. Bring out the starchy white table linens and top them with shallow trays of baby's tears or sprouted grasslike oats or cracked wheat in which you nestle your favorite decorated eggs (marbleized with tea or other natural dyes, brightly hued with commercial dye, or intricately painted Russian style). Or even better, feature the naturally speckled tiny eggs of quail or other fowl.

To make Easter entertaining easier, do as much as possible ahead, as suggested in the timetable. Enlist help from family or guests during the final hour or so of preparation so that the day can be a holiday for the cook as well.

Begin with steamed mussels redolent of garlic and herbs, accompanied with baguettes to scoop up every drop of the broth.

The showstopping main course comes to the table as a golden puff of crust decorated with pastry leaves. The top is cut off to reveal a presliced roasted leg of lamb. Tiny new potatoes cooked with fresh rosemary and tender asparagus shoots dripping with pistachio-flavored butter are the seasonal accompaniments. Spinach salad topped with sliced shallots and crumbled blue cheese refreshes the palate after the main course.

The feasting closes with crisp cooky Easter baskets made ahead and filled at serving time with ice cream and seasonal fruits.

Opposite: Steamed Mussels Provençal open an Easter feast set on a white damask-covered table. Butter piped onto a tulip petal echoes the casual arrangement of mixed spring flowers.

Right: Tiny quail eggs and huge goose eggs gathered in a vetiver basket and ceramic bowl add to the seasonal look.

SHOPPING LIST

1 head garlic
1 small onion
1 bunch celery
24 to 32 thin-skinned red
    potatoes (1-inch diameter
    or smaller)
3 pounds asparagus
3 quarts spinach leaves
10 to 12 shallots or 2 small
    red onions
Fresh parsley (about ¾ cup
    chopped)
Fresh sage (1½ tablespoons
    minced)
Fresh rosemary (1½
    tablespoons minced)
2 lemons (for juice)
Seasonal fruits (to make about
    4 cups)
2 cups (1 lb.) butter or
    margarine
2 quarts fresh mussels in the
    shell
Leg of lamb, boned and tied
    (about 4 pounds)
Dry white wine or
    regular-strength chicken
    broth (1 cup)
Regular-strength beef broth (1
    cup)
1 can (1 lb.) tomatoes
1 package active dry yeast
Pistachio nuts (¾ cup)
Chopped nuts (1 cup)
4 ounces blue cheese or
    unripened chèvre (goat
    cheese)
2 baguettes or French bread
Vanilla ice cream (about 2
    quarts) or 2 cups whipping
    cream
2 bottles Gamay Beaujolais
    Blanc
2 or 3 bottles Petite Sirah

*Reassembled sliced Roast
Lamb in Crust is a
showstopping main dish. Offer
some of the crust along with
the meat.*

Staples

Cayenne (⅛ teaspoon)
Pepper (⅜ teaspoon)
Salt
Garlic salt
Dry sage (about 1½ teaspoons) if fresh is not available
Dry rosemary (about 3½ teaspoons) if fresh is not available
Dry marjoram (¾ teaspoon)
Dijon mustard (1 tablespoon)
Vanilla (2 teaspoons)
White wine vinegar (6 tablespoons)
Olive oil or salad oil (about 2 cups)
All-purpose flour (8½ cups)
Cornstarch (1 teaspoon)
Brown sugar (½ cup)
Light corn syrup (½ cup)
Sugar (for whipped cream and coffee if desired)
Coffee

ALTERNATIVES

—Substitute clams for mussels or start with a crab or shrimp cocktail instead.
—Cut large thin-skinned potatoes into bite-size pieces if small potatoes aren't available.
—Cashews can fill in for pistachios.

Calorie counters

—Eliminate crust on roast.
—Skip the pistachio butter with asparagus; drizzle them with lemon juice instead.
—Delete the crumbled cheese in salad dressing.
—Serve the fresh fruit in cups instead of in cooky baskets, and, of course, without the ice cream or whipped cream.

Budget watchers

—Choose clams instead of mussels if there is a difference in price.
—Substitute a boned pork loin for the lamb. Roast as directed for lamb, until thermometer registers 170° (30 to 35 minutes per pound).
—Serve fresh green beans instead of asparagus.
—Use red onion instead of shallots.

EASY TIMETABLE

Up to a week ahead
—Bake cooky baskets.

Two days ahead
—Roast and chill leg of lamb.
—Make and chill dough for crust.
—Make salad dressing.
—Chill white wine.

One day ahead
—Punch down chilled dough.
—Scrub new potatoes.
—Wash and chill spinach leaves.
—Prepare dessert fruits.

Day of the party
—Complete lamb in crust and bake.
—Roast potatoes.
—Whip cream.

Just before the party
—Prepare steamed mussels.
—Cook asparagus and make pistachio butter.
—Open red wine.

During the party
—Toss spinach salad.
—Assemble cooky baskets.
—Make coffee.

Top: New Potatoes Rosemary, Pistachio-buttered Asparagus.

Above: Easter baskets made of cooky dough are filled with ice cream and fresh fruit.

LATE NIGHT ROMANCE
An elegant supper for 2

*American Golden Caviar
on Pan-fried Potato Slices
with Sour Cream*

*Young Asparagus and Shrimp
with Homemade Mayonnaise*

Champagne or Sparkling Wine

Chocolate Truffles

Recipes on Page 93.

LATE NIGHT ROMANCE

Many of life's most memorable occasions are those times when we entertain that special person. Here's a late night supper for after the theater or when the children are tucked safely in bed.

Pull out your most beautiful table accessories, china, glassware, and silver. Don't forget the soft music, flowers, and candlelight.

The menu is also appropriate for midday meals and can easily be multiplied for more guests.

Fresh golden caviar, sometimes called California caviar, actually comes from the Midwest; it is packaged and distributed frozen. A container keeps in the freezer for several months, and the caviar can withstand thawing and refreezing. To serve, spoon into a bowl that will nestle in ice inside a larger bowl.

Unless you're on a really hedonistic binge, the truffle recipe will make enough for several occasions. Truffles keep in the refrigerator for about 2 weeks.

SHOPPING LIST

1 large thin-skinned potato
1 pound asparagus
Cherry tomatoes (optional)
1 lemon (for juice)
1 to 3 eggs
Whipping cream (about 2 tablespoons)
Sour cream
About 2 ounces fresh golden caviar
1 to 1½ cups cooked medium-size shrimp in shells
4 ounces semisweet chocolate
1 bottle champagne or sparkling wine

Staples

Dijon mustard (1 teaspoon)
White wine vinegar (1 tablespoon) if lemon juice is not used
Salad oil (1 cup)
Salt
Ground sweet chocolate or cocoa (2 tablespoons)

ALTERNATIVES

—Any canned pasteurized caviar can be substituted for the golden caviar.
—Tender green beans can stand in for asparagus.

Calorie counters

—Spoon caviar on thinly sliced rounds of cucumber.
—Drizzle asparagus and shrimp with a bit of oil and fresh lemon juice instead of mayonnaise.
—Go with seasonal fruit instead of chocolate truffles.

Budget watchers

—Try inexpensive lumpfish caviar.
—Choose a sparkling wine, inexpensive champagne, dry white wine, chilled mineral water, or sparkling apple juice.

EASY TIMETABLE

Up to two weeks before
—Make chocolate truffles.

Two days ahead
—Make and chill mayonnaise.

One day ahead
—Chill champagne.
—Cook and chill asparagus.

Day of the party
—Place caviar on ice.

Just before the party
—Fry potatoes.
—Arrange asparagus and shrimp plates.

Opposite: Champagne accompanies a late supper of American Golden Caviar on Pan-fried Potato Slices, served alongside Young Asparagus and Shrimp with Homemade Mayonnaise.

Left: Chocolate Truffles guarantee a decadently rich ending.

ENTERTAINING WITH FRENCH FLAIR

Warm or cold lunch or supper for 6

Carrot and Orange Soup

*Oven-baked
Fish, Shrimp, Eggs,
and Vegetables with Aioli Sauce*

French Bread

*Dry White Burgundy or
Entre-Deux-Mers*

Floating Islands

Coffee

Recipes on Pages 94–97.

ENTERTAINING WITH FRENCH FLAIR

Transport your guests to the Riviera with a make-ahead meal that's equally enjoyable warm or cold, as lunch or supper, indoors or out—whatever the unpredictable spring weather calls for.

Cheerful Mediterranean colors—sky blue, sunny yellow, and earthy terra-cotta—in table coverings and napkins, dishes, flowers, and decorations set the tone for this leisurely, casual dining experience and enhance the cheerful hues of the food.

Brightly colored carrot soup enlivened with freshly squeezed orange juice and served icy cold is the right beginning if the weather is warm. Reheat if the day or evening turns cool.

Aioli sauce, redolent of garlic, is a tasty dip for barely cooked vegetables, hard-cooked eggs, and crusty bread, as well as the suggested fish and shrimp. It's equally good with cooked meat: poached chicken, smoked turkey, roast beef, or ham.

The French dessert classic is guaranteed to bring delight at meal's end. It looks and tastes complex, but the components can be made ahead and assembled about 4 hours before serving time.

Opposite: Carrot and Orange Soup in the foreground. Fish filets and vegetables are to be dipped in garlicky Aioli Sauce.

Above: Spoon a portion of Floating Island custard and a meringue onto each plate.

SHOPPING LIST

6 large artichokes
2 pounds carrots
12 thin-skinned potatoes (*each* about 1½-in.-dia.)
1 medium-size cauliflower
1 pound green beans or asparagus spears
3 onions (1 large; 2 medium)
3 large leeks or 8 green onions
2 large shallots or 1 small onion
1 or 2 heads garlic
6 medium-size juice oranges
3 lemons (for juice)
2 tablespoons butter or margarine
14 eggs
3 cups half-and-half or milk
2 pounds fish fillets (about 1 in. thick) or 1 whole fish (4 to 5 lbs.)
1 pound unshelled large shrimp
2 cans (14½ oz. *each*) regular-strength chicken broth
1 loaf (1 lb.) French bread
Grand Marnier or other orange-flavored liqueur (2 tablespoons)
2 or 3 bottles dry White Burgundy or Entre-Deux-Mers plus 1½ cups dry white wine for poaching

Staples

Sugar (1¼ cups plus 1 teaspoon)
Olive oil (1 cup)
Olive or salad oil (5 tablespoons)
White wine vinegar (⅓ cup) if lemon juice is not used
Tomato paste (1 tablespoon) or catsup (2 tablespoons)
Whole black peppers (12)
Whole allspice (4)
Bay leaves (3)
Dry thyme (½ teaspoon)
Dill weed (½ teaspoon)
Cream of tartar (¼ teaspoon)
Vanilla (1½ teaspoons)
Salt and pepper

ALTERNATIVES

—Raw vegetables can be used in place of the cooked ones. Consider fennel (sweet anise), bell peppers, cucumbers, radishes, and celery.

Calorie counters
—Omit fish, shellfish, and meat.
—Offer ripe fruit instead of the floating islands.

Budget watchers
—Omit costly shrimp, or replace it with cooked chicken.

EASY TIMETABLE

One day ahead
—Make and chill carrot and orange soup.
—Make and chill *aioli* sauce.
—Cook and chill eggs.
—Cook and chill vegetables if you'll serve them cold.
—Cook and chill fish if you'll serve it cold.
—Make and chill custard and meringues for floating islands.
—Chill wine.

Day of the party
—Four hours before serving, assemble and complete floating islands.

Just before the party
—Reheat soup if desired.
—Let *aioli* sauce warm to room temperature.
—Cook fish if you'll serve it warm.
—Complete warm sauce for fish.
—Cook shrimp.
—Cook vegetables if you'll serve them warm or at room temperature.

During the party
—Heat bread if desired.
—Make coffee.

SHOWY SALAD IN AN EDIBLE BOWL

Supper for 4

*Chicken and Pea Pod Salad
in Pastry Bowl*

French Colombard or Chenin Blanc

Raspberries with Almond Cream

Iced Coffee

Recipes on Page 98.

SHOWY SALAD IN AN EDIBLE BOWL

''Spectacular'' describes the look of this showstopping main-dish salad; ''easy'' describes its preparation.

The big pastry salad bowl is merely cream puff batter baked in one large round that can be made ahead of time. Keep overnight at room temperature or pop into the freezer for longer storage. A brief reheating revives the chewy crust.

Crisp, barely cooked edible-pod peas line the boat and a creamy chicken salad tops them. Vary the meal by substituting any favorite main-course salad filling.

Raspberries speak the language of summer. Coupled with an extremely easy almond cream, they make a perfect conclusion to the meal.

Repeat the cool green of the pea pods with an indoor oasis of potted greenery, or set up the little supper on a terrace or other outdoor entertaining area.

SHOPPING LIST

Green onions (3 to 4 for ½ cup sliced)
¼ pound edible-pod peas
Fresh coriander (cilantro) or parsley (about 4 sprigs)
1 lime (for juice)
2 cups raspberries
5 eggs
5 tablespoons butter or margarine
1 small package (3 oz.) cream cheese
1 cup whipping cream
1 cup sour cream
3-pound broiler-fryer chicken or 2 whole breasts (1 lb. each)
1 can (8 oz.) water chestnuts
Almond-flavored liqueur (2 tablespoons)
Almonds for garnish (optional)
2 bottles White wine

Staples

All-purpose flour (⅔ cup)
Sugar (2 teaspoons)
Powdered sugar (½ cup)
Curry powder (2 teaspoons)
Ground ginger (½ teaspoon)
Salt
Pepper

ALTERNATIVES

—If you can't find fresh edible-pod peas, use frozen thawed ones.
—Strawberries can substitute for raspberries.

Calorie counters
—Serve the raspberries plain or with a sprinkling of sugar and a hint of cream.

Budget watchers
—Go with strawberries instead of raspberries.
—Almond flavoring can be used instead of the liqueur.

EASY TIMETABLE

Up to a month before
—Bake and freeze pastry bowl.

One day ahead
—Make and chill chicken salad.
—Chill wine.

Day of the party
—Cook and chill edible-pod peas.
—Make and chill almond cream.
—Make and chill coffee.

Just before the party
—Recrisp pastry bowl and assemble salad.
—Assemble dessert and refrigerate.

Opposite: Bright gerberas accent the supper table for a summer main course Chicken and Pea Pod Salad in Pastry Bowl. Cut the chewy crust into wedges to serve.

Left: The perfect ending to a hot day is Iced Coffee, and Raspberries with Almond Cream.

PICNICKING MADE EASY

An ice chest buffet for 8 to 10

Avocado-Shrimp Cocktail

Add-on Vichyssoise
Bread Sticks and Butter
Sparkling Water

Nectarines in Sweet White Wine
Crisp Cookies
Pinot Blanc or White Zinfandel

Recipes on Page 99.

Quite a few of the parties in this book can adapt to the picnic genre, but none could be easier than this three-course buffet served right out of ice chests.

Each course of this festive picnic is attractively packed in its own chest. Foods in watertight containers nestle on crushed ice that not only keeps the meal cold, but doubles as an attractive base for serving, eliminating the need for a picnic table. Serve each course, with fresh spoons, in clear plastic disposable cups or bowls.

Start by filling chests with bottled sparkling water and wine. On the top of one chest, arrange the components of a make-your-own shrimp cocktail—cooked shrimp, sauce, avocado, fresh coriander (cilantro), and lime wedges. At the site, just open the top and let the guests put together their own first course.

The main-course chest contains some of the beverages, plus butter for the breadsticks and a hearty vichyssoise to which guests add slivers of ham, gratings of fresh nutmeg, and snips of fresh chives.

At dessert time another chest reveals a bowl of juicy sliced nectarines (turned in about ¼ cup of lemon juice to preserve their color) and a fruity-flavored sweet white wine. Spoon the fruit into individual dishes or glasses and pour the wine over it. Accompany with cookies. Sip the wine, dunk the cookies, and finish the fruit with a spoon.

Pack the breadsticks, cookies, corkscrew, bottle opener, nutmeg grater, kitchen scissors (for chives), a small knife, cups, and spoons in a basket or canvas tote. Don't forget blankets, spreads, or other ground covers. Pillows make for comfort; a kite or game makes for a fun venture.

Opposite: Contemporary picnic accessories beautify a buffet served directly from ice chests. Add-on Vichyssoise topped with slivered ham, chives, and nutmeg is picture-pretty. Guests combine ingredients for an Avocado-Shrimp Cocktail. Crisp Cookies are dunked into the Nectarines in Sweet White Wine.

SHOPPING LIST

1 medium-size green pepper
Green onions (3 to 4)
1 medium-size onion
4 medium-size thin-skinned potatoes
4 or 5 medium-size leeks
1 cucumber
2 medium-size ripe avocados
Fresh oregano (1½ teaspoons chopped)
Fresh coriander (cilantro), 1 cup leaves
Chives (about 36)
3 or 4 limes (1 for juice)
1 or 2 lemons (for juice)
8 to 10 large ripe nectarines or peaches
1½ pounds medium-size cooked shrimp
1 pound sliced boiled ham
1 cup (½ lb.) butter or margarine
1 cup unflavored yogurt
1 cup sour cream
3 cans (6 oz. *each*) tomato-based vegetable juice
3 cans (14½ oz. *each*) regular-strength beef broth
About 20 breadsticks
Crisp cookies (about 2 to 2½ dozen)
3 to 5 bottles Pinot Blanc or White Zinfandel
1 or 2 bottles fruity-flavored sweet or slightly sweet white wine, such as late-harvest Johannisberg Riesling or a Gewürztraminer
10 individual bottles sparkling water
Crushed ice to half-fill 3 chests

Staples
Worcestershire (2 tablespoons)
Prepared horseradish (1 teaspoon)
Dry oregano (½ teaspoon)
2 whole nutmegs

ALTERNATIVES

—Three medium-size onions can be substituted for leeks.

Calorie counters
—Increase the yogurt in the vichyssoise to 2 cups; omit the sour cream.
—Serve nectarines without the wine.

EASY TIMETABLE

One day ahead
—Make and chill shrimp cocktail sauce.
—Make and chill vichyssoise and toppings.
—Pack all nonperishables in basket or hamper.
—Chill wines and sparkling water.

Day of the picnic
—Slice and chill nectarines or peaches.

Just before leaving for picnic
—Pack ice chests.

AN AFTERNOON OF CHEESE AND WINE

A tasting of cheeses and wines
for 10 to 100

Hot Chèvre Toast

Brie in Wine Aspic
Decorated with
Edible Flowers and Herbs

Layered Cheese Torta
with Fresh Basil and Pine Nuts

Blue Cheese with Warm Walnuts

Cheese Tray with Summer Fruits

Sliced   *Assorted*
Baguettes   *Crackers*

Coffee

Recipes on Pages 100–101.

AN AFTERNOON OF CHEESE AND WINE

Potluck Wines

*(Guests are asked to bring an assigned type of wine
to ensure a wide range for tasting and comparison.
Choose from: Chardonnay, Chenin Blanc, Gewürztraminer,
Johannisberg Riesling, Pinot Blanc, Sauvignon Blanc,
Barbera, Cabernet Sauvignon, Gamay, Gamay Beaujolais,
Grenache Rosé, Merlot, Petite Sirah, Pinot Noir, Zinfandel,
Sparkling and Dessert Wines)*

"A book of verses underneath the bough, a jug of wine, a loaf of bread—and thou. . . ." Omar Khayyám's ancient recipe for a perfect afternoon was missing only one thing: cheese!

For a new twist on easy entertaining with the classic combination of cheese, bread, and wine, make it a potluck and ask your friends to bring the wine. The results will be far more interesting than if you buy the wines yourself. And it makes such a party quite affordable. You can choose a theme when you issue the invitations: all chardonnays, all red varietals, all Napa Valley vineyards, all Italian wines, all sparkling wines, all wines of a certain vintage, perhaps a few dessert wines, or whatever realm of the grape you'd like to explore. In addition to having a great time, everyone is likely to learn something about wine.

Choose as many items as you wish from our menu to suit the size of your crowd. For a group of 10, you'll probably want to offer only 3 of the items. Each of the recipes serves 10. Increase the offerings and multiply the recipes as your guest list expands.

If the party is outdoors, be sure to put the cheeses under some sort of shade. Place the cheeses on cutting boards of wood, plastic, or marble that can withstand knife scratches. Lay appropriate cheese knives alongside each type and place baguettes or crackers within easy reach of each cheese presentation.

Decorate the wine bar so that it is just as festive as the cheese table. As at a professional wine tasting, have enough glasses so that each person can have one for whites and another for reds. Provide pitchers filled with water for rinsing glasses, and residue bowls for disposing of excess wine after tasting. Provide tubs or buckets of crushed ice to keep whites, rosés, and light reds appropriately chilled.

To bring the party to a close, pack up the wine and offer freshly brewed coffee.

Opposite: Cheese buffet includes (clockwise from top) Blue Cheese with Warm Walnuts, Summer Fruits, Layered Cheese Torta with Fresh Basil and Pine Nuts, Brie Decorated with Edible Flowers and Herbs in Wine Aspic, and Hot Chèvre Toast.

SHOPPING LIST

*For each 10 guests
(by recipe)*

Chèvre toast
¾ pound chèvre (goat cheese)
1 long baguette (about 1 lb.)

Brie in wine aspic
2 small wheels (about 8 oz. *each*) Brie
Dry white wine (2 cups)
Unflavored gelatin (1 envelope)
1 long baguette (about 1 lb.)

Cheese torta
1 small (3 oz.) and 1 large (8 oz.) package cream cheese
About 3 ounces Parmesan or Romano cheese (⅔ cup grated)
1⅓ cups (⅔ lb.) unsalted butter
Fresh basil (about 2 cups leaves)
Olive oil (3½ tablespoons)
Pine nuts (about ¼ cup)
1 long baguette (about 1 lb.) or crackers
Salt
Pepper

Blue cheese with walnuts
2 pounds blue cheese
2 cups (8 oz.) walnut halves
Water crackers or other unsalted crackers (about 7 oz.)

Cheese tray with summer fruits
Allow about ⅛ pound cheese per person.
Allow about ¾ cup assorted fruit per person.

EASY TIMETABLE

Up to five days ahead
—Make and chill layered torta.

Day of the party
—Make aspic; decorate and chill brie.
—Prepare chèvre toast.

Just before the party
—Prepare tub of ice and water for chilling wines.
—Heat walnuts for blue cheese.
—Arrange cheese and fruit tray.
—Slice baguettes.

During the party
—Broil chèvre toast and pass.

**POTLUCK
FISHERMAN'S STEW**

A beach party for 10
that multiplies;
everyone brings a fish to add
to your simmering pot

Raw Vegetables with Dipping Sauce

Fisherman's Stew

Toast Rounds   Garlic Mayonnaise

Dry White Wine

Melons

Recipes on Page 102.

Turn-of-the-century Italian-immigrant fishermen get the credit for inventing the delicious Western soup cioppino in the same way that French fishermen invented bouillabaisse. Each fisherman threw something into a communal pot of simmering flavorful broth. Today there are countless versions; the common theme is a mixture of whatever fresh seafood is available.

Here is a big fish stew that's a bit French bouillabaisse, a bit Italian cioppino, and a whole lot of fun for everyone.

Invite each guest to bring a pound of fresh seafood: fish fillets or shellfish. Any firm-fleshed fresh fish works well in the stew. You provide the whole fish, a big kettle of simmering broth (to receive the fish), and the rest of the meal. If you want to expand the party for more than 10, you can cook the stew in up to a 50-quart kettle (borrowed from a friendly restaurant or a school, perhaps) or divide the broth and fish equally among several small kettles.

Preparation of the vegetables can be done at home or at the beach while you wait for the guests to arrive. About an hour before serving, start a fire. Unless the site has fire rings with grates, you might find it easier to take along portable stoves or barbecue grills. Otherwise, you can position several heavy steel rods (rebars) over the ring to support the big pot. (Rods should be a little longer than the diameter of the ring.)

This is the time of year to cut into juicy melons—cantaloupe, casaba, Crenshaw, honeydew, and the old picnic classic, watermelon. Use large galvanized tubs or new plastic garbage cans full of crushed ice to chill wine, beer, and sodas. It takes about 30 minutes in a mixture of ice and a little water.

In addition to the food, beverages, tubs for chilling drinks, and heat sources and cooking fuel, you'll need to pack ground covers for sitting, a corkscrew, bottle opener, soup ladles, knives for cutting melons, containers for vegetables and dips, large disposable soup bowls, plastic spoons, throw-away wine glasses, and big garbage bags. You may need to include insect repellant and portable lighting if the party will continue into the evening. Game equipment makes the afternoon even more fun.

Opposite: Guests help themselves to cooked fish and shellfish and simmering broth.

SHOPPING LIST

For each 10 guests (multiply by 2 for 20 and so on.)

Assorted vegetables for dipping (enough to make 7 to 8 cups)
6 medium-size leeks
2 large onions
1 head garlic
Fresh parsley (10 sprigs)
Fresh thyme (1 tablespoon)
1 orange (for grated peel)
5 lemons (for wedges)
Assorted melons (at least 10 wedges)
Ingredients for favorite dip (to make 1½ to 2 cups)
1 quart clam juice
1 quart regular-strength chicken broth
2 large cans (1 lb. 12 oz. *each*) tomatoes
4 or 5 baguettes (1 for toast rounds; rest for eating as is)
1 to 3 eggs (for mayonnaise)
6½ cups (about 1.5 L.) dry white wine for broth
2 or 3 jugs (1.5 L. *each*) dry white wine for drinking

Fish and seafood—guidelines for guests
2 to 3 pounds assorted fish fillets
1 to 2 pounds shrimp (in shells)
1½ to 2 pound live lobster
About 3 pounds oysters, clams, or mussels (in shells)
2 to 3 pound whole fish

Staples
Olive oil or salad oil (¼ cup)
White wine vinegar (1 tablespoon)
Bay leaves (3)
Dry thyme (1 teaspoon) if fresh is not available.
Fennel seed (¼ teaspoon)
Cayenne (⅛ teaspoon)
Dijon mustard (1 teaspoon)
Liquid hot pepper seasoning

ALTERNATIVES

—Use 3 large onions in place of leeks.
—Regular French bread can be substituted for long, skinny baguettes.

Calorie counters
—Skip the garlic mayonnaise.
—Omit the vegetable dip.

Budget watchers
—Serve iced tea, sodas, or beer instead of wine.
—Limit dessert to watermelon.

EASY TIMETABLE

Up to two weeks before
—Make and chill garlic mayonnaise.

One day ahead
—Clean vegetables for dipping and refrigerate each type in a separate container.
—Prepare dip for vegetables.
—Make toast rounds and pack airtight.

At the beach
—Build fire and prepare stew broth.
—Chill beverages in tubs of ice.
—Arrange vegetables and dipping sauce.
—Add fish and seafood according to recipe.
—Slice melons.

DINNER
UNDER THE STARS
For 6

*Calamari-Kiwi Salad
with Watercress*
Sauvignon Blanc

*Mesquite-grilled Beef Tenderloin
in Cabernet Sauvignon Marinade*
Skillet Potatoes Anna
*Sautéed Red Bell Peppers
and Onions*
Selected Mustards
Crusty French Bread
Cabernet Sauvignon

Sherried Cream with Red Grapes

Recipes on Pages 103–105.

Long days lend themselves to warm outdoor dining under a starlit canopy. Take advantage of the season and set a table on the patio or deck, beside the pool, or in the garden. Tiny white Christmas lights strung in nearby trees echo the summer sky. Star charts and perhaps a telescope add to the theme.

Open the Sauvignon Blanc as guests arrive and continue it with the opening course, which can be served on small plates as a stand-up appetizer or after guests are seated at the table.

Dinner starts with an unusual combination of squid and kiwi. When called by its Italian name, *calamari*, squid sounds like the delicacy it is. Once you learn to clean the slippery little creatures, you'll find it very easy. In this recipe, gentle poaching brings out the fine texture and delicate flavor of the squid.

Until recently, kiwis were costly imports from New Zealand. Now California growers are making the fuzzy little fruits more readily available across the country.

Grilling outdoors is a favored summertime entertainment. Aromatic smoke curling up around the beef carries appetizing promises. (Information on grilling with mesquite and other fragrant woods is given on page 155.)

Red bell peppers are showier and sweeter than those picked still green. When cooked ahead, the pepper and onion sauté can be reheated in a frying pan placed on the outdoor grill, adding to the festive spirit of outdoor cooking.

If you've hesitated to buy red grapes because of the pesky little seeds, you've welcomed the introduction of seedless red grapes. Several varieties are now making their way to produce shelves, but 'Flame' is the current favorite. Dessert combines red seedless grapes with a sherried cream elegantly served in stemmed glasses.

Opposite: Marinated beef tenderloin hot off mesquite coals is sliced and served with a sauce of Cabernet Sauvignon Marinade and favorite mustards.

Top right: No accompaniment could be easier or tastier than Skillet Potatoes Anna, cooked and served in a heavy skillet.

SHOPPING LIST

1 head garlic
5 red bell peppers (4 large, 1 medium-size)
5 onions (4 large, 1 small)
5 or 6 large russet potatoes
2 or 3 kiwis
About 2¼ cups seedless red grapes
Fresh basil (2 tablespoons chopped), optional
Fresh parsley (¼ cup chopped)
Watercress (about 12 sprigs)
1 cup (½ lb.) butter or margarine
3 cups milk
3 eggs
3¾ pounds whole small squid or 1½ pounds cleaned mantels
A 4-pound piece beef tenderloin or filet
1 can (14½ oz.) regular-strength chicken broth
Dry white wine for poaching (2¼ cups)
Cream sherry or apple juice (6 tablespoons)
2 bottles Sauvignon Blanc
2 or 3 bottles Cabernet Sauvignon

Staples
Sugar (½ cup plus ¾ teaspoon)
Cornstarch (3 tablespoons)
Olive oil (a generous ½ cup)
Bay leaf
Salt
Pepper

Calamari and kiwi team up for an unusual and refreshing salad perfect for a warm summer night.

ALTERNATIVES

—Look for frozen squid if fresh are not available. Substitute cooked shrimp or crab if necessary.
—Choose any tender cut of steak (porterhouse, sirloin, rib) in place of the filet.
—Green or yellow bell peppers may be used in place of red.
—Use seedless green grapes if red ones are not in the market, or slice and seed regular red grapes.

Calorie counters
—Serve baked potatoes instead of skillet potatoes.
—Eliminate sherried cream and offer plain grapes or other fresh fruits.

Budget watchers
—Skip the first course and white wine.
—Choose a less tender cut of steak (such as chuck, sirloin tip, or round). Brush each side lightly with water, sprinkle with ½ teaspoon meat tenderizer per pound of meat, and pierce with a fork at ½-inch intervals. Stand steak on edge in a V-shaped rack in a roasting pan. Place in a 200° oven for 45 minutes per pound before transferring to the grill to brown (3 to 5 minutes per side).
—Serve a good red jug wine instead of the more expensive Cabernet Sauvignon.

Top Right: Sautéed Red Bell Peppers and Onions can be made ahead and reheated on the grill when the beef is almost done.

Right: Seedless red grapes smothered in sherried cream and served in stemmed glasses bring the meal to an elegant conclusion.

EASY TIMETABLE

Up to three days before
—Sauté peppers and onions.

One day ahead
—Clean, cook, and chill squid.
—Chill white wine.
—Marinate beef.

Day of the party
—Make and chill sherried cream with grapes.
—Combine squid with sauce.

Just before the party
—Put skillet potatoes in oven.
—Build mesquite fire, allow to burn until glowing and covered with gray ash, and begin cooking beef.
—Arrange salad on plates.
—Open Cabernet Sauvignon to breathe.

During the party
—Heat peppers and onions on grill.
—Heat bread if desired.

A RED, WHITE, AND BLUE LUNCH

Patriotic holiday for 8 to 10

Roasted Red Pepper
and Tomato Salad

White Cheese Platter
(Feta, White Cheddar, Jarlsberg, Jack)

Pine Nut Sticks

Dry White Wine

Blueberry Meringue Torte
with Rum Custard

Recipes on Pages 106–107.

Our Fourth of July party features a red pepper and tomato salad, a white cheese platter and white wine, and a blueberry torte. Pine nuts, a major food of native Americans, flavor firecracker-shaped bread.

Decorate your indoor or outdoor setting with flags of all sizes and red, white, and blue bunting or ribbon streamers. Have some recorded patriotic music echoing in the background throughout the afternoon.

To stage a personal fireworks display, give your guests sparklers to wave.

SHOPPING LIST

6 large red bell peppers
5 large firm-ripe tomatoes
1 head garlic
Fresh parsley (1 tablespoon chopped)
1 or 2 lemons (for peel)
2 cups blueberries
11 eggs
1½ cups whipping cream
1½ cups milk
1 can (3½ oz.) whole pitted large ripe olives
1 can (2 oz.) rolled anchovies
1 package active dry yeast
About ⅔ cup pine nuts
Rum (2 tablespoons) or rum extract (½ teaspoon)
4 or 5 bottles dry white wine

Staples

Olive oil (¼ cup plus 2 tablespoons)
Salad oil (2 tablespoons)
Sugar (1¼ cups plus 1 tablespoon)
All-purpose flour (about 2½ cups)
Ground cumin (1 teaspoon)
Anise seed (½ teaspoon)
Cream of tartar (½ teaspoon)
Vanilla (1 teaspoon)
Salt
Coarse salt (2 tablespoons)
Pepper

ALTERNATIVES

—Roasted red peppers are available in jars; green ones can be used at the expense of the color scheme.
—Frozen blueberries can fill in for fresh.

Calorie counters

—Serve lightly sugared blueberries with just a bit of cream instead of the torte.

EASY TIMETABLE

Up to five days ahead
—Make meringues and store airtight.

Up to two days ahead
—Roast and chill red peppers.
—Make pine nut sticks.

One day ahead
—Assemble blueberry torte.
—Chill wine.

Day of the party
—Make pepper and tomato salad.

Opposite: A light summer holiday meal centers around Roasted Red Pepper and Tomato Salad garnished with hard-cooked eggs and olives, and accompanied with firecracker-shaped Pine Nut Sticks.

Left: Blueberry Meringue Torte with Rum Custard rounds out the patriotic color-inspired party menu.

**A COOL LUNCH
FOR A
SUMMER DAY**
Just for 2

Salmon Tartare
Fresh Chives   *Toast Triangles*
Grey Riesling

*Vanilla Fig Compote
with Ice Cream*

Recipes on Page 108.

A COOL LUNCH FOR A SUMMER DAY

When the summer sun reaches its peak, plan a lunch retreat in the coolest spot you can find. What could be more refreshing for warm-weather dining than a lime-enhanced cool salmon tartare, a light variation on the classic beef dish, and a dessert of luscious ripe figs.

Figs appear in the nation's markets in two waves: June brings a rather small crop of large fruit; August and September, a larger crop of smaller figs. Sweet fresh figs make great snacks and desserts as they are or with a little sugar and cream. For a more festive presentation serve the compote in vanilla syrup with an echo of vanilla ice cream.

SHOPPING LIST

1 shallot
Fresh marjoram or dill (1 teaspoon minced)
6 chives
2 limes
1 lemon (or 3 lemons if limes are not available)
4 small or 2 large figs
½ cup raspberries or blackberries
¾ pound salmon fillets (fresh or frozen)
1 can (7 oz.) roasted red pepper or whole pimiento
1½ teaspoons capers
Bread for toasting
1 pint vanilla ice cream
Dry red wine (⅓ cup)
1 bottle Grey Riesling

Staples

Dry marjoram or dill weed (½ teaspoon) if fresh is not available
Sugar (¼ cup)
Vanilla bean (⅓) or vanilla extract (½ teaspoon)

ALTERNATIVES

Calorie counters
—Serve ripe fresh figs by themselves as dessert.

EASY TIMETABLE

One day ahead
—Make and chill vanilla syrup.
—Freeze salmon if fresh.
—Chill wine.

Day of the party
—Make and chill salmon tartare.
—Heat vanilla syrup; add figs and berries.

Just before the party
—Arrange tartare on plates.
—Make toast.

During the party
—Assemble dessert.

Opposite: Clear glass plates on a glass table set with lush ferns create a cool oasis for a lunch of Salmon Tartare.

Left: Figs and raspberries gently stirred in vanilla syrup are spooned over ice cream.

WELCOME AUTUMN WITH A GARLIC FESTIVAL

Garlic and onion
team up in a buffet for 8

Garlic-Jelly Cream Cheese
Unsalted Crisp Crackers

Garlic Soup

Garlic Tart

Baked Garlic Sausages
with Mustard, Horseradish,
and Pickles

Green Salad

Crusty Bread

Barbera   Cider

Apples

Recipes on Pages 109–110.

WELCOME AUTUMN WITH A GARLIC FESTIVAL

A festive buffet celebrating the harvest of "the stinking rose" seems an appropriate ending to summer and welcome to autumn.

Decorate the buffet with braided garlic heads. (You can use the garlic for months to come.) Scatter local signs of Indian summer or early autumn, such as colorful dried leaves, among the braids.

Garlic jelly spooned over cream cheese begins the feast as guests arrive. Offer cider or favorite drinks and crisp crackers with the pungent appetizer spread. Make the garlic jelly ahead. You'll have enough for many uses; or you might present a jar to each guest or couple as they leave the party.

Garlic teams up with its onion relative in a slow sauté to bring out the sweetness of the bulbs and form the basis for three buffet dishes. To avoid a bitter flavor, do not let the garlic scorch as it cooks.

Ladle the soup from a tureen into mugs that travel along with the dinner plates from buffet to small tables set up for dining. Place carafes of the red wine and cider on each table, as well as a basket of crusty bread. Decorate the tables with apples (which will serve as dessert) and more garlic heads.

SHOPPING LIST

Garlic braids and at least 12 heads (for decorations, jelly, and cooking)
5 pounds onions
Salad greens
8 to 12 apples
¼ cup (⅛ lb.) butter or margarine
1 cup milk
1 cup sour cream
1 large package (8 oz.) cream cheese
8 ounces Swiss cheese
3 eggs
⅓ to ½ pound smoked pork chops or ham
8 garlic (knackwurst) sausages
8 to 12 dill pickles
½ cup Dijon mustard
½ cup prepared horseradish
1 package (about 7 oz.) unsalted crackers
3 cans (14½ oz. *each*) regular-strength beef broth
2 pouches (3 oz. *each*) liquid pectin or 2 boxes (1¾ to 2 oz. *each*) dry pectin
7 canning jars (½-pt. size)
Port (3 tablespoons)
3 or 4 bottles Barbera
1 gallon apple cider

Staples

Ingredients for favorite salad dressing
White wine vinegar (3 cups)
Salad oil (2 teaspoons)
Sugar (6 cups)
All-purpose flour (¼ cup)
Ground nutmeg (⅛ teaspoon)
Dry mustard (1 teaspoon)
Caraway seed (¼ teaspoon)
Food coloring (optional)
Salt

Opposite: A late afternoon buffet features (clockwise from front) Garlic Tart, Garlic Soup, Cider, and Baked Garlic Sausages.

Left: Homemade Garlic Jelly spooned over cream cheese.

ALTERNATIVES

—Substitute any good heat-and-serve sausage for the knackwurst.

Calorie counters
—Skip the appetizer.

EASY TIMETABLE

More than a month ahead
—Make garlic jelly.

Up to a week ahead
—Make and freeze garlic tart.

Two days ahead
—Sauté and chill garlic and onions.

One day ahead
—Chill cider.

Day of the party
—Make garlic soup.

Just before the party
—Bake garlic sausages.
—Reheat garlic tart.
—Open red wine to breathe.
—Spoon garlic jelly over cream cheese.

**SIMPLY DELICIOUS
DINNER**

For 4

*Harvest Chicken
with Vegetables
and Roasted Potatoes*

*Dry Chenin Blanc
or Gamay Beaujolais*

*Bartlett or Comice Pears
with Gorgonzola*

Coffee

Recipe on Page 111.

SIMPLY DELICIOUS DINNER

Here's one of those meals that is so easy and so good it's destined to become part of any busy cook's repertoire. A whole rosemary-fragrant chicken roasts with colorful vegetables in one pan while potatoes bake alongside. All you do is stir the vegetables occasionally while you set a casual but stylish table.

Dessert is another simple classic: whole Bartlett or Comice pears to peel (if you wish), quarter, core, and spread liberally with creamy Gorgonzola cheese.

Opposite: Present the Harvest Chicken surrounded with Vegetables and Roasted Potatoes.

Below: Spread ripe pears with creamy Gorgonzola or other blue cheese for a simple, delicious dessert with coffee.

SHOPPING LIST

4 thin-skinned potatoes (about 3 in. long)
3 large carrots
4 small patty pan squash
3 medium-size crookneck squash
2 large red or green bell peppers
1 head garlic
1 large onion
6 to 8 cherry tomatoes
10 to 12 sprigs fresh rosemary
4 ripe Bartlett, Comice, or other pears
3½- to 4-pound broiler-fryer chicken
⅓ to ½ pound Gorgonzola
1 or 2 bottles dry Chenin Blanc or Gamay Beaujolais

Staples
Dry rosemary (1 teaspoon) if fresh is not available
Coffee

EASY TIMETABLE

One day ahead
—Chill white wine.

Just before the party
—Cook chicken, vegetables, and potatoes.
—Arrange pears and cheese.

During the party
—Make coffee.

AN AUTUMN BRUNCH
Woodland brunch for 2

Sweet Sausage Balls
Jack Cheese
Buttermilk and Currant Scone
Sweet Butter
Champagne or Sparkling Wine
Coffee or Tea

Ripe Persimmons

Recipes on Page 112.

Stretch the traditional picnic season with a visit to view autumn color. Prepare the sausage balls the day before; the next morning, bake the big scone while you wrap a piece of cheese and some butter. Pour coffee or tea into a thermos and slip the chilled wine into a small ice chest or wine cooler. Pack it all in a hamper along with champagne glasses, plates, utensils, cups, and a knife—and head for the woods.

Or enjoy the brunch as a cozy indoor picnic. An arrangement of vivid-leafed branches adds an outdoorsy note to your table.

SHOPPING LIST

2 or 3 ripe persimmons (firm if flat-bottomed 'Fuyu' variety; very soft if oval 'Hachiya' variety)
1 orange (for peel)
4 mild Italian or fennel sausages
½ cup (¼ lb.) butter or margarine
¼ pound jack cheese
¼ cup buttermilk
3 tablespoons currants
Dry white wine for poaching (1 cup)
Champagne or sparkling wine

Staples
All-purpose flour (1 cup)
Sugar (about 2 tablespoons, plus enough for coffee, if desired)
Baking powder (1 teaspoon)
Baking soda (⅛ teaspoon)
Ground cinnamon (⅛ teaspoon)
Coffee
Cream or milk for coffee

ALTERNATIVES

—Choose your favorite breakfast sausage if Italian sausages are not available.
—Any semisoft mild cheese can substitute for the jack.
—Bring grapes or apples if persimmons aren't available.

Calorie counters
—Substitute a low-fat cheese.
—Serve the scone with whipped butter, a light-style margarine, or plain.

Budget watchers
—Sparkling apple juice adds elegant fizz at little cost.

EASY TIMETABLE

One day ahead
—Prepare and chill sausage balls.
—Chill champagne.

Just before leaving for the picnic
—Pack cheese, butter, and persimmons.
—Pack champagne in cooler.
—Cook sausage balls and pack in thermos.
—Bake scone and wrap in foil.
—Make coffee or tea and pack in thermos.

Opposite: Ready to be packed into a picnic hamper are (clockwise from top) Sweet Sausage Balls, Buttermilk and Currant Scone, Sweet Butter, Jack Cheese, and Ripe Persimmons.

Left: Japanese-type persimmons are cut into segments to be dipped into orange-flavored liqueur.

BIG BURGER
BEFORE THE BIG GAME

Tailgate cookout for 8

Anaheim Chilies
with String Cheese

Platter Burger
with Mexican Seasonings
on Round French Bread Loaf

Green Salad with Sunflower Seed

Ice Cold Beer or Iced Tea

Chocolate-Nut Squares

Recipes on Pages 113–114.

This showstopping burger for 8 is platter-sized to fit on a large round of French bread. Season the meat with Mexican spices; cook it on a grill, using two rimless baking sheets as spatulas; and top it with cheese, chilies, tomatoes, and avocado.

We've staged the party as a tailgate cookout, but it's equally at home in the backyard.

CHECKLIST

☐ Portable grill

☐ Charcoal, starter, and matches

☐ Ice chest packed with beer or iced tea and with watertight containers holding:

☐ Anaheim (California) chili slices

☐ string cheese

☐ avocado topping

☐ Cheddar cheese slices

☐ chilies, sliced tomatoes, olives

☐ Seasoned ground beef

☐ Buttered bread round

☐ Salad greens, sunflower seed, favorite salad dressing, bowl, and serving pieces

☐ Chocolate-nut squares in a box

☐ Two rimless baking sheets; waxed paper

☐ Disposable plates, utensils, glasses, and napkins

☐ Folding table and cloth

☐ Bottle opener for beer (if needed)

SHOPPING LIST

Salad greens
6 to 8 green or red Anaheim chilies
1 small onion
1 head garlic
2 medium-size ripe avocados
1 lemon (for juice)
2 medium-size tomatoes
6 to 8 ounces string cheese
8 ounces Cheddar cheese slices
1¼ cups (⅝ lb.) butter or margarine
3 eggs
2½ pounds ground lean beef
1 round loaf (24 oz.) French bread
1½ cups (about ½ lb.) filberts or almonds
3 ounces semisweet chocolate
¼ cup taco sauce
2 cans (4 oz. each) whole green chilies
1 small can (3¼ oz.) whole pitted ripe olives
2 or 3 six-packs beer

Staples
Dry oregano leaves (2 teaspoons)
Chili powder (2 tablespoons)
Ground cumin (1 teaspoon)
Sunflower seed (½ cup)
Salt
Garlic salt
Liquid hot pepper seasoning
Powdered sugar (about 1½ cups)
Cocoa (3 tablespoons)
Tea

ALTERNATIVES

—Green or red bell peppers can be used instead of Anaheim chilies; substitute mozzarella if you can't find string cheese.
—If large round loaves of French bread are not available, shape the burger to fit a long loaf.

Calorie counters
—Eliminate the cheese and enjoy the peppers alone.
—Serve fresh fruit for dessert instead of the chocolate-nut squares.

EASY TIMETABLE

One day ahead
—Bake chocolate-nut squares.
—Prepare and chill Anaheim chilies.
—Pack and chill chilies, tomatoes, and olives for burger.
—Season ground beef.
—Wash, dry, and chill salad greens.
—Make salad dressing and pack watertight.
—Mix butter and chili powder and prepare bread round.
—Pull apart string cheese.

Day of the party
—Prepare and chill burger patty.
—Make avocado topping.
—Make iced tea.
—Pack all perishables and beverages in ice chests.

At the site
—Shape burger patty.
—Arrange appetizer platter.
—Toss green salad.

During the party
—Cook and assemble the big burger.

Opposite: Decorate the table or tailgate with team colors. Strips of String Cheese are piled onto Anaheim Chilies, and the Platter Burger is cut into wedges.

Left: Filberts and almonds are combined in this version of Chocolate-Nut Squares.

DINNER AT EIGHT

Formal dinner for 8

*Oysters on the Half Shell
with Ginger-Vinegar Sauce*

Cocktails or Chardonnay

Chilled Beet Soup

Chicken with a Pocketful of Leeks

Green Beans   Two-Tone Rice

Sauvignon Blanc

*Green Salad
(optional)*

*Chocolate-Almond Torte
with Whipped Cream*

Coffee

Liqueurs

Recipes on Pages 115–117.

DINNER AT EIGHT

Almost everyone enjoys an occasional dress-up evening. Our menu for eight is easy as can be, but is glamorous enough for the most elegant of presentations.

It's time to polish the silver, wash the good china and crystal, iron the heirloom cloths, and perhaps reintroduce your friends or family to a bit of formality.

Start with cocktails or white wine in the living room—or on the terrace if the weather permits. The oyster bar is optional; you could pass any favorite fancy tidbit instead.

Dinner is served in four courses. Should it be a cool autumn evening, the soup can be heated just before serving. Steam or boil green beans, toss in butter or margarine, and garnish with nuts or lemon zest. Arrange dinner plates and salad plates in the kitchen, but present the dessert whole and slice it at the table. After coffee, offer a choice of liqueurs in the living room.

Opposite: Arriving guests enjoy Oysters on the Half Shell with Ginger-Vinegar Sauce, garnished with pickled ginger and lemon.

Below: First course at the table is Chilled Beet Soup topped with sour cream, green apple, and a sprig of fresh dill.

SHOPPING LIST

6 or 7 lemons
Small piece of fresh ginger root
Fresh dill (1 tablespoon chopped)
Fresh tarragon (1 tablespoon leaves)
Green onions (6 to 8 for ¾ cup sliced)
About 7 medium-size beets
1 large apple
4 or 5 large leeks
1 large onion
2½ to 3 pounds green beans
Salad greens (optional)

2 cups buttermilk
½ pint sour cream
2 cups whipping cream
2 cups (1 lb.) butter or margarine
5 eggs
4 whole chicken breasts (about 1 lb. each)
24 to 40 small oysters in shells
1 cup rice wine vinegar
5 cans (14½ oz. *each*) regular-strength chicken broth
About ¼ cup pickled ginger (optional)
¾ cup wild rice
¾ cup long grain rice
5 ounces semisweet or bittersweet chocolate

8 to 10 unblanched almonds
1 box zwieback crackers
Mirin (sweet rice wine) or cream sherry, (4 to 6 tablespoons)
Dry white wine for cooking (½ cup)
Cocktail ingredients or 2 bottles Chardonnay
2 to 4 bottles Sauvignon Blanc
Liqueurs
Bag of crushed ice

Staples
White wine vinegar (1 cup) if rice vinegar is not available
Oil and vinegar for salad dressing (optional)
Dry dill weed (1 teaspoon) if fresh is not available
Dry tarragon (1 teaspoon) if fresh is not available
Cream of tartar (¼ teaspoon)
Sugar (1½ cups, plus enough for coffee and whipped cream if desired)
Powdered sugar (1 tablespoon)
Instant coffee (1 teaspoon)
Cocoa (for dusting cake)
Coffee
Salt
Pepper

ALTERNATIVES

—Chicken breasts can be filled with sautéed mushrooms or onions when leeks are not available.

Calorie counters
—Serve poached pears or seasonal fruits instead of the chocolate dessert.

Budget watchers
—Serve a favorite appetizer instead of the oysters.
—Skip the liqueurs.

EASY TIMETABLE

One day ahead
—Make ginger-vinegar sauce for oysters.
—Make and chill beet soup.
—Sauté leeks.
—Prepare, stuff, and chill uncooked chicken breasts.

Day of the party
—Slice lemon wedges for oyster bar.
—Set up ingredients for cocktails and after-dinner liqueurs.
—Bake chocolate-almond torte.
—Chill white wine

Just before the party
—Open oysters and place on ice.
—Transfer soup to serving tureen.
—Whip cream for torte.
—Cook rice.
—Cook chicken breasts.
—Cook green beans.

During the party
—Make coffee.

Opposite: Chicken with a Pocketful of Leeks is an elegant main course with Green Beans with pine nuts and Two-Tone Rice, a mixture of white and wild rice.

Top right: Offer whipped cream with the Chocolate-Almond Torte.

A BIG BUFFET
THAT CAN GROW
Supper party for 25 to 125

*Cold Sliced Turkey,
Ham, Mortadella, and Roast Beef*

Cheese Tray

*Condiments:
Mayonnaise, Mustard,
Whole Cranberry Sauce
Vegetable Tray Salad
Parsley-Potato Salad
Fresh Fruit Salad
Pasta and Pepper Salad*

Pumpkin Bread	*Double Cheese Bread*
French Bread	*Butter*

Dry White and Red Jug Wines

Sparkling Water   Apple Cider

*Spice Cake with Caramel Icing
Seed Cake   Pork Sausage Cake
Coffee and Tea*

Recipes on Pages 118–120.

A BIG BUFFET THAT CAN GROW

Big parties—office bashes, club events, church socials, neighborhood gatherings, reunions, or holiday parties—have a habit of expanding at the last minute. It seems that everyone wants to bring along their house guests, visiting relatives, new friends, old friends, or special someone.

To help you cope with such possibilities, here is a buffet supper that can easily expand with just a little advance notice. The chart on page 57 shows how much food you'll need for every 25 guests. Recipes are scaled to 12 servings; twice the amount will serve 25. Duplicate, rather than multiply, recipes to be assured of good results.

The menu centers around cold sliced meats and cheeses, breads and condiments, make-ahead salads, and cakes for dessert. For super-easy entertaining everything, or at least part, could be purchased from delicatessens and bakeries.

However, if you want to do it all yourself, the secret is in working ahead. The cakes and breads can all be made weeks in advance and frozen, some actually improving in flavor as they mellow. The meats can be cooked ahead, sliced, and frozen if held for more than a day or two. Salads can be refrigerated for at least a day.

If the guest list outgrows your supply of dishes, glasses, and flatware, use high-quality paper partyware, or rent from a party supplier. The suggestions on page 150 will help you in dealing with a large crowd.

Opposite: Buffet features (clockwise from top) Cheese Tray, Parsley-Potato Salad, Assorted Cold Sliced Meats, and Pasta and Pepper Salad.

Below: Icing-dipped almonds garnish Spice Cake. Recipe makes more icing than shown here, and can completely cover cake.

TO PUT TOGETHER

Cold sliced meats
—Generously fill trays, making as many as you'll need. Line trays with lettuce leaves or garnish with parsley or watercress.

Butter
—Soften cubes and pack into a crock, smoothing top so that it looks attractive.

Condiments
—Limit the mustard selection to Dijon, which goes with everything. You can buy cranberry sauce or serve homemade.

Breads
—Purchase French bread or other local specialties. Try a few made-ahead loaves of the two recipes given, or substitute your own favorites.

Salads
—Choose vegetables and fruits that hold up well and do not wilt or darken. Go with equal quantities of at least three of the salads listed, or substitute your own favorites or good ones made by local suppliers.

Cheeses
—Limit the selection to 3 or 4 whole or large chunks of cheeses like Jarlsberg, Edam, Gouda, or jack. For large parties, buy bigger pieces instead of adding more variety. Place them all on the buffet at the beginning of the party, with knives for guests to cut the cheeses themselves. (Chunks of cheese stay fresher longer than slices or cubes.)

Cakes
—Slice cakes immediately before the party, keeping slices together for an attractive presentation and to preserve freshness. Provide cake servers so guests can help themselves.

Beverages
—Chill bottles in large plastic garbage cans or bags filled with ice. For serving, place bottles in tubs filled with ice. Borrow or rent electric coffee makers; remember that it takes 45 minutes to 1 hour for large machines to complete coffee. Put out plenty of disposable cups and spoons for self-service. If you choose to serve hot tea, have a coffee maker or large thermos filled with hot water and provide a selection of tea bags.

Autumn desserts include (clockwise from top) Double Cheese Bread, Seed Cake, Pork Sausage Cake, and sliced Pumpkin Bread served with Cranberry Sauce.

A BIG BUFFET THAT CAN GROW

Quantities required for buffet supper party

Number of guests	25	50	75	100	125
Cold sliced cooked meats (pounds)	8	16	24	32	40
Chunks of cheese (pounds)	7	14	21	28	35
Mayonnaise, as a condiment (cups)	1½	3	4½	6	7½
Dijon mustard (cups)	½	1	1½	2	2½
Whole cranberry sauce (cups)	3	6	9	12	15
Salads (gallons)	3	6	9	12	15
Breads (5- by 9-inch loaves)	2–3	3–4	4–5	5–6	6–7
Butter (pounds)	½	1	1½	2	2½
Cakes (10- to 12-cup size or 9-inch-diameter two-layer cakes)	2–3	4–5	6–7	8–9	10–11
Wine (cases)	1	2	3	4	5
Mineral water (quarts or liters)	6	12	18	24	30
Coffee (cups ground; use 1 cup per 2½ quarts of water)	3½	7	10½	14	17½

SHOPPING LIST FOR 25

For salads
4 large cucumbers
2 pounds beets
2 pounds carrots
6 large ripe avocados
2 large red or green bell peppers
4 pounds thin-skinned potatoes
1 large onion
1 head garlic
Fresh parsley (1¼ cups chopped)
Fresh tarragon (¼ cup chopped)
3 ounces (⅔ cup grated) Parmesan cheese
1 cup sour cream
1 pound small shell macaroni

Staples for salads
Mayonnaise (1 cup)
Salad oil (2 cups; or 3 cups if olive oil is not used)
Olive oil (1 cup)
Tarragon-flavored vinegar (1 cup)
White wine vinegar (about 1 cup)
Sugar (1 tablespoon)
Dry tarragon (2 tablespoons) if fresh is not available
Dry basil (2 tablespoons)
Salt
Pepper

For breads and cakes
1 lemon (for grated peel)
1 pound bulk pork sausage
15 eggs
3⅔ cups (about 2 lbs.) butter or margarine
1⅔ cups (plus ⅔ cup if used instead of white wine) milk
1 cup sour cream
⅓ cup half-and-half or whipping cream
About 6 ounces (1½ cups shredded) sharp Cheddar cheese
1 package (4 oz.) crumbled blue cheese
1 can (1 lb.) pumpkin
3 cups raisins
1½ cups chopped walnuts
1 cup pieces plus 1 cup chopped walnuts or pecans
Blanched almonds, pecan halves, holly leaves, and candied (glacé) whole cherries, for decoration
White wine (⅔ cup for double-cheese bread)

Staples for breads and cakes
Granulated sugar (9⅔ cups)
Brown sugar (2½ cups)
Powdered sugar (about 2¼ cups)
All-purpose flour (15⅓ cups)
Whole-wheat flour (1 cup)
Baking powder (about 3 tablespoons)
Baking soda (1 tablespoon)
Ground allspice (2 teaspoons)
Ground cinnamon (about 2 tablespoons)
Ground cloves (1 tablespoon)
Ground ginger (1½ teaspoons)
Ground nutmeg (½ teaspoon)
Pumpkin pie spice (2 teaspoons)
Poppy seed (2 tablespoons)
Sesame seed (1 tablespoon)
Caraway seed (1 tablespoon)
Anise seed (1 tablespoon)
Instant coffee (2 teaspoons)
Salt

EASY TIMETABLE

More than a month ahead
—Bake and freeze breads and cakes.

Up to three days ahead
—Cook and chill turkey, ham, and beef.

Two days ahead
—Soften butter and pack in crocks.

One day ahead
—Make and chill vegetable, pasta, potato, fruit salads.
—Slice meats; wrap tightly and chill.
—Buy cooked meats.

Day of the party
—Thaw breads and cakes.
—Chill white wine, sparkling water, and cider in tubs of ice.
—Assemble and garnish cold meat trays.

Just before the party
—Prepare cheese tray.
—Slice breads and cakes.
—Spoon mayonnaise, mustard, and cranberry sauce into bowls.
—Make coffee and tea.

During the party
—Replenish trays as needed.

WESTERN HARVEST
THANKSGIVING
Holiday buffet for 10 to 12

*Chilled Artichokes
with Herbed Goat Cheese*

*Roasted Squab or Quail
with Pears and Red Wine Sauce*

Wild Rice with Mushrooms

*Butter-steamed Brussels Sprouts
and Red Bell Peppers*

*Spaghetti Squash
with Orange-Filbert Butter*

Pueblo Bread

Chardonnay and/or Merlot

Fruit Salad Platter

*Nut Mosaic Tart
with Whipped Cream*

Custard Persimmon Pie

*Late-Harvest Riesling
or Sparkling Wine*

Coffee

Recipes on Pages 121–124.

American Thanksgiving traditions would be quite different had our forebears landed on the western shore instead of in New England. Pilgrim prayers of thanks for a harvest to see them through a bitter winter could have been for artichokes, persimmons, and quail instead of corn, pumpkins, and turkey.

Our holiday feast echoes tradition, but showcases the bounty of the West, which appears in markets everywhere this month.

For openers, artichokes team up with domestic goat cheese. Turkey is replaced by farmed quail or squab accompanied by pears poached and sauced in red wine. (Both of these birds are being grown commercially and shipped fresh or frozen.) Wild rice and mushrooms replace the traditional stuffing. We suggest a rich Chardonnay or a hearty red Merlot; or serve both and let guests decide which they prefer with the game.

Approximate the shiny glaze traditional on brick-oven-baked pueblo bread by placing a pan of water in a conventional oven. For 10 to 12 guests, make the recipe twice.

Light spaghetti squash strands tossed in fruit- and nut-flavored butter take the place of heavy sweet potatoes or yams. Brussels sprouts from the Pacific coastal fog belt pair up with sweet red bell peppers grown in California's hot farming valleys.

A colorful fruit salad platter features avocados, papayas, and red seedless grapes in a dressing of pineapple, lime, and mint; it's so good you won't miss the cranberries, although they would be appropriate because they're now being grown in the Northwest, too.

Climax the feast with a tart that's a rich mosaic of the West's nut harvest—Arizona pecans, California almonds and pistachios, Hawaii macadamias, Oregon filberts, and walnuts gathered from California, Oregon, and Washington. Accompany it with the custard persimmon pie—reminiscent of pumpkin pie—or persimmon pudding from a favorite recipe. After the dessert, pour a sweet late-harvest wine or a sparkling wine made in the champagne manner; both represent the harvest of western vineyards.

Adorn the table with a cornucopia brimming with western fruits, vegetables, and nuts. Brightly hued pottery dishes are appropriate, as are soft pastels reminiscent of the desert. Add a touch of early Spanish, Mexican, or West Coast Indian art if you have such accessories.

Opposite: Our Western Harvest feast features Roasted Quail (legs tied with blanched green onion tops) with Pears and Red Wine Sauce on a bed of Wild Rice and Mushrooms.

Right: Nut Mosaic Tart and Custard Persimmon Pie adorned with pastry leaves are rich dessert choices.

SHOPPING LIST

5 or 6 small artichokes
12 to 14 cherry tomatoes
1 large onion
5 or 6 shallots or 2 small red onions
2½ pounds small mushrooms (1 in. diameter or smaller)
2 pounds Brussels sprouts
2 large red bell peppers
2 spaghetti squash (about 3 lbs. each)
6 medium-size Bosc or Comice pears or 12 Seckel or other miniature pears
2 large oranges
2 limes
1 large pineapple
2 large papayas
1 pound seedless red grapes
2 large avocados
Fresh mint
1 cup (about ⅓ lb.) shelled filberts
3 cups (about 1 lb.) assorted shelled nuts, whole or halves (almonds, walnuts, filberts, macadamias, pistachios, or pecans; use one kind or equal parts of 3 varieties)
1 package yeast (active dry or compressed)
6 ounces unripened domestic chèvre (goat cheese) with herb coating
5 cups (2½ lbs.) butter or margarine
2 cups whipping cream
4 eggs
10 to 12 squab or 20 to 36 quail
6 cups regular-strength chicken broth
1 can (14½ oz.) regular-strength beef broth
2 cups (about ¾ lb.) wild rice
1 cup honey
1 bottle dry red wine (for sauce)
3 or 4 bottles Chardonnay or Merlot (or 2 of each)
2 bottles late-harvest Riesling or 3 bottles sparkling wine

Staples

White wine vinegar (½ cup)
Olive oil or salad oil (⅓ cup)
Bay leaves (2)
Whole black peppers (2 teaspoons)
Dry basil (1 teaspoon)
Dry mint leaves (2 tablespoons) if fresh is not available
Dry thyme leaves (¾ teaspoon)
Ground nutmeg (½ teaspoon)
Prepared mustard (1 teaspoon)
Salt
Pepper
Granulated sugar (about 1 cup)
Brown sugar (2 tablespoons)
Vanilla (1 teaspoon)
All-purpose flour (6⅓ cups)
Coffee

ALTERNATIVES

—French goat cheese (such as Bucheron) can be used in place of domestic; if neither is available, Boursin or another creamy herbed cheese is good.
—Rock Cornish hens can replace squab or quail.
—Substitute green for red bell peppers.
—Though it's not as much fun, winter squash can fill in for spaghetti squash; mash and mix with flavored butter.
—-Green seedless grapes are usually available even if red ones are scarce.

Calorie counters
—Provide a little lemon-flavored butter for dipping artichoke leaves.
—Enjoy a ripe persimmon instead of the rich tart.
—Relax; it's a holiday!

Budget watchers
—Roast Rock Cornish hens instead of costly quail or squab.
—Serve a good dry jug wine throughout the meal.
—Bake a pumpkin pie instead of the nut tart or persimmon pie.

EASY TIMETABLE

One day ahead
—Cook and chill artichokes.
—Steam and chill Brussels sprouts.
—Cut and chill pineapple and prepare dressing for fruit salad.
—Chill Chardonnay and dessert wine.
—Roast nuts for tart.
—Make and chill tart shell.
—Purée persimmons (for optional pie).

Day of the party
—Poach pears in red wine.
—Prepare and chill fruit salad platter.
—Whip cream for tart.
—Bake tart.
—Bake persimmon pie (optional).

Just before the party
—Blend goat cheese and assemble appetizer platter.
—Roast birds and keep warm.
—Cook wild rice and mushrooms.
—Bake squash and make orange-filbert butter.
—Cook Brussels sprouts and peppers.
—Open Merlot to breathe.

During the party
—Finish sauce for birds and pears.
—Add avocado and dressing to salad platter.
—Make coffee.

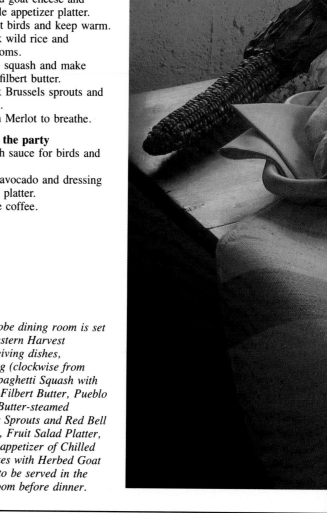

This adobe dining room is set with Western Harvest Thanksgiving dishes, including (clockwise from front) Spaghetti Squash with Orange-Filbert Butter, Pueblo Bread, Butter-steamed Brussels Sprouts and Red Bell Peppers, Fruit Salad Platter, and the appetizer of Chilled Artichokes with Herbed Goat Cheese to be served in the living room before dinner.

BIG BREAKFAST BONANZA

Supersize pancake for 6

Freshly Squeezed Orange Juice
Big Dutch Baby Pancakes
Powdered Sugar　　Lemon Wedges
Warm Honey and Syrups
Sliced or Sautéed Fresh Fruits
Sliced Ham
Coffee or Tea

Recipes on Page 125.

BIG BREAKFAST BONANZA

West Coast cooks have several versions of these spectacular oven pancakes that have come to be known as Dutch Babies. The egg-rich batter puffs up during its half hour in the oven and makes the most dramatic presentation when cooked in a big pan. But if you don't have a large enough pan, several small pancakes are equally delicious.

A few minutes before the pancake is ready, seat everyone at the table and pour the fresh juice. You don't want anyone to miss the spectacular presentation when the pan filled with the puffy Dutch Baby (soon to deflate) comes to the table.

Cut the pancake into wedges and serve with powdered sugar and lemon wedges. Also offer warm honey and your favorite syrups, fresh sliced or sautéed seasonal fruits, and sour cream or yogurt. For a group of hearty eaters, pop a second pancake into the oven when you take out the first one.

For breakfast entertaining, set the table the night before and have all the ingredients prepared, measured, and ready before going to bed.

Giant Dutch Babies make great lunch or supper entrées as well.

SHOPPING LIST

2 lemons or limes
About 24 oranges
3 or 4 large apples or pears,
    or about 4 cups sliced
    fresh fruit
1¼ cups (⅝ lb.) butter or
    margarine
3 cups milk
12 eggs
½ cup sour cream or yogurt
1½ pounds sliced baked ham
Maple and/or fruit syrups
Honey

Staples

All-purpose flour (1½ cups)
Granulated sugar
Powdered sugar (about ½ cup)
Cinnamon
Ground nutmeg
Coffee or Tea
Cream or milk for beverage

ALTERNATIVES

Calorie counters
—Lightly sprinkle powdered sugar on the pancake and drizzle with lemon juice; or top with plain fresh fruit and a dab of yogurt.
—Skip the ham.

EASY TIMETABLE

One day ahead
—Select pan or pans and assemble ingredients.

Just before the party
—Squeeze orange juice.
—Warm ham slices.
—Warm honey and syrups.
—Make coffee.
—Cut and sauté the fruit.
—Make pancake batter and bake pancake.

Opposite: As guests finish one Big Dutch Baby Pancake with fresh fruits and sliced ham, a second pancake comes piping hot from the oven in a paella pan.

Left: Hefty glasses of Freshly Squeezed Orange Juice begin the Big Breakfast Bonanza.

WINTER WARM-UP
Cold-day lunch or dinner for 6

Hot Buttered Cauliflower Soup
Crusty Bread

Spinach-filled Pasta Roll
with Tomato-Cream Sauce
Watercress and Apple Salad
Chianti Classico or Barbera

Chestnuts in Port
Espresso

Recipes on Pages 126–127.

WINTER WARM-UP

Crisp weather calls for the warmth of friends and nourishing fare. This Italian-inspired menu features the produce of winter: cauliflower in a creamy soup topped with swirls of melting butter, spinach stuffed into an easily prepared pasta roll accompanied or followed by a simple salad of watercress and crunchy apples, and fresh chestnuts saturated with port.

Omit the little bit of prosciutto or ham in the spinach stuffing and you have a perfect vegetarian menu.

No recipe is necessary for the salad. On each salad plate simply arrange sprigs of watercress with slices of cored red and green apples. Drizzle with good-quality olive oil and a bit of raspberry vinegar or red wine vinegar; or use your favorite vinaigrette. Sprinkle generously with freshly ground black pepper.

Wine-muddled chestnuts are a perfect ending after the rich pasta course. Serve with port if you desire. Pass warm moistened cloth napkins to clean hands after peeling and eating the nuts.

Establish the Italian atmosphere with traditional red, green, and white decorations or set the table with ultramodern accessories in the style of industrial Milan.

SHOPPING LIST

1 medium-size cauliflower (about 1½ lbs.)
2 large leeks
2¼ pounds spinach
2 onions (1 large; 1 small)
1 pound mushrooms
1 large carrot
About 3 cups watercress
3 medium-size apples (2 red, 1 green)
1 pound chestnuts
⅓ cup pine nuts
4 eggs
1½ cups whipping cream
1 cup (½ lb.) butter or margarine
1 pound ricotta cheese
6 ounces Parmesan cheese
1 ounce prosciutto
2 cans (14½ oz. *each*) regular-strength chicken broth
1 can (28 oz.) whole pear-shaped tomatoes
1 large loaf crusty bread
Ruby or Tinta port (½ cup)
2 or 3 bottles Chianti Classico or Barbera

Staples
All-purpose flour (about 1⅓ cups)
Sugar (¼ cup plus ½ teaspoon, and enough for espresso)
Olive oil or salad oil (2 teaspoons plus enough for salad dressing)
Raspberry vinegar or red wine vinegar (for salad dressing)
Ground nutmeg (¾ teaspoon)
Salt
Pepper (¼ teaspoon)
Ground dark-roast coffee for espresso

Opposite: Hot Buttered Cauliflower Soup begins a cold-day lunch that features Spinach-filled Pasta Roll.

Left: Chestnuts glazed in port top off the meal.

ALTERNATIVES

—If fresh chestnuts are not available, serve glacéed chestnuts.

Calorie counters
—Don't sugar chestnuts, or serve pears or segmented oranges instead.
—Omit butter in soup.
—Skip the bread.

Budget watchers
—Use cooked ham rather than prosciutto.
—Serve fresh fruit instead of chestnuts.

EASY TIMETABLE

Up to three days ahead
—Make soup.

One day ahead
—Make spinach filling for pasta roll.
—Make tomato-cream sauce.
—Wash and crisp watercress.

Day of the party
—Make pasta, assemble roll, and cook.

Just before the party
—Reheat soup.
—Bake pasta roll.
—Reheat tomato-cream sauce.
—Complete salad.
—Open wine.

During the party
—Heat bread if desired.
—Roast chestnuts.
—Complete chestnuts in port.

COME FOR CHOCOLATE AND COFFEE

A tasting for 10 to 50

Tasting of several brands of bittersweet, semisweet, milk, and white chocolate

Spirited Chocolate Fondue with Seasonal Fruits, Nuts in Their Shells, and Dried Fruits

Assorted Fancy Cookies

Dry Red Wine (Cabernet Sauvignon, Pinot Noir, or Zinfandel)

Coffee Bar Several Roasts with Assorted Liqueurs and Toppings

Recipes on Page 128.

Who could resist an invitation to a chocolate tasting? Guests not only get to sample a variety of chocolates, but to taste several red wines that are highly touted companions to chocolate desserts. At the end of the evening a coffee bar allows each person to compare several roasts spiced with a selection of additions and toppings.

The flavor and texture of chocolate depends on the type of cacao beans blended by the manufacturer and how long the chocolate is treated to the conching process (heating the chocolate and grinding it between rollers). The longer chocolate is conched, the smoother and more expensive it is.

Select domestic or imported (from Belgium, France, Germany, Holland, Italy, and Switzerland) chocolates: bittersweet, semisweet, milk, and white. Provide as many as your budget allows. Check grocery stores, fancy food delicatessens, and candy shops.

Chop chocolate into small chunks, arrange them separately and by varieties (such as all milks) side by side, and number each mound. Provide a chart and pencils for judging. Rate according to:

☐ **Appearance.** Shiny to dull.
☐ **Aroma.**
☐ **Flavor.** Including off-flavors and aftertaste.
☐ **Melting point.** How quickly it dissolves on your tongue.
☐ **Sweetness.** Too sweet or too bitter.
☐ **Texture.** Creamy, grainy, waxy, or lumpy.

Should you choose to serve the red wines, make them available during the chocolate tasting and with the fondue.

Leftover chocolate samples can be used in the fondue, which is quick to make after the tasting. In the likely case that all the chunks will be eaten, purchase enough extra chocolate for the fondue. Before the party starts, cut the seasonal fruits into bite-size pieces and arrange them—as well as the nuts, dried fruits, and cookies—in baskets or on trays.

Opposite: Chocolates are featured with fresh and dried fruits, nuts, and cookies for dipping in Spirited Chocolate Fondue. The chalkboard suggests coffee bar recipes.

Buy at least three different roasts of coffee, plus a decaffeinated type. Make them in electric coffee makers just as the chocolate tasting begins, or brew and pour into thermal pots to keep them warm. Label each type so that guests can serve themselves.

Put out cups or mugs from the household miscellany, or rent matching ones. Provide the toppings, seasonings, liqueurs, and spirits listed in the recipe. Write out several recipes on a chalkboard or posterboard behind the coffee bar to get the guests started with their concoctions.

SHOPPING LIST

For each guest you will need

¼ pound of chocolate for tasting and fondue
4 pieces each of fresh fruit (such as strawberries, coconut, pineapple, kiwis, pears, tangerines, oranges, apples—brush cut surfaces of apples and pears with lemon juice to prevent darkening) and dried fruits, nuts, and cookies
⅓ bottle dry red wine
2 cups coffee
1 tablespoon grated semisweet chocolate for coffee
1 tablespoon unwhipped cream
1 stick cinnamon

Additionally you will need

Bowl or shaker of sugar for coffee
Container of lemon-zest strips (allow 1 lemon for 10 guests)
Bowl of cardamom pods
Several whole nutmegs and grater
3 or 4 bottles of different liqueurs
1 bottle brandy or Cognac
1 bottle light or dark rum
1 bottle whiskey (Irish, Scotch, Canadian, American rye, or bourbon).

EASY TIMETABLE

One day ahead
—Chop chocolate samples and store airtight.
—Assemble ingredients for coffee bar.

Day of the party
—Cut and chill fresh fruit.
—Whip cream for coffee.
—Put out chocolates for the tasting (with chart and pencils for notes).

Just before the party
—Arrange fresh and dried fruits, nuts, and cookies in serving pieces.
—Heat water under chafing dish.
—Open red wines to breathe.
—Make coffees.

During the party
—Make chocolate fondue.

HOLIDAY FIESTA
A Mexican-American party for 12

Stuffed Cheese Appetizer

*Tomatillo, Jicama,
and Apple Salad*

Chile con Queso

Mexican Chili-Cheese Logs

*Turkey in Molé Sauce
with Warm Tortillas*

Guacamole

*White   Margarita
Sangria Punch   Wine Punch*

Tropical Fruits

Walnut Butter Cookies

Coffee

Recipes on Pages 129–132.

For an unusual, fun-filled evening of Christmas cheer, stage a Mexican-American holiday fiesta.

Welcome guests with illuminated walkways (fill paper bags halfway with sand to hold a votive candle; light just before party time.) Festoon the house with colorful decorations. Hang ribbons, crepe-paper streamers or garlands, and a piñata if available. Make big bouquets of holiday greens mixed with bright flowers.

Sing carols and trim the tree if you like—both activities fit the Mexican tradition. Climax the evening with the breaking of the piñata. (Choose a place where nothing else is likely to be damaged as well.) Provide bags or little baskets for guests to take home the candies and treats they catch.

Recipes serve 12; for a larger party, duplicate the recipes once or twice rather than multiplying them. All dishes have steps that can be completed ahead. A few will need last-minute reheating or garnishing. Provide plenty of colorful paper napkins—most of the dishes are finger foods.

Tropical fruits are the perfect ending. Crack open fresh coconuts for guests to break apart. Slice pineapples, mangos, and papayas if you can find them, and don't forget the bananas.

If it's a family affair, provide a fruit punch or citrus juice in addition to the wine-based punches.

Opposite: Turkey in Molé Sauce is wrapped with Guacamole in Warm Tortillas. Mexican paper doilies and a pine cone basket of fresh fruits decorate the table.

Right: White Sangria Punch and Margarita Wine Punch enliven the festivities.

Buffet includes (clockwise from top) Chile con Queso with vegetables for dipping; Tomatillo, Jicama, and Apple Salad; Stuffed Cheese Appetizer; and Mexican Chili-Cheese Logs.

SHOPPING LIST

(Per 12 guests)

3 tart, green-skinned apples
2 medium-size avocados
1 large tomato
12 to 16 fresh green California (Anaheim) chilies
4 onions (3 medium-size; 1 large)
1 head garlic
1 lemon
4 or 5 limes
1 small (1½ lbs.) jicama or a 1½-pound piece of a larger root
12 tomatillos
Fresh cilantro (coriander) leaves (½ cup chopped plus ½ cup whole)
Assorted tropical fruits for dessert (⅓ to ½ lb. per person)
Assorted vegetables for dipping (5 or 6 pieces per person)
1¾ to 2 pounds jack, teleme, or Longhorn Cheddar cheese
10 ounces sharp Cheddar cheese
1¼ cups (⅝ lb.) butter or margarine
4 eggs
1 pound ground lean pork
1¼ pounds bulk pork sausage
1 pound ground turkey
1 turkey breast (4½ to 5 lbs.) or 2 broiler-fryer chickens (3½ to 4 lbs. *each*)
2 cans (14½ oz. *each*) pear-shaped tomatoes
1 large can (7 oz.) chopped green chilies (plus 2 more cans if fresh chilies are not available)
2 cans (4 oz. *each*) whole green chilies
½ cup taco sauce
1 small can (5⅓ oz.) evaporated milk
1 jar (4 oz.) Spanish-style pimiento-stuffed olives

1 can (4 oz.) sliced ripe olives
1 can (14½ oz.) regular-strength beef broth
2 cans (14½ oz. *each*) regular-strength chicken broth
¼ cup sesame seed
½ cup raisins
2 ounces semisweet chocolate
1 dozen corn tortillas or 1 bag (7½ oz.) tortilla chips
2 dozen flour or corn tortillas
1 cup chopped walnuts
3 cans (6 oz. *each*) frozen limeade concentrate
3 cans (6 oz. *each*) frozen lemon-limeade concentrate
1 can (12 oz.) frozen lemonade concentrate
1 can (6 oz.) frozen orange juice concentrate
2 jugs (1.5 L. *each*) dry white wine

Staples
Salad oil (¼ cup, plus enough to fry tortillas)
Wine vinegar (2 teaspoons)
Cornstarch (1 tablespoon)
Granulated sugar (2 teaspoons, plus extra for coffee if desired)
Powdered sugar (1¼ cups)
Cake flour (2 cups)
Firm-textured bread slices (2)
Ground coriander (¼ teaspoon)
Chili powder (¼ cup)
Ground cinnamon (1¼ teaspoons)
Ground allspice (¼ teaspoon)
Ground cumin (¾ teaspoon)
Cumin seed (¾ teaspoon)
Ground cloves (1 teaspoon)
Cayenne (½ teaspoon)
Garlic powder (¼ teaspoon)
Liquid hot pepper seasoning
Instant minced onion (2 tablespoons)
Dry oregano leaves (1½ teaspoons)
Beef bouillon cube
Vanilla (1 teaspoon)
Salt
Coarse salt
Green food coloring (optional)
Coffee
Cream for coffee

ALTERNATIVES

—A well-stocked supermarket should have all the Mexican products you'll need.

Calorie counters
—There are plenty of foods on the menu for dieters. Go easy on the guacamole and skip the cookies.

Budget watchers
—You could offer domestic beer instead of the wine punch, or serve a fruit punch without alcohol.
—Serve tangerines, tangelos, or oranges instead of the tropical fruits.

EASY TIMETABLE

More than a month ahead
—Make and freeze chili-cheese logs.
—Freeze ice rings for punches.
—Make and freeze walnut butter cookies.

Up to a week ahead
—Make and chill molé sauce.

Two days ahead
—Cook turkey or chicken for molé.
—Make and chill meat and sauce for stuffed cheese appetizer.

One day ahead
—Start *chile con queso.*
—Prepare and chill raw vegetable dippers.
—Fry tortillas for stuffed cheese appetizer.

Day of the party
—Make and chill quacamole.
—Slice and chill some of the tropical fruits.
—Combine ingredients for punches.
—Prepare tomatillo, jicama, and apple salad.

Just before the party
—Assemble stuffed cheese appetizer.
—Add cheese to *chile con queso.*
—Fill punch bowls.
—Make coffee.

FIRESIDE DINNER
For 2

Tangerine Sauced
Roasted Duckling
with
Baked Whole Onions and Yam Chunks

Zinfandel

Endive Salad

Liqueured Coffee
with Whipped Cream

Recipes on Page 133.

After the rush of the holidays, the time is right for a quiet evening by the fire. Or plan the meal as a Valentine treat.

A special friend or two are bound to enjoy crisp-skinned ducks in tangerine sauce served with chunks of roasted yams and succulent whole baked onions. Who would guess it's so easy on the cook?

Drizzle leaves of Belgian endive with a bit of walnut oil and a squeeze of fresh lemon juice, or make your favorite dressing.

Linger by the fire with a cup of cream-topped liqueured coffee. See page 128 for some suggested variations, or create your own.

Opposite: Baked Whole Onions (cut in half) and Yam Chunks surround Tangerine Sauced Roasted Duckling.

Above: Endive leaves are topped with the white part of green onions, walnuts, and lemon peel for an easy and elegant salad.

SHOPPING LIST

3 or 4 onions (2 or 3 medium-size; 1 small)
About 1½ pounds yams
1 head Belgian endive
2 or 3 tangerines
1 lemon (optional) for salad
1 cup whipping cream
1 duckling (4½ to 5 lbs.)
1½ tablespoons honey
Walnut oil (optional) for salad
1 bottle Zinfandel
Liqueur for coffee

Staples
Sugar (to sweeten whipped cream if desired)
Cornstarch (2 teaspoons)
Bay leaf
Salt
Pepper
Coffee

ALTERNATIVES

—You could serve a chicken rather than the duck.
—A salad of watercress or butter lettuce could replace the endive.

Calorie counters
—End the meal with plain coffee.
—Serve chicken instead of duck.

Budget watchers
—Roasted chicken would be less expensive.
—Prepare a salad of watercress or butter lettuce.
—Skip the liqueur unless you have it in stock.

EASY TIMETABLE

One day ahead
—Wash and chill endive leaves.

Day of the party
—Start tangerine sauce.
—Whip and chill cream for coffee.

Just before the party
—Roast duckling, yams, and onions and complete tangerine sauce.
—Open Zinfandel to breathe.

During the party
—Dress endive salad.
—Make coffee.

CHINESE NEW YEAR CELEBRATION

Guest-participation
dinner for 8 to 10

Winter Melon Soup with Crab

Coriander Chicken Salad

Sweet and Sour Deep-fried Fish
Peking Beef with Chinese Pea Pods

Eight Immortal Jai

Steamed Rice

Gewürztraminer

Almond Custard
with Loquats or Mandarins

Almond Cookies

Tea

Recipes on Pages 134–137.

A Westernized celebration of the turning of the Chinese lunar calendar enlivens an otherwise bleak January.

Our streamlined version of a six-course banquet is filled with Chinese symbolism: Winter melon represents the season, while the crab added to the soup promises a fertile new year. Chicken and lettuce cut into long, thin strips mean a long life. The whole fish stands for totality and its red sauce offers good luck. The stir-fry vegetable dish commemorates eight ancient monks (called immortal jai). The combination of beef with edible-pod peas signifies the philosophy of balance, as does the contrast of orange loquats or mandarin oranges with white cubes of almond custard. Add a bowl of whole tangerines and traditional paper packets of money for each guest to take home, and your table is blessed with luck and prosperity.

A quick look at the menu might lead you to think that this party doesn't qualify as easy entertaining. Rest assured that the soup, salad, and dessert can be completed ahead. You can also make sauces for the fish and jai, marinate the beef, and cut all the vegetables. The secret of successful Chinese cooking is to have all the ingredients ready to add to each dish. Assemble components on the counter just before party time for last-minute help from a fellow cook or a team to finish the three main dishes, which are served together. While one cook fries the fish, another stir-fries vegetables and then beef in the same pan. You'll need two woks, or two large frying pans, or one of each. Plan on about 15 minutes in the kitchen during the party.

You can present the meal in courses—soup followed by chicken salad; then the fish, vegetables, and beef; and finally the dessert. Wine and tea accompany the entire meal. Chinese tradition also allows for everything to be placed on the table at one time and enjoyed together. The choice is yours.

Chinese-American homes are decked with branches of flowering quince and pyramids of tangerines and oranges at this time of year. Red and gold—popular colors for the occasion—might guide your tablesetting. Be sure to include chopsticks for everyone, but have forks in reserve for the timid. Tradition calls for firecrackers, but if local fire laws rule them out, you can settle for sparklers.

Don't forget to check on the symbol of the new year and include the dog, pig, lion, dragon, monkey, or whatever among your characters.

Opposite: Winter Melon Soup with Crab, served from a carved whole winter melon, dramatically begins the celebration.

Above: Almond Custard with Mandarin Oranges and Almond Cookies offers a happy ending to the meal. Traditional tangerines and Chinese money packets promise luck and prosperity.

SHOPPING LIST

—You should be able to find everything you need in a well-stocked supermarket, but if you live near a Chinese community, don't miss out on the authenticity and fun of shopping at an Oriental grocery.

—Whatever purchases are left after the banquet can be used to prepare both Oriental and Western dishes. Hoisin sauce is an excellent condiment or a basting or barbecue sauce for pork and poultry. Both soaked black mushrooms and cloud ears can be chopped and used in salads or sautéed in butter to serve over cooked eggs, vegetables, or meats. Winter melon and dried lotus seeds are good soup additions. Salted Tientsin (Tianjin) preserved vegetables add interest to soups and salads. Substitute Oriental sesame oil for part of the oil in salad dressings, marinades, or stir-fry dishes. Kanten (agar-agar), made from seaweed, can be used in place of gelatin. (One package of gelatin equals about half a stick of kanten.)

Oriental market
1 well-shaped winter melon (10 lbs.)
¾ pound Chinese edible-pod peas
½ to ¾ cup soy sauce
About ⅓ cup Oriental sesame oil
1 tablespoon hoisin sauce
1 can (about 7 oz.) bamboo shoots
1 can (about 2¼ oz.) water chestnuts
1 can (16 oz.) loquats or 2 cans (11 oz. *each*) mandarin oranges
½ cup dried lotus seeds
About 8 dry Oriental mushrooms
¾ ounce dry black fungus (cloud ears)
1 teaspoon Chinese five spice powder
1 tablespoon Tientsin preserved vegetables (optional)
About ⅜ ounce white kanten (agar-agar)
Almond cookies
Green tea

Other markets
Small piece of fresh ginger
½ pound zucchini (if winter melon is not available)
1 or 2 lemons
¼ pound mushrooms (if dry Oriental mushrooms are not available)
2 heads iceberg lettuce
Fresh coriander (Chinese parsley) leaves (¼ cup chopped plus sprigs for garnish)
2 to 3 green onions (¼ cup sliced)
1 small green bell pepper
1 small tomato
1 pound broccoli
3 or 4 carrots
2 small onions
1 head garlic

1 package (10 oz.) frozen peas
5 cans (14½ oz. *each*) regular-strength chicken broth
2 to 3 cups long- or medium-grain rice
½ cup sesame seed
3 envelopes unflavored gelatin (if kanten is not available)
1 small can (5⅓ oz.) evaporated milk
½ cup unsweetened pineapple juice
½ pound boneless pork chops
1 whole red snapper or rock cod (2 to 2½ lbs.)
¼ pound crab meat
About 1 ounce cooked ham
1 broiler-fryer chicken (3¼ to 3½ lbs.)
1 pound lean beef steak
Dry sherry (⅓ cup)
3 or 4 bottles Gewürztraminer

Staples
Dry mustard (1 tablespoon)
Salad oil (2 to 3 cups)
Sugar (about 1½ cups)
Ground cinnamon (½ teaspoon) if five spice is not available
Cornstarch (about ¾ cup)
Catsup (generous ½ cup)
Red wine vinegar (⅔ cup)
Worcestershire (2 teaspoons)
Liquid hot pepper seasoning
Almond extract (1 teaspoon)

ALTERNATIVES

—Each recipe gives available alternatives for Oriental products and vegetables.

Calorie counters
—Everything should be allowed in normal servings; go easy on the sweet and sour sauce, white rice, and almond cookies.

Budget watchers
—There are no singularly expensive items; the cost is in stocking Oriental products, but keep in mind that they can be used later.
—Omit wine and serve only tea, or pour a good dry white jug wine.

EASY TIMETABLE

Two days ahead
—Marinate and chill chicken.

One day ahead
—Cook chicken, strip meat, and chill.
—Make chicken salad dressing.
—Prepare, marinate, and chill beef.
—Rinse and dry fish, rub with sherry, and chill.
—Make and chill almond custard.
—Chill Gewürztraminer.

Day of the party
—Make soup.
—Cook winter melon shell (optional).
—Make and chill sweet and sour sauce.
—Make sauce for eight immortal jai.
—Complete dessert.

Just before the party
—Arrange chicken salad on platter.
—Reheat soup and pour into melon shell or tureen.
—Cook rice.
—Make green tea.

During the party
—Fry fish and place on warm platter while you reheat and finish sweet and sour sauce.
—Cook and combine pea pods and beef.
—Stir-fry eight immortal jai.

Opposite: Main dishes for the banquet include (clockwise from top) Steamed Rice, Peking Beef with Chinese Pea Pods, Sweet and Sour Deep-fried Fish, Eight Immortal Jai, and Coriander Chicken Salad.

WINTER SALAD SUPPER
A buffet for 12

Jicama with Oranges

*Beets and Pears
with Dandelion Greens*

Parsnips with Crackling Pork

*Soy-braised Onions
with Daikon and Carrot*

Turnips with Mustard Greens

Celery Root with Green Beans

Cold Sliced Roast Beef or Turkey

Baguettes and Butter

Assorted Cheeses

Sauvignon Blanc and Zinfandel

Mulled Cider

*Fresh Orange Baba-rin
(optional)*

Recipes on Pages 138–140.

We end a year of entertaining with a celebration of the garden bounty available even in midwinter. Salad parties are normally warm-weather treats, but for this chilly-evening buffet, humble root vegetables star in a collection of sophisticated salads as fresh and party-worthy as any of their fair-weather counterparts.

Set up the salad platters in the kitchen or other cozy place, near a roaring fire. Add cold sliced roast beef, turkey, or other favorite meats; cheeses; and baguettes and a crock of butter. Apple cider slowly simmered with cinnamon, cloves, and other winter spices is the perfect accompaniment.

Dessert is not essential because several of the salads include fruit, but we've included a recipe for a "soggy cake" (page 140) as an optional addition to the menu if your crowd favors sweets. It's dubbed a baba-rin—a name that, like the cake, combines savarin (a very light,

porous, yeast-raised cake traditionally soaked with a liqueur-flavored syrup) with baba (about the same, but with raisins). This refreshing orange-flavored dessert has some characteristics of each of the two cakes, yet contains no liqueur or raisins. To serve 12 people, you'll need to make two cakes.

Opposite: Clockwise from top: Cold Sliced Turkey, Celery Root with Green Beans, Beets and Pears with Dandelion Greens, and Jicama with Oranges.

Below: Clockwise from top: Soy-braised Onions, Parsnips with Crackling Pork, Turnips with Mustard Greens, and Assorted Cheeses.

SHOPPING LIST

3 medium-size oranges (1 for juice)
1 or 2 limes (for juice)
1 or 2 lemons (for juice)
1 medium-size pear
1 small red-skinned apple
¾ pound jicama
2 medium-size beets (about 3-in. diameter)
1 piece daikon (about 6 in. long and 1½ in. thick)
2 medium-size carrots
2 medium-size turnips (about 2½-in. diameter)
1 celery root (1½ to 1¾ lbs.)
1 small red onion
1 pound small white onions
¾ pound tender parsnips
1 small red bell pepper
¼ pound green beans
1 head butter lettuce (or 2 or 3 heads if mustard greens are not used in Jicama with Oranges recipe)
About 4 cups mustard greens
Dandelion greens (to make 3 cups shredded)
1 head garlic
1 small piece fresh ginger (about 1 in. long)
Fresh coriander (cilantro), 1 to 2 tablespoons leaves
Fresh parsley (2 teaspoons chopped)
1 cup (½ lb.) butter or margarine
Assorted cheeses
½ pound boneless pork shoulder

12 thin slices dry salami
Beef or turkey for roasting (allow ¼ lb. boneless cooked meat per person)
About 2 tablespoons chopped walnuts
1 can (2 oz.) anchovy fillets
1 jar (2 oz.) diced pimiento (if red bell pepper is not available)
3 or 4 baguettes
1 gallon apple cider
4 or 5 bottles Sauvignon Blanc and/or Zinfandel

Staples

Dijon mustard (2 teaspoons)
Distilled white vinegar (2¼ cups, plus 1½ tablespoons if white wine vinegar is not used)
White wine vinegar (1½ tablespoons)
Salad oil (about 1 cup)
Soy sauce (¾ cup)
Honey (2 teaspoons)
Sugar (about ¾ cup)
Sesame seed (2 teaspoons)
Dry thyme leaves (¾ teaspoon)
Pepper
Cinnamon sticks and other winter spices (for mulled cider)

Ingredients for 2 Fresh Orange Baba-rins (optional)

12 oranges (for juice and grated peel) plus 6 to 8 large oranges (for sectioning)

1½ cups (¾ lb.) butter or margarine
14 eggs
2 cups milk
2 cups whipping cream
2 packages active dry or compressed yeast
3½ cups sugar
4 cups all-purpose flour
1 teaspoon coriander seed
Salt

ALTERNATIVES

—If your market doesn't have jicama root, use fresh apples. (Dip in lemon juice to retain white color.)
—If you can't find dandelion greens, shredded curly endive or escarole can substitute.
—Turnips or rutabagas can fill in for parsnips or daikon. (For the sake of variety, however, don't substitute turnips in more than one salad.)
—If celery root is not available, prepare more of the other salads or add a favorite recipe of your own.

Calorie counters

—Here's a party where you can indulge—except for the butter, of course.

Budget watchers

—Serve just mulled cider, or substitute a good dry white or red jug wine for the varietals.

EASY TIMETABLE

One day ahead

—Slice and chill oranges and jicama.
—Roast beef or turkey while you cook vegetables.
—Cook, slice and chill beets.
—Cook and chill crackling pork.
—Slice, cook, and chill parsnips.
—Cook soy-braised onions and store, covered, at room temperature.
—Shred and chill daikon and carrots.
—Cook and chill turnips.
—Cook and chill celery root and green beans separately.
—Wash, dry, and chill all greens.
—Make mustard vinaigrette for beets.
—Make anchovy dressing.
—Chill Sauvignon Blanc.
—Bake cake and pour orange syrup over (optional).
—Make and chill orange custard (optional), but do not add cream.

Day of the party

—Whip cream, fold into orange custard, and chill (optional).

Just before the party

—Warm cider with spices.
—Open Zinfandel to breathe.
—Complete jicama and orange salad.
—Complete beet and pear salad.
—Complete onion, daikon, and carrot salad.
—Complete celery root and green bean salad.
—Warm cracklings and complete parsnip salad.
—Reheat turnips and complete salad with mustard greens.

During the party

—Slice oranges and assemble cake (optional).

Recipes
FOR EASY ENTERTAINING

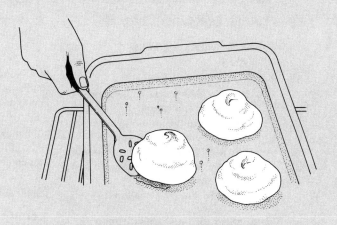

SPRING GARDEN SUPPER

For 4
(Pictured on Pages 6–7)

Fresh Tiny Peas in the Pod
Fruity Chenin Blanc

Young Vegetable Platter
with Sliced Ham and Green Sauce
Croissants with Sweet Butter
Chilled Dry Zinfandel Rosé

Lemon Ice
Coffee

Fresh Tiny Peas

32 to 40 tender young pea pods

Rinse and drain pea pods and serve in a bowl or basket, accompanied by a chilled fruity wine. Shell peas to eat. Allow 8 to 10 pea pods per serving.

Young Vegetable Platter

3 or 4 medium-size leeks
Water
1 pound slender asparagus
½ pound edible-pod or sugar snap peas or green beans
1 medium-size (about 1⅔ lbs.) green cabbage, preferably Savoy
¾ to 1 pound thinly sliced cooked ham or plain or smoked turkey, chicken, or pheasant
Green Sauce (recipe follows)

Trim tough tops and roots from leeks and pull off coarse outer layer. Split lengthwise and rinse under cool running water. Tie each half leek together at midsection with twine or a strip of leek green that has been blanched in boiling water for about 45 seconds.

Snap tough ends from asparagus, pull strings from peas, and cut cabbage through core into 4 to 6 wedges.

In a 5- to 6-quart pan on highest heat, bring 3 quarts water to a boil. Cook vegetables uncovered (use a wire basket for easy removal), one kind at a time, pushing down into liquid, until bright green and just barely tender when pierced; 3 to 4 minutes for leeks, about 4 minutes for cabbage, about 3 minutes for asparagus, and 2 to 3 minutes for peas.

Remove vegetables from water (use a slotted spoon or lift out basket) and immerse at once in ice water. When cold, lift out and drain. (If done as early as the day before, cover and chill.)

Arrange vegetables on a platter with ham or other meat and accompany with Green Sauce. Serves 4.

Green Sauce

1 egg
3 tablespoons fresh lemon juice
½ cup packed watercress leaves
1 tablespoon fresh tarragon *or* ½ teaspoon of the dry herb
2 teaspoons Dijon mustard
1 cup salad oil

In a blender at high speed or in a food processor, whirl egg, lemon juice, watercress, tarragon, and mustard until fairly smooth. Slowly pour in oil. (If made ahead, cover and chill as long as overnight.) Makes about 1⅔ cups.

Lemon Ice

2 to 3 cups Sugar Syrup (recipe follows)
2 cups fresh lemon juice mixed with 2 cups water

Mix Sugar Syrup to taste with lemon juice and water.

Pour mixture into container of regular or self-refrigerated ice cream maker and freeze according to manufacturer's directions. Serve when just frozen, or firm by packing with 1 part salt to 8 parts cracked ice, or store covered container in the freezer up to one month. Firming takes 1 to 2 hours. (To make hard ice easy to scoop, let it stand at room temperature to soften slightly, about 10 minutes for a full batch.) Makes about 1½ quarts.

Sugar Syrup

2½ cups *each* sugar and water

In a 2- to 3-quart pan, bring sugar and water to boil over high heat; boil 5 minutes. Let cool. Use, or cover and chill indefinitely. Makes 3 cups.

Sushi Selections

⅓ cup seasoned rice vinegar for sushi
or 4 teaspoons sugar dissolved in
⅓ cup distilled or white wine
vinegar

2 medium-size carrots, peeled,
cut into 3- to 4-inch pieces,
and then cut lengthwise into fine
julienne strips
Water
About 1 pound spinach, stems
discarded, leaves washed

2 small ripe avocados

½ cup fresh lemon juice

½ English cucumber, peeled, cut into
3- to 4- inch pieces, and then cut
lengthwise into fine julienne strips

1 bag (3½ oz.) fresh enoki mushrooms, brown ends trimmed off

½ pound each cooked and shelled crab
and cooked and shelled
medium-size prawns or small
whole shrimp

½ pound boned, skinned, thinly sliced
yellowfin tuna, sea bass, halibut,
or snapper (or some of each)

¼ pound thinly sliced smoked salmon

¼ cup (2 oz.) salmon caviar

In a 2- to 3-quart pan, bring sushi
vinegar to a boil. Add carrots; cook
and stir just until tender-crisp to bite,
about 30 seconds; drain. Remove
from pan and set aside.

Rinse cooking pan. Add 1 inch water
and bring to a boil. Gently push
spinach down into water. Cook and
stir just until limp, about 1 minute;
drain and set aside.

Halve, pit, and peel avocados. Slice
lengthwise into strips about ⅛ inch
thick. Place in a bowl with lemon
juice; moisten each slice to prevent
browning. Set aside.

On a large tray, separately arrange
carrots, spinach, avocado, cucumber,
mushrooms, crab, prawns, tuna,
salmon, and salmon caviar. (If made
ahead, cover and chill up to 5
hours.) Serve slightly cool or at room
temperature. Serves 6.

Sushi Rice

3 cups short-grain rice
Water

⅓ cup seasoned rice vinegar for sushi
or 4 teaspoons sugar dissolved in
⅓ cup distilled or white wine
vinegar

In a 3- to 4-quart pan, cover rice
with water and stir; drain. Rinse
repeatedly until water is clear; drain.

Add 3½ cups water to rice. Cover
and bring to a boil over high heat.
Reduce heat to low and cook without
stirring until all water is absorbed,
about 15 minutes.

Stir in vinegar. Spread rice equally
on 2 rimmed 10- by 15-inch baking
pans. Stirring, cool quickly until no
longer steaming, fanning with a piece
of cardboard or a hand-held hair
dryer on cool setting. Let stand to
cool to room temperature. (If made
ahead, cover tightly and hold at room
temperature up to 1 day.) Spoon rice
into a serving bowl. Serves 6.

Seaweed Wrappers

1½ ounces roasted or unroasted nori
(dark green paper-thin sheets of
seaweed)

Roasting (more accurately, toasting)
brings out the green color and makes
nori crisper. To toast your own, draw
a sheet of nori back and forth over a
low gas flame or electric burner set
on low until nori becomes quite crisp
(see page 84). With scissors, cut
roasted nori into 4- to 5-inch squares.
(If made ahead, let cool; then package airtight for several hours.) Stack
nori on a plate or in a basket. Makes
enough for 6 servings.

Wasabi Paste

3 tablespoons wasabi powder (Japanese hot horseradish)
3½ teaspoons water

Stir wasabi powder with water until smooth. Divide into 6 equal portions. Pinch into small cones and place one cone on each serving plate. Serves 6.

Toasted Sesame Seed

¼ cup sesame seed

In a 10- to 12-inch frying pan over medium-high heat, stir sesame seed until golden, 3 to 5 minutes. Reserve 4 teaspoons toasted seed for Sesame Sauce. Spoon remainder into 1 or 2 small serving bowls.

Sesame Sauce

1 cup mayonnaise
4 teaspoons *each* honey and toasted sesame seed (directions precede)
1½ teaspoons Oriental sesame oil

Stir together mayonnaise, honey, sesame seed, and sesame oil. Spoon into 1 or 2 small serving bowls. Makes about 1 cup sauce.

MAKING SUSHI

Move unroasted seaweed sheet (nori) back and forth over low gas flame or electric burner set on low until seaweed is crisp.

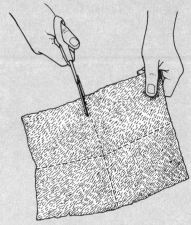

With scissors, cut toasted seaweed into 4- to 5-inch squares.

Hold a piece of seaweed in your palm, spoon a small quantity of sushi rice into the center, and top sparsely with one or a combination of items from the sushi tray, adding wasabi, sesame sauce, or toasted sesame seed to taste.

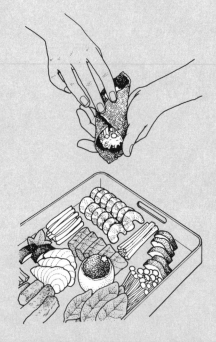

Bring corners of seaweed around to enclose the filling. Dip bite by bite into soy sauce.

BIRDWATCHER'S BREAKFAST

An early morning party for 6
(Pictured on Pages 12–13)

Orange and Grapefruit Segments
Soft-cooked Eggs
Beehive Bread
Wildflower Honey   Sweet Butter
Coffee or Tea

Golden Beehive Bread

- 1 **package active dry yeast**
- ¼ **cup warm water (about 110°)**
- ½ **cup (¼ lb.) butter or margarine, at room temperature**
- ½ **cup sugar**
- 1 **tablespoon grated lemon peel**
- ⅓ **cup warm milk (about 110°)**
- ½ **teaspoon salt**
- 5 **eggs**
- 5½ **to 6 cups all-purpose flour**
- 1 **egg beaten with 1 tablespoon milk**

In a large bowl, add yeast to water; let stand about 5 minutes. Stir in butter, sugar, lemon peel, milk, salt, and eggs until blended. Gradually beat in 5 cups of the flour; then turn onto a floured board and knead, adding more flour as required, until dough is smooth and elastic. Turn over in a greased bowl, cover with plastic wrap, and let rise in a warm place until doubled.

Punch dough down; then knead briefly on a floured board to release air. Return to greased bowl; turn dough over. Cover with plastic wrap; chill 1 to 24 hours.

Wrap the outside of a 2- to 2½-quart ovenproof glass or metal mixing bowl (about 9 inches in diameter and 4 inches deep) with foil, folding excess inside. Grease foil generously and invert bowl on a greased 12- by 15-inch baking sheet.

Punch dough down and knead briefly on a floured board. Divide dough into 20 equal pieces. Working with 1 or 2 pieces at a time (keep remaining dough covered and chilled), roll each portion into a rope about ⅜ inch thick and 18 to 20 inches long.

Pinch ends of 2 ropes together and twist. Starting at bowl rim, wrap twist around bowl. When adding a new twist, pinch ends together to join them.

Keep bowl in refrigerator to prevent uneven proofing as you roll ropes. With a 2½-quart bowl, you may not quite cover the entire bowl, but you can leave a small opening at the top of the hive. (Extra dough can be formed into rolls: Shape into 2-inch balls and let rise on greased baking sheet until almost doubled; bake in a 375° oven until browned, 15 to 20 minutes.)

Cover shaped dough loosely with plastic wrap and let rise in a warm place until puffy, 20 to 30 minutes. Gently brush with egg and milk mixture.

Bake in a 350° oven until well browned, 25 to 30 minutes. Let cool on bowl on a rack for about 10 minutes. Crumple a large piece of foil into a loose ball of the same diameter as the depth of the bowl; set foil ball in the center of a rack.

Gently remove bread from bowl, using a small spatula if needed to free bread; set bread over foil ball so that it supports top of hive (loaf is fragile when hot) until bread is almost cool. Serve warm, or if you will transport it, cooled.

If made ahead, cool, wrap well, and freeze. Thaw, uncovered, at room temperature; then place on a baking sheet in a 350° oven; heat until warm, 7 to 10 minutes. Serve open side down for a beehive or open side up for a basket (trim bottom, if needed, so that basket rests flat). To eat, tear off serving-size pieces. Makes 1 large loaf.

SHAPING BEEHIVE BREAD

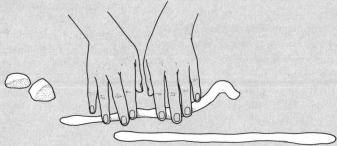

Divide dough into 20 equal pieces. Working with 1 or 2 pieces at a time, roll each portion into a rope about ⅜ inch thick and 18 to 20 inches long.

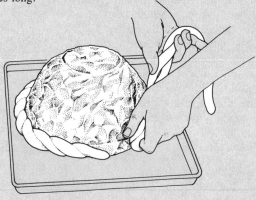

Pinch ends of 2 ropes together and twist. Starting at the rim of a greased, foil-covered bowl, wrap twist around bowl. When adding a new twist, pinch ends together to join.

Gently remove baked bread from bowl and set over foil ball to support top of hive until bread is almost cool.

Wheat-flecked Beehive Bread

2 packages active dry yeast
2 cups warm water (about 110°)
2 tablespoons honey
1 teaspoon salt
¼ cup (⅛ lb.) butter or margarine, at room temperature
2 cups whole-wheat flour
½ cup wheat germ
3½ to 4 cups all-purpose flour
1 egg beaten with 1 tablespoon milk

Sprinkle yeast over water in a large bowl; let stand about 5 minutes to soften. Stir in honey, salt, and butter. Beat in whole-wheat flour and wheat germ. Gradually beat in 3 cups of the all-purpose flour. Turn dough out onto a floured board and knead until smooth and elastic, adding more flour as required to prevent sticking. Turn dough over in a greased bowl, cover with plastic wrap, and keep in a warm place until almost doubled, about 45 minutes.

Punch dough down; knead briefly on a floured board to release air. Return to greased bowl, turning to grease top. Cover with plastic wrap and chill 1 to 24 hours.

Shape and bake as directed for Golden Beehive Bread. Because whole-wheat dough is more elastic, make each dough rope about ¼ inch thick and 25 inches long. Makes 1 large loaf.

SALAD-SANDWICH BUFFET

A do-it-yourself lunch for 8
(Pictured on Pages 14–17)

Curried Chicken Salad

Tuna Salad

Marinated Mushroom Salad
Celery Root Salad

Ratatouille Salad

*Thinly Sliced Ham
and Swiss Cheese*

Mayonnaise   Mustard

Butter or Leaf Lettuce

Buttered Baguettes

Chablis or Iced Tea

Homemade Fresh Banana Gelato

Curried Chicken Salad

- ½ cup mayonnaise
- ½ teaspoon garlic salt
- 1 teaspoon curry powder
- ⅛ teaspoon cayenne
- ½ teaspoon prepared mustard
- 2 teaspoons fresh lemon juice
- 2 tablespoons finely chopped Major Grey's or other mango chutney
- 3½ cups cold cooked chicken, cut into about ½-inch chunks
- ⅔ cup thinly sliced celery
- 2 thinly sliced green onions, tops included
- 1 small apple, diced
- 3 tablespoons toasted sliced almonds

In a medium-size bowl, combine mayonnaise, garlic salt, curry powder, cayenne, mustard, lemon juice, and chutney. Add chicken, celery, green onions, and apple, and stir to blend. Cover and chill if made ahead. Just before serving, sprinkle top with almonds. Makes 4½ cups.

Tuna Salad

- 1 cup tomato-based chili sauce
- ¼ cup fresh lemon juice
- 2 cloves garlic, minced or pressed
- 1 teaspoon dry basil *or* 1 tablespoon of the fresh herb
- 2 teaspoons prepared horseradish
- 1 small onion, chopped
- ½ cup whole pitted ripe olives
- 2 cans (about 7 oz. *each*) solid light tuna, including oil
  Peperoncini (Italian pickled peppers), if desired

Stir together chili sauce, lemon juice, garlic, basil, and horseradish. Add onion and olives. Cover and chill if made ahead.

Just before serving, add tuna and mix gently just until lightly coated with sauce. Garnish with several peperoncini if desired. Makes 4 cups.

Marinated Mushroom Salad

- 1¼ pounds small mushrooms, washed, and ends trimmed
  Salted water
- 6 tablespoons olive oil
- 2 tablespoons fresh lemon juice
- 1 clove garlic, pressed
- ½ teaspoon *each* crushed whole black pepper, coriander seed, and mustard seed
- 1 small onion, finely chopped
- ½ cup chopped parsley
  Salt

Place mushrooms in boiling salted water to cover and simmer, uncovered, 5 minutes. Drain and let cool.

Mix together olive oil, lemon juice, garlic, pepper, coriander seed, and mustard seed. Add the mushrooms, onion, and parsley, and salt to taste; stir to blend. Cover and marinate at room temperature, stirring occasionally, for at least 2 hours. (If made ahead, refrigerate; remove early enough for oil to come to room temperature before serving.) Serve in marinade. Makes 3½ cups.

Celery Root Salad

- 6 tablespoons olive oil
- 3 tablespoons white wine vinegar
- 1 teaspoon each sugar and caraway seed
- 1 clove garlic, minced or pressed
  Salt
- 1¼ pounds (about 2 medium-size) celery root, peeled, washed, and cut into thin matchstick-size pieces (about 3½ cups)
- ¼ cup mayonnaise

Combine olive oil, vinegar, sugar, caraway seed, garlic, and salt to taste. Stir in celery root. Cover and marinate at room temperature, stirring occasionally, for about 2

PREPARING CELERY ROOT

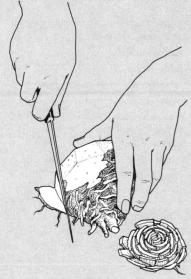

Cut off top of celery root. Peel away outside of root.

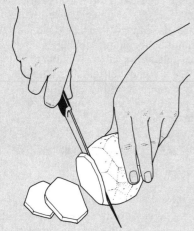

Slice into ⅛-inch rounds.

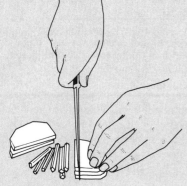

Cut through several slices at a time into matchstick pieces.

hours. (If made ahead, refrigerate; remove early enough for oil to come to room temperature before serving.) Just before serving, pour salad into a strainer or colander to drain off excess marinade; reserve for dressing green salads if desired. Mix celery root with mayonnaise. Makes 3 cups.

Ratatouille Salad

- 1 medium-size onion, finely chopped
- 1 clove garlic, minced or pressed
- 3 tablespoons olive oil
- 1 small (about ¾ lb.) eggplant, cut into 1-inch cubes
- 1 medium-size zucchini, cut into ½-inch-thick slices
- 1 medium-size green pepper, cored, seeded, and cut into ¼-inch strips
- ¼ cup chopped parsley
- 1 can (14½ oz.) pear-shaped tomatoes including liquid
- 1 teaspoon *each* dry basil and salt
- ⅓ cup grated Parmesan cheese

In a 10- to 12-inch frying pan over medium heat, cook onion and garlic in olive oil, stirring, until limp. Add eggplant, zucchini, green pepper, parsley, tomatoes and their liquid, basil, and salt. Break tomatoes into small pieces with a spoon.

Cover and simmer, stirring occasionally, until all vegetables are tender when pierced, about 25 minutes. Cook, uncovered, stirring occasionally, over high heat until most of the liquid has evaporated. Cool, cover, and chill if made ahead. Serve at room temperature with Parmesan cheese to sprinkle over individual servings. Makes 4 cups.

Fresh Banana Gelato (Italian ice cream)

- 3 cups milk
- ¾ cup sugar
- ½ vanilla bean (a 2- to 3-inch section) *or* 1 teaspoon vanilla extract
- 3 thinly pared strips of lemon peel (each about 2 inches long)
- 6 egg yolks
- 3 medium-size ripe bananas
- 3 tablespoons fresh lemon juice

In a 3- to 4-quart pan, combine milk, sugar, lemon peel, and vanilla bean (or omit vanilla bean and substitute vanilla extract, as directed below). Stir over medium heat just until sugar is dissolved.

Gradually whisk 1 cup of the warm milk mixture into egg yolks in a bowl; then pour egg mixture into pan, whisking. Continue to cook, stirring constantly, until liquid coats the back of a metal spoon in a thin, even, smooth layer; this takes about 10 minutes. (Do not bring to scalding or custard will curdle.)

Pour through a fine wire strainer into a large bowl; discard peel. (Rinse vanilla bean, let dry, and save for later use as long as it has a strong vanilla fragrance.) If you did not use vanilla bean, add vanilla extract to gelato base at this point. Cool to room temperature.

Smoothly mash or purée bananas and combine with lemon juice. Stir 1 cup of the cooled gelato mixture into the bananas until well blended; then gradually stir in remainder. Freeze in a regular or self-refrigerated ice cream maker, following directions provided by the manufacturer. Serve when just frozen, or firm by packing with 1 part salt to 8 parts cracked ice, or placing in a covered container in the freezer; firming takes 1 to 2 hours. If made ahead and hard-frozen, let the ice cream soften slightly at room temperature (about 10 minutes for a full batch) before scooping. Freeze no longer than 1 month. Makes about 1½ quarts.

AFTER THE EGG HUNT

Easter dinner for 8
(Pictured on Pages 18–21)

*Steamed Mussels Provençal
with Baguettes and Butter*
Gamay Beaujolais Blanc

Roast Lamb in Crust
New Potatoes Rosemary
Pistachio-buttered Asparagus
Petite Sirah

*Spinach Salad with Shallots
and Crumbled Cheese*

Seasonal Fruits in Cooky Baskets
Coffee

Steamed Mussels Provençal

3 cloves garlic, minced or pressed
1 small onion, chopped
½ cup chopped celery
3 tablespoons butter or margarine
1 can (1 lb.) tomatoes
⅛ teaspoon cayenne
**1 cup dry white wine or regular-
strength chicken broth**
½ cup minced parsley
⅛ teaspoon pepper
**2 quarts fresh mussels in shells,
cleaned**
**About ½ cup melted butter or
margarine**

In a 4- to 5-quart pan over medium heat, cook garlic, onion, and celery in the 3 tablespoons butter, stirring occasionally, until soft. Add tomatoes, with their liquid, and cayenne; simmer, covered, for 15 minutes. Add wine, parsley, and pepper; cook, covered, until the mixture boils.

Add mussels, cover, and simmer gently until the mussels open, about 8 to 10 minutes; discard any that don't open.

With a slotted spoon, transfer mussels to individual bowls; ladle cooking broth evenly over servings or into small cups. Serve with melted butter for dipping mussels. Serves 8 as a first course, 2 or 3 as an entrée.

CLEANING MUSSELS

Touch the edge and inside muscle of an open mussel. A fresh one will close immediately.

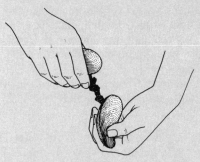

Pull off the beard which connects uncleaned mussels.

With a sharp knife, scrape off encrustations on shell. Then scrub with a brush.

Rinse thoroughly in several changes of cold water, or under cold running water.

Roast Lamb in Crust

- **1 boned and tied leg of lamb (4 lbs.)**
- **1 package active dry yeast**
- **2½ cups warm water (110°)**
- **2½ teaspoons salt**
- **2 tablespoons olive oil or salad oil**
- **7½ to 8 cups all-purpose flour**
- **4 cloves garlic, minced**
- **1½ tablespoons *each* minced fresh sage and rosemary leaves *or* 1½ teaspoons *each* of the dry herbs, crumbled**
- **½ teaspoon salt**
- **¼ teaspoon pepper**
- **⅓ cup finely chopped parsley**
- **1 teaspoon cornstarch mixed with ⅔ cup water**
- **1 cup regular-strength beef broth**

Place lamb, fat side up, on a rack in a roasting pan measuring about 11 by 14 inches; insert a meat thermometer in thickest part of lamb. Bake in a 325° oven until thermometer registers 150° for medium-rare lamb (20 to 25 minutes per pound). Cool at room temperature 1 hour; then cover meat and pan drippings separately and chill up to 2 days.

For the crust, dissolve yeast in water in a large mixing bowl; stir in the 2½ teaspoons salt and the oil. With a heavy-duty mixer or a heavy spoon, beat in enough of the flour (about 7 cups) to make a stiff dough. Turn dough out onto a floured board and knead until smooth and satiny, adding flour as required to prevent sticking. Turn dough over in a greased bowl, cover with plastic wrap, and let rise in a warm place until doubled, about 1½ hours. If made ahead, punch dough down, cover, and chill. Punch down again after 24 hours; dough will keep up to 48 hours.

Mix together garlic, sage, rosemary, salt, pepper, and parsley. If made ahead, cover and chill.

About 2 to 3 hours before serving, remove roast and dough for crust from refrigerator. Cut strings off

LAMB IN CRUST

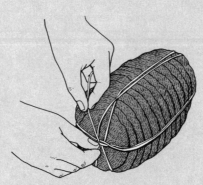

Cut roasted meat into slices ¼ to ⅓ inch thick. Reassemble roast and wrap string around it 2 or 3 times to hold slices together.

Spread half the parsley mixture in a strip about the width of the roast down the center of the rolled dough and set meat on top. Sprinkle remaining parsley mixture over roast. Brush edges of dough with water.

Fold sides of dough over roast.

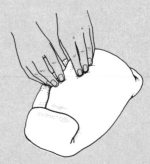

Dough edges should overlap slightly at center; press together. Fold in ends and pinch to seal.

Place roast, seam-side down, in a greased, shallow baking pan. After dough rises, decorate top with leaves cut from scraps of dough. Prick in 3 or 4 places around sides with a fork.

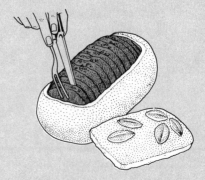

To serve, cut off top crust with a sharp knife, cut and discard top string, and lift out meat slices.

roast and trim off excess fat. Cut meat into ¼- to ⅓-inch-thick slices. Reassemble roast and wrap string around it 2 or 3 times to hold slices together. Using a tape measure or string, measure circumference of roast at thickest point; also measure its length.

Punch dough down, turn out onto a lightly floured board, and roll to make a rectangle about ¼ inch thick. Cut the rectangle 2 inches longer than the roast's circumference and 3 inches wider than its length. Cover and chill trimmings up to 24 hours longer to make Seasoned Bread Rounds (recipe follows) for another day.

Using half of the parsley mixture, spread a strip about the size of the roast down the center of dough, and set meat on top. Sprinkle remaining parsley mixture over meat. Brush edges of dough with water and fold sides of dough over roast so that edges overlap slightly at the center; press together. Fold in ends and pinch to seal.

Place roast, seam side down, in a greased shallow 10- by 15-inch baking pan. Let stand, lightly covered, in a warm place until dough is slightly puffy, 30 minutes to 1 hour. Meanwhile, bring cornstarch-and-water mixture to a boil, stirring; let cool.

Brush dough with half of the cornstarch mixture. With a fork, prick dough around the sides in 3 or 4 places. If desired, roll out a portion of dough about ⅛ inch thick and cut out decorative shapes. Brush bottoms with water and press gently into crust. Bake in a 375° oven for 15 minutes. Again brush dough with cornstarch mixture; return to oven and bake until golden brown, 35 to 40 minutes longer.

Meanwhile, lift fat from reserved pan drippings and combine drippings with beef broth to make pan-juice gravy. Just before serving, heat to boiling.

To serve, cut top off crust with a sharp knife, lift out meat slices, and cut or break crust into serving pieces. Pass pan-juice gravy to spoon over meat and crust. Serves 8.

New Potatoes Rosemary

24 to 32 small (1- or 2-inch diameter) thin-skinned red potatoes (about 4 cups), scrubbed
   About ¾ cup olive oil
½ cup minced red onion or shallots mixed with 2 tablespoons fresh lemon juice
6 to 8 sprigs (3- to 4-inch) fresh rosemary or 2 teaspoons of the dry herb
   Salt

Arrange potatoes in a single layer in a shallow rectangular or oval 9- by 13-inch pan. Pour oil around to make a ¼-inch-deep layer. Stir in onion lemon-juice mixture and top with about 4 sprigs of fresh rosemary.

Bake in a 400° oven, shaking occasionally to rotate potatoes in oil, until the largest give readily when pressed, 25 to 40 minutes.

Serve garnished with additional fresh rosemary sprigs. Salt to taste. Serves 8.

Seasoned Bread Rounds

Form leftover dough for crust into 2-inch balls. On a greased 10- by 15-inch baking sheet, flatten them into 5- to 6-inch rounds. Sprinkle lightly with garlic salt and minced fresh or crumbled dry rosemary (or make extra parsley-garlic mixture for the Roast Lamb in Crust). Press seasonings into the bread rounds and brush with olive oil or salad oil. Let stand in a warm place until slightly puffy, about 20 minutes. Bake in a 375° oven until golden, about 20 minutes. Serve warm.

Pistachio-buttered Asparagus

3 pounds asparagus, tough ends snapped off
   Water
¾ cup (⅜ lb.) butter or margarine
2 tablespoons fresh lemon juice
¾ teaspoon dry marjoram
¾ cup chopped pistachio nuts

In a 5- to 6-quart pan, cook asparagus, uncovered, in boiling water to cover until just barely tender when pierced, 5 to 8 minutes. Drain and arrange on serving platter.

Meanwhile, melt butter with lemon juice, marjoram, and pistachios until sizzling; pour over the cooked asparagus and serve. Serves 8.

Spinach Salad with Shallots and Crumbled Cheese

⅛ cup finely slivered shallots or red onion
½ tablespoon Dijon mustard
¼ cup white wine vinegar
½ cup salad oil
3 quarts small spinach leaves, rinsed, dried, and chilled
½ cup (4 oz.) crumbled blue cheese or California chèvre (goat cheese)

Combine shallots, mustard, vinegar, and oil. Cover and keep as long as 2 days.

Mix spinach with shallot dressing just before serving and sprinkle with crumbled cheese. Serves 8.

Seasonal Fruits in Cooky Baskets

½ cup (¼ lb.) butter or margarine

½ cup each firmly packed brown sugar and light corn syrup

7 tablespoons all-purpose flour

1 cup finely chopped nuts

2 teaspoons vanilla

Vanilla ice cream or sweetened whipped cream

3 to 4 cups fresh seasonal fruit, cut in bite-size pieces if necessary

In a 1- to 2-quart pan, melt butter over low heat. Add brown sugar and corn syrup. Cook over high heat, stirring constantly, until liquid boils; remove from heat and stir in flour and nuts until blended. Stir in vanilla.

Grease and flour 12- by 15-inch or 14- by 17-inch baking sheets. (They must be flat, not warped.) For each cooky, place 2 to 3 tablespoons of the batter about 8 inches apart on the sheet. (Depending on pan size and cooky size, you can bake only 1 or 2 cookies at a time.) If the batter has cooled and does not flow easily, evenly press or spread it out to a 4-inch circle. Bake in a 325° oven (you can bake 2 pans at a time, staggering the pans in the oven and changing them halfway to ensure even browning) until a rich golden brown all over, about 12 minutes. Let cool on pan on a wire rack until cooky firms up slightly, about 1 minute.

When cooky edges are just firm enough to lift, loosen edges from pan with a wide spatula; then slide spatula under entire cooky to remove. Lift cooky—it should still be hot and flexible (somewhat stretchy), but cooled until firm enough to move and not pull apart. Turn cooky over and drape over a glass that measures about 2 inches across the bottom. With your hand, gently cup cooky around the base;

make bottom flat and flare cooky out at sides. (If cooky becomes too firm to shape, return to the oven a few minutes until pliable.) Let shaped cooky cool until firm, about 2 minutes. Gently remove. Repeat, using remaining batter, and greasing and flouring baking sheets each time.

Use baskets at once, or store airtight in rigid containers at room temperature for up to 1 week; freeze for longer storage. Immediately before serving, place a small scoop of ice cream or whipped cream in each basket and top with fruit. Serve immediately. Serves 8 to 12.

SHAPING COOKY BASKETS

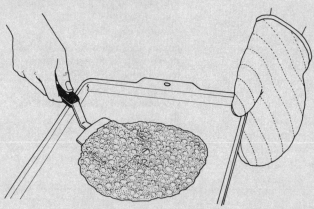

Cool cooky just until firm enough to move and not pull apart, but still hot and flexible. When edges of cooky are just firm enough to lift, loosen edges from pan with a wide spatula, then slide spatula under entire cookie to remove from sheet.

Turn cooky over and drape over a glass that measures about 2 inches across the bottom. With your hand, gently cup cooky around the base, flatten bottom, and flare out at sides to form a basket. Let shaped cooky cool until firm, about 2 minutes. Gently remove from the glass.

To serve, place a small scoop of ice cream in each basket and top with fruit.

LATE NIGHT ROMANCE

An elegant supper for 2
(Pictured on Pages 22–23)

*American Golden Caviar
on Pan-fried Potato Slices
with Sour Cream*

*Young Asparagus and Shrimp
with Homemade Mayonnaise*

Champagne or Sparkling Wine

Chocolate Truffles

Young Asparagus and Shrimp with Homemade Mayonnaise

1 **pound asparagus, tough ends snapped off**
Water
1 **to 1½ cups medium-size shrimp, cooked in their shells**
Cherry tomatoes (optional)
Homemade Mayonnaise (recipe follows)

Gently flick off asparagus scales with a paring knife, or if you wish, peel the stalk. (The flavor will be less pronounced and slightly sweeter if stalks are peeled.)

In a 10- to 12-inch frying pan, lay spears parallel (no more than 2 or 3 layers deep) in boiling water to cover. Boil until easily pierced, 5 to 8 minutes. Drain at once. Plunge the hot spears into a bowl of ice water; when cool, drain and chill. If made ahead, refrigerate as long as overnight.

For each serving, arrange half of the chilled spears on a plate. Spoon half of the shrimp on top; if desired, garnish with cherry tomato flowers or whole cherry tomatoes. Pass Homemade Mayonnaise. Serves 2.

Homemade Mayonnaise

1 **whole egg *or* 3 egg yolks (yolks yield a thicker, more golden sauce)**
1 **teaspoon Dijon mustard**
1 **tablespoon white wine vinegar or fresh lemon juice**
1 **cup salad oil**
Salt and fresh lemon juice to taste

In a blender or food processor, combine egg or yolks, mustard, and the 1 tablespoon vinegar. Whirl on high speed until well blended. Slowly add oil in a thin stream. If desired, mix in salt and lemon juice. Use, or cover and refrigerate up to a week. Makes 1½ cups, enough for 4 servings.

Chocolate Truffles

4 **ounces semisweet chocolate, coarsely chopped**
2 **tablespoons whipping cream**
About 2 tablespoons ground sweet chocolate or cocoa

Place semisweet chocolate and cream in a 1- to 1½-quart pan over lowest possible heat. (If heat is too high, the chocolate separates.) Stir constantly until chocolate is melted and well blended with cream. Cover and chill just until chocolate-cream is firm enough to hold its shape, about 40 minutes.

Meanwhile, spread ground chocolate on a small plate or on a piece of waxed paper. Using your fingers or 2 spoons, quickly shape about 1 teaspoon of the chocolate-cream at a time into a ball; then roll in the ground chocolate until completely coated. Arrange truffles in a single layer in a shallow container. Cover and refrigerate until firm to serve, or store up to 2 weeks. Makes about 12 truffles.

Carrot and Orange Soup

2 tablespoons butter or margarine
1 pound carrots, thinly sliced
1 large onion, sliced
3 cups regular-strength chicken broth
1 teaspoon sugar
½ teaspoon dill weed
1½ cups fresh orange juice
   Salt

Melt butter or margarine in a 5- to 6-quart pan. Add carrots and onion. Cook, stirring, until onion is limp. Add chicken broth, sugar, and dill weed. Cover and simmer 35 minutes or until carrots are very tender when pierced.

Whirl half the mixture at a time in a blender until smooth. (Or lift vegetables from broth and whirl in food processor, adding only enough broth to make a smooth purée; return purée to broth and stir to blend.) Stir in orange juice. Cover and chill. Season to taste with salt. Serve chilled or reheat just to simmering. Makes about 6½ cups or 6 first-course servings.

Oven-poached Fish

   Water
2 medium-size onions, sliced
12 whole black peppers
4 whole allspice
⅓ cup fresh lemon juice or white wine vinegar
2 bay leaves
   About 1 teaspoon salt
1 cup dry white wine or water
2 pounds fish fillets (about 1 in. thick), such as lingcod or rockfish, *or* 1 whole fish (about 4 to 5 lbs.), such as rockfish, cleaned and dressed
3 large leeks *or* 8 green onions
2 to 3 tablespoons olive oil or salad oil
   Salt and pepper

In a 3- to 4-quart pan, combine 2 quarts water, onions, peppers, allspice, lemon juice, bay leaves, 1 teaspoon salt, and wine. Cover and simmer 20 to 30 minutes. Strain, reserving liquid for poaching.

Arrange fish fillets in a single layer in a greased 2½- to 3-inch-deep, 12- by 15-inch baking pan. (If using a

COOKING A WHOLE FISH

Wrap whole fish snugly in cheesecloth, folding edges together on top of fish.

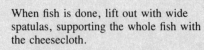

When fish is done, lift out with wide spatulas, supporting the whole fish with the cheesecloth.

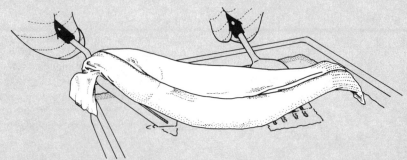

whole fish, wrap snugly in cheesecloth, folding edges together on top of fish.) Bring poaching liquid to a boil and pour over fish—it should just cover fish; if needed, add equal parts of hot water and dry white wine.

Cover pan tightly and place in a 425° oven. Cook until fish is opaque throughout; allow 12 to 15 minutes per inch of thickness, measured at thickest part.

When fish is done, lift out fillets with a wide spatula; support a whole fish with the cheesecloth. Drain well and arrange on a rimmed serving platter; gently pull cheesecloth from beneath whole fish. Cover and keep warm for up to 30 minutes; or if made ahead, cool, cover, and chill as long as overnight. Reserve poaching liquid.

While fish cooks, trim off most of the green parts of leeks, split in half lengthwise, and rinse well between layers; then slice thinly. (Or thinly slice green onions.) Heat olive oil in a 10- to 12-inch frying pan over medium heat. Add leeks and cook, stirring, until limp. Set aside if made ahead of time.

Before serving, add ½ cup of the reserved poaching liquid (discard remainder or reserve for soup) to leeks. Bring to a boil and add salt and pepper to taste. Spoon hot sauce over hot or cold fish. Serves 6.

Eggs

6 eggs
Water

In a 2- to 3-quart pan, cover eggs with 1 inch water. Bring to a boil on high heat; then at once reduce heat so that water temperature is just beneath an active bubble and cook for 12 minutes. Drain and immerse immediately in cold water to cool. Serve at room temperature or chilled; shell at table. Serves 6.

Aioli Sauce

7 or 8 large cloves garlic, minced or pressed
Yolk of 1 hard-cooked egg
1 raw whole egg
1 tablespoon fresh lemon juice
1 cup olive oil
Salt

In a blender or food processor, combine garlic, hard-cooked egg yolk, whole egg, and lemon juice. Whirl until blended. With motor at high speed, gradually add olive oil, pouring in a thin stream. Add salt to taste.

Serve, or cover and chill if made a day ahead. Let warm to room temperature before serving. Makes 1½ cups, enough for 6 servings.

Shrimp

1 pound unshelled large shrimp (about 15 shrimp)
2 tablespoons olive oil *or* salad oil
2 large shallots *or* 1 small onion, chopped
1 or 2 cloves garlic, minced or pressed
1 bay leaf
½ teaspoon dry thyme
1 tablespoon tomato paste *or* 2 tablespoons catsup
½ cup dry white wine
Salt

Devein shrimp by inserting a slender pick through shell at joints in back and gently pulling out sand veins.

In a 10- to 12-inch frying pan, heat olive oil over low heat. Add shallots and garlic; cook, stirring, until limp. Add bay leaf, thyme, and the shrimp. Cook, stirring, until shrimp turns pink, 5 to 7 minutes.

With a slotted spoon, lift out shrimp. Stir tomato paste and wine into pan. Boil, uncovered, over high heat until juices thicken slightly. Stir in shrimp to coat, and salt to taste. Serves 6.

DEVEINING SHRIMP

Insert a slender pick through joint in back of shell.
Carefully pull out the dark sand vein.

Vegetables

6 large artichokes, well washed
1 pound green beans or asparagus spears
12 small thin-skinned potatoes (about 1½-in. diameter), scrubbed
6 slender carrots, peeled
1 medium-size cauliflower (about 1½ lbs.), cored but left intact
Water

Trim thorny tops from artichokes; with scissors snip off thorns on remaining leaves and trim woody end of stems. Snap ends and any strings from green beans (or tough ends from asparagus).

Arrange vegetables on one or more racks and cook over boiling water, covered, until tender when pierced. Add vegetables in sequence according to cooking time. Allow about 30 minutes for artichokes; about 20 minutes for potatoes; about 15 minutes for cauliflower and carrots; and 10 minutes for asparagus and beans.

Serve warm or cool; if made ahead, cover and chill as long as overnight. Serves 6.

Floating Islands

6 eggs
1¼ cups sugar
1½ teaspoons vanilla
3 cups half-and-half or milk
2 tablespoons Grand Marnier or other orange-flavored liqueur
¼ teaspoon cream of tartar
Boiling water

Separate 4 of the eggs; put whites in large bowl of electric mixer and set aside. Place yolks in the top of a double boiler and add remaining 2 eggs, ⅓ cup of the sugar, and the vanilla; mix thoroughly. In a 1½- to 2-quart pan, heat half-and-half or milk to scalding, and stir slowly into egg mixture.

Nest double boiler in gently simmering water and cook custard, stirring constantly, until it coats a metal spoon in a velvety smooth layer; expect custard to thicken in 10 to 15 minutes, but cooking time varies with the rate of heat.

At once, set top of double boiler with the custard into ice water to stop the cooking; stir frequently until the sauce has cooled. Stir Grand Marnier into custard.

Pour custard into a 2- to 3-quart serving bowl (glass shows off the dessert best, but any favorite bowl can be used), cover, and chill in the refrigerator as long as overnight.

With an electric mixer at high speed, whip the reserved egg whites and cream of tartar until foamy. Continue beating at high speed, gradually adding ⅔ cup of the sugar, until stiff peaks form when beater is withdrawn.

Place a large, shallow pan (about 12 by 15 inches) in a 400° oven and pour in about 1 inch boiling water. With a spoon, drop large scoops of beaten egg whites (make 6 in all) into the water, keeping them slightly apart. Bake, uncovered, for 5 to 8 minutes or until the meringues are golden.

Turn off oven, open door, and pull rack with meringues partway out. With a slotted spoon, lift meringues, one at a time, from water. (Empty the pan of water when it has cooled.)

You can mound the meringues onto the chilled custard; or, if made in advance, you can set them side by side in a rimmed pan (sides of the pan should be higher than the meringues). Cover with plastic wrap (wrap should not touch meringues) and chill until next day—then place them on the chilled custard.

As long as 4 hours before serving, you can complete the dessert. Place remaining ¼ cup sugar in a 5- to 6-inch frying pan and set on high heat. Shake and tilt pan to mix sugar as it begins to liquefy and caramelize; do not stir and do not let scorch. When sugar is melted, pour at once over meringues, letting caramel drizzle down on all sides. As a precaution against breakage if you use a glass bowl, do not pour the caramel directly on the glass; the caramel should cause no problem if it flows from the meringues and then against bowl sides. Serve, or cover and keep cold.

To serve, break through the caramel with a large spoon and place about ½ cup of the custard and a meringue puff in each individual bowl. Serves 6.

MAKING FLOATING ISLANDS

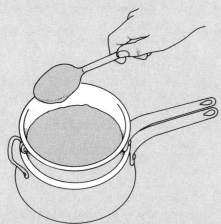

Nest double boiler in gently simmering water and cook custard, stirring constantly, until it coats a metal spoon in a velvety smooth layer.

At once set top of double boiler with the custard into ice water to stop the cooking. Stir frequently until sauce cools.

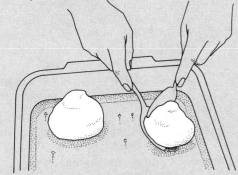

With a spoon, drop large scoops of meringue (6 in all) into boiling water, keeping them slightly apart. Bake 5 to 8 minutes or until meringues are golden.

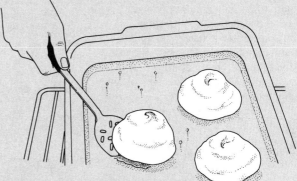

Turn off oven, open door, and pull rack with meringues partially out. With slotted spoon, lift meringues, one at a time, from water.

As long as 4 hours before serving, lay meringues onto chilled custard in a clear glass bowl.

Pour caramelized sugar over meringues, being careful not to pour hot caramel directly onto chilled glass bowl.

SHOWY SALAD IN AN EDIBLE BOWL

Supper for 4
(Pictured on Pages 26–27)

*Chicken and Pea Pod Salad
in Pastry Bowl*

French Colombard or Chenin Blanc

Raspberries with Almond Cream

Iced Coffee

Raspberries with Almond Cream

1 small package (3 oz.) cream cheese
½ cup powdered sugar
2 tablespoons almond-flavored liqueur
1 cup whipping cream
2 cups fresh raspberries
   Almonds for garnish (optional)

In a 2- to 3-quart deep bowl, beat together cream cheese, sugar, and liqueur with electric mixer at high speed until smooth. Still beating, pour in cream in a steady stream. (Mixture should be the consistency of stiffly whipped cream at all times; if it looks soft, stop adding cream and continue to beat until mixture thickens.) If made ahead, cover and refrigerate up to 6 hours.

Line the bottom of each of 4 dessert bowls with a scant ½ cup of the raspberries. Mound almond cream equally over each. Top with remaining berries, and garnish with whole almonds, if desired. Serves 4.

Chicken and Pea Pod Salad in Pastry Bowl

3 cups boned and skinned cooked chicken, cut in bite-size pieces
1 can (8 oz.) water chestnuts, drained and sliced
½ cup thinly sliced green onion
2 hard-cooked eggs, coarsely chopped
1 cup sour cream
1 teaspoon fresh lime juice
2 teaspoons *each* sugar and curry powder
½ teaspoon ground ginger
   Salt and pepper to taste
¼ pound edible-pod peas
   Water
   Pastry Bowl (recipe follows)
   Fresh coriander (cilantro) or parsley

Combine chicken, water chestnuts, green onion, and eggs. In a small bowl, stir together sour cream, lime juice, sugar, curry powder, and ginger. Pour dressing over chicken mixture and mix well. Season with salt and pepper. Cover and chill; assemble salad, or store up to 24 hours.

Remove tips and strings from peas. Drop into a 1- to 1½-quart pan of rapidly boiling water and boil for 1½ minutes. Drain, plunge into cold water, and drain again. (Or place in a shallow baking dish, cover, and cook in a microwave oven at full power for 1½ minutes; drain.) Cover and chill if cooked ahead.

To serve, arrange pea pods in bottom and up the sides of pastry bowl. Pile chicken salad on top and garnish with fresh coriander. Serves 4.

Pastry Bowl

⅔ cup water
5 tablespoons butter or margarine
¼ teaspoon salt
⅔ cup all-purpose flour
3 eggs

In a 1½- to 2-quart pan, combine the water, butter, and salt. Quickly bring to a boil, stirring to melt butter. Add flour all at once and cook, stirring vigorously, until mixture forms a ball and leaves the sides of the pan. Remove from heat and beat in eggs, one at a time, until mixture is smooth and glossy. Spoon into a greased 9-inch cheesecake pan with a removable bottom or spring-release sides. Spread evenly over bottom and up sides of pan.

Bake crust in a 400° oven for 40 minutes or until puffed and brown. Turn off oven. Prick with a wooden pick in 10 to 12 places and leave in closed oven for about 10 minutes to dry; then remove pan from oven and cool completely. Remove crust from the pan.

If you make the pastry bowl a day ahead, cover loosely with foil and store at room temperature. (For longer storage, wrap completely in foil and freeze; thaw completely before recrisping.) To serve, recrisp pastry, uncovered, in a 400° oven for 10 minutes. Cool; then line with pea pods, add the salad, and garnish. Serves 4.

Avocado-Shrimp Cocktail

3 cans (6 oz. *each*) tomato-based vegetable juice

1 medium-size green bell pepper, seeded and chopped

¼ cup chopped green onion

2 tablespoons *each* Worcestershire and fresh lime juice

1 teaspoon prepared horseradish

1½ teaspoons chopped fresh oregano leaves *or* ½ teaspoon of the dry herb

1½ pounds medium-size cooked shrimp

2 or 3 limes, cut into wedges

About 1 cup fresh coriander (cilantro) leaves, rinsed

2 medium-size ripe avocados

In a 1- to 1½-quart container with a spillproof top, combine vegetable juice, green pepper, green onion, Worcestershire, lime juice, horseradish, and oregano. Secure lid and pack in ice chest (or you can refrigerate the sauce as long as overnight and then pack in the ice chest).

Put shrimp and lime wedges in separate watertight containers; pack in ice chest. Set coriander and avocados on the ice.

To serve, cut avocados into halves and remove pits. Score avocado flesh into cubes. Spoon shrimp into individual cups or bowls; liberally ladle sauce onto shrimp. Add, as desired, avocado chunks scooped from the shell, cilantro leaves, and a squeeze of lime. Serves 8 to 10.

Add-on Vichyssoise

4 or 5 medium-size leeks

½ cup (¼ lb.) butter or margarine

1 medium-size onion, coarsely chopped

4 medium-size thin-skinned potatoes, peeled and cut into chunks

3 cans (14½ oz. *each*) regular-strength beef broth

1 cucumber, peeled, seeded, and cut into chunks

1 cup *each* unflavored yogurt and sour cream

1 pound boiled ham

2 whole nutmegs

36 to 40 chives, rinsed

Trim root ends, tough outer leaves, and tops from leeks. Cut in half lengthwise and wash well. Coarsely chop and put into a 5- to 6-quart pan along with butter and onion.

Cook, stirring, over medium heat until leeks are very limp and slightly tinged with brown, about 30 minutes. Add potatoes, broth, and cucumber; cover and simmer over medium heat until potatoes mash easily, about 25 more minutes. Remove from heat, uncover, and let cool to lukewarm.

In a blender, whirl potato mixture, yogurt, and sour cream, a portion at a time, until smooth; pour into a 1-gallon container with a spillproof top. Cover and chill at least 3 hours (or as long as overnight); then pack in ice chest.

Sliver ham and arrange with nutmeg (also a nutmeg grater) in a watertight container; pack in ice chest. Lay chives on ice.

To serve, ladle soup into individual bowls or cups; then top as desired with ham, a grating of nutmeg, and snipped pieces of chives. Serves 8 to 10.

Nectarines in Sweet White Wine

8 to 12 nectarines or peeled peaches

¼ cup lemon juice

Crisp cookies

1 bottle sweet and fruity white wine such as a late-harvest Johannisberg Riesling or Gewürztraminer

Slice nectarines or peaches, turn in lemon juice, place in waterproof container, and pack in ice chest. To serve, spoon fruit into bowls and bathe with the fruity white wine. Sip the wine and eat the fruit with a spoon. Accompany with your favorite plain, crisp cookies. Serves 8 to 10.

CLEANING LEEKS

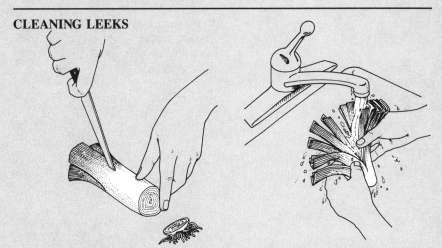

Insert knife through white part of leek just below leaves and cut in half lengthwise through leaves.

Rinse thoroughly between leaves.

AN AFTERNOON OF CHEESE AND WINE

A tasting of cheeses and wines
for 10 to 100
(Pictured on Pages 30–31)

Hot Chèvre Toast

*Brie in Wine Aspic,
Decorated with Edible Flowers
and Herbs*

*Layered Cheese Torta
with Fresh Basil and Pine Nuts*

Blue Cheese with Warm Walnuts

Cheese Tray with Summer Fruits

*Sliced   Assorted
Baguettes   Crackers*

Hot Chèvre Toast

**1 long baguette (about 1 lb.) cut
    into ½-inch-thick slices**
¾ pound chèvre (goat) cheese

Place bread slices in a single layer on an ungreased 10- by 15-inch baking pan. Broil 4 inches from heat until light golden. Turn slices over; top with a thick slice of chèvre. (If done ahead, cover pan with plastic wrap to prevent drying and set aside.) To serve, broil until cheese is hot. Arrange hot toast on a platter for passing. Serves about 10.

Blue Cheese with Warm Walnuts

2 cups (8 oz.) walnut halves
**2 pounds blue cheese
    Water crackers or other unsalted
    crackers**

Spread walnuts out on an ungreased 9-inch-square baking pan. Bake, uncovered, in a 300° oven until skins peel off easily, 20 to 25 minutes. Shake pan occasionally to turn nuts. Cool slightly; rub nuts gently with your fingers to remove skins. If made ahead, store airtight up to 1 week. Reheat in 300° oven for 5 to 8 minutes.

Pour warm nuts onto a board; set out cheese, crackers, and knives for spreading. Serves about 10.

Decorated Brie in Aspic

Choose edible decorations from fresh herbs such as chives, dill, sage, thyme, or rosemary; tiny spinach leaves; green onions; or petals from well-rinsed, pesticide-free borage, nasturtiums, pansies, roses, citrus, primroses, carnations, chrysanthemums, geraniums, or violets. Plan your design by arranging decorations before applying aspic.

**2 cups dry white wine or regular-
    strength chicken broth**
**1 envelope unflavored gelatin
    Brie or other flat-surfaced cheese
    with edible rind, chilled
    Decorations**

In a 2- to 3-quart pan, combine wine and gelatin; let stand about 5 minutes. Place over medium heat and stir until gelatin dissolves.

Set pan in ice water and stir liquid occasionally (but slowly so bubbles don't develop), until it begins to thicken and looks syrupy.

Set cheese on wire rack in a rimmed pan. Arrange decorations on cheese to determine a pattern, then set decorations aside. Spoon aspic over top and sides of the cheese, and when slightly tacky (just a few minutes) add the decorations. Chill uncovered, about 15 minutes.

Spoon aspic over top and sides of cheese again; you may need to add several more coats, chilling between each layer, to cover all exposed portions. Invert a bowl over cheese without touching and chill until ready to serve, up to 36 hours.

You can store unused aspic (including drips from under the rack), covered, in the refrigerator for several days. Reheat to melt, then chill until syrupy.

Makes enough aspic to coat six 3- by 5-inch rectangles of cheese with 3 layers of aspic.

Layered Cheese Torta with Fresh Basil and Pine Nuts

1   small (3 oz.) and 1 large (8 oz.)
    package cream cheese, at room
    temperature
1⅓ cups (⅔ lb.) unsalted butter, at
    room temperature
    Water
    Pesto Filling (recipe follows)
    Fresh basil sprigs
    Pine nuts

With an electric mixer, beat cream cheese and butter until very smoothly blended; scrape mixture from bowl sides as needed.

Cut two 18-inch squares of cheesecloth; moisten with water, wring dry, and lay out flat, one on top of the other. Smoothly line a 4- to 5-cup straight-sided plain mold (such as a loaf pan, terrine, charlotte mold, or clean flowerpot) with the cheesecloth; drape excess over rim of mold.

With your fingers or a paddle (such as a rubber spatula) make an even layer with ⅙ of the cheese. Cover with ⅕ of the pesto filling, extending it evenly to sides of mold. Repeat until mold is filled, finishing with cheese. If you want thinner or thicker layers, divide cheese and filling so that you will have a bottom and top layer of cheese—in a wide mold you may need to make fewer layers.

Fold ends of cheesecloth over torta and press down lightly with your hands to compact. Chill until torta feels firm when pressed, about 1 hour. Then invert onto a serving dish and gently pull off cheesecloth. (If cloth is not removed, it will act as a wick and cause filling color to blend into cheese.)

Serve, or wrap airtight with plastic wrap and refrigerate up to 5 days. Just before serving, garnish top with a sprig of fresh basil and a sprinkling of pine nuts. Present torta with sliced baguettes or crackers; let guests serve themselves. Serves 10.

Pesto Filling

1⅔ cups lightly packed fresh basil
    leaves
⅔ cup (about 3 oz.) freshly grated
    Parmesan or Romano cheese
3½ tablespoons olive oil
2½ tablespoons pine nuts
    Salt and pepper

In a blender or food processor, whirl to a paste basil leaves, cheese, and olive oil. Stir in pine nuts and salt and pepper to taste.

FORMING A CHEESE TORTA

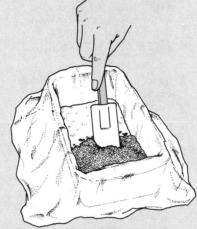

With your fingers or a paddle, make an even layer with ⅙ of the cheese in a cheesecloth-lined pan. Cover with ⅕ of the basil filling. Continue layering until cheese and filling are all used.

Fold ends of cheesecloth over torta and press down lightly with your hands to compact.

Invert chilled, firm torta onto a serving dish and gently pull off cheesecloth.

Just before serving, garnish top with sprigs of fresh basil and a sprinkling of pine nuts.

Raw Vegetables with Dipping Sauce

Clean and prepare an assortment of seasonal raw vegetables from the garden or market, allowing about ¾ cup per person. Consider carrot sticks, celery hearts, green onions, radishes, cauliflowerets, sliced squash, cherry tomatoes, small whole mushrooms, red or green bell pepper strips, sliced turnips, jicama, green beans, and edible-pod peas. Pack each type of vegetable in locking plastic bags or watertight containers and transport in an ice chest.

Prepare your favorite dipping sauce, or use the Green Sauce on page 82; you'll need 1½ to 2 cups. Pack in a watertight container for the ice chest.

At the beach, place the sauce in a bowl in the center of a tray or basket and surround with vegetables grouped by type.

Toast Rounds

1 long baguette (about 8 oz.), thinly sliced

Arrange bread slices in a single layer on baking sheets. Place in a 350° oven and bake until lightly toasted, about 15 minutes. Let cool; use or package airtight as long as overnight.

Potluck Fisherman's Stew

You can multiply this recipe up to 5 times, to serve as many as 50 people. For large groups, cook the stew in a 50-quart kettle, or cook the leek-onion-garlic mixture in one 12- to 14-quart kettle and then divide it equally among additional kettles before adding the remaining ingredients.

¼ cup olive oil or salad oil
6 medium-size leeks, well rinsed and sliced (white part only)
2 large onions, chopped
2 large cloves garlic, minced or pressed
2 large cans (1 lb. 12 oz. *each*) tomatoes, cut in chunks
6½ cups (1.5 L.) dry white wine
1 quart clam juice
1 quart regular-strength chicken broth
3 bay leaves
1 tablespoon fresh thyme leaves or 1 teaspoon of the dry herb
½ teaspoon grated orange peel
½ teaspoon fennel seed, crushed
¼ teaspoon cayenne pepper
10 pounds assorted fish and shellfish (Example: 2 pound lobster; 2 pounds oysters, clams, or mussels; 1 to 2 pounds shrimp; 2 to 3 pounds fish fillets; 2 to 3 pound whole fish)
Lemon wedges
Parsley or other fresh herbs

In a 12- to 14-quart kettle, pour in olive oil. Add leeks (reserving a few slices to garnish the stew), onions, and garlic. Cook, stirring, until onions are soft. Add tomatoes and their liquid, wine, clam juice, chicken broth, bay leaves, thyme leaves, orange peel, fennel seed, and cayenne. Bring to a boil.

Wrap any whole fish (cleaned and scaled) in cheesecloth slings. (Cut off heads and tails if necessary to fit pans; discard, or wrap in another cheesecloth sling and use to flavor broth.) Lower whole fish or whole lobster into the boiling broth. Cover and simmer gently for 5 minutes.

Then add any clams or mussels, scrubbed clean, along with assorted fish fillets or steaks (½ to 1 inch thick). Cover, bring back to simmering, and cook for 5 minutes.

Add cleaned and coarsely chopped squid, cleaned and deveined shrimp, and oysters (scrub if in shells); cover and simmer about 5 minutes longer, or until clams, mussels, and oysters pop open and all fish is no longer translucent in thickest part when prodded apart. Slide pan to side of fire to keep warm.

Lift out the whole fish, if used, in the cheesecloth sling (discard head and tail) and lay on a shallow baking pan or rimmed platter. Carefully remove and discard cheesecloth. With slotted spoon or wide spatula, lift out remaining fish, discarding any shellfish that haven't popped open, and place alongside whole fish. Garnish with reserved sliced leeks, lemon wedges, and parsley sprigs.

Have guests spread Toast Rounds with Garlic Mayonnaise (recipes follow) and set in their soup bowls, then choose an assortment of fish and seafood, and ladle the hot broth over all. Serves 10.

Garlic Mayonnaise

1 egg *or* 3 egg yolks
1 tablespoon white wine vinegar *or* fresh lemon juice
1 teaspoon Dijon mustard
4 to 6 cloves garlic
1 cup salad oil *or* olive oil
Liquid hot pepper seasoning

In a blender or food processor, whirl eggs, vinegar, mustard, and garlic until blended. On high speed, add oil—just a few drops at a time at first, then increasing to a slow, steady stream. Add liquid hot pepper seasoning to taste.

Use, or cover and chill as long as 2 weeks. Keep cold until ready to serve. Makes 1½ cups. To make more, prepare 1 batch at a time.

DINNER
UNDER THE STARS
For 6
(Pictured on Pages 34–37)

*Calamari-Kiwi Salad
with Watercress*

Sauvignon Blanc

*Mesquite-grilled Beef Tenderloin
in Cabernet Sauvignon Marinade*

Skillet Potatoes Anna

*Sautéed Red Bell Peppers
and Onions*

Selected Mustards

Crusty French Bread

Cabernet Sauvignon

Sherried Cream with Red Grapes

Mesquite-grilled Beef Tenderloin in Cabernet Sauvignon Marinade

A 4-pound large-end section of beef tenderloin (or beef filet), trimmed of excess fat
1   **cup Cabernet Sauvignon (or other dry red wine)**
    About ¼ cup olive oil
1   **small onion, chopped**
¼   **cup chopped parsley**
1   **clove garlic, minced or pressed**
1   **bay leaf**
½   **teaspoon salt (optional)**
½   **teaspoon pepper**

Place beef in a large, heavy plastic bag set in a pan. Stir together wine, olive oil, onion, parsley, garlic, bay leaf, salt, and pepper. Pour over beef in bag; twist end of bag to close, and secure it with a wire tie. Let stand at room temperature at least 3 hours or refrigerate overnight; turn bag several times to distribute marinade.

Ignite enough mesquite or long-burning charcoal briquets to make a solid single layer on fire grate of barbecue. When coals are just barely covered with gray ash, spread out evenly in a single layer and position cooking grill 6 inches above coals.

Lift beef from marinade and set on grill. Cook, turning every 5 minutes for even browning, until a meat thermometer inserted in center registers 130° for rare, 35 to 40 minutes, or until as done as you like it. (If the tenderloin drips fat it may flame up, so have a water spray bottle close at hand to extinguish the flame.)

The marinade can be saved for use with other meats or vegetables to be grilled later in the week. Or you may choose to strain it and boil to reduce it to about ½ cup. To thicken slightly, add 1½ tablespoons butter (in one piece) and stir constantly until blended into sauce. Set container of sauce in hot water to keep warm until ready to serve with the meat.

Transfer beef to a platter and let stand at least 10 minutes before serving. Cut on a slight diagonal into ½-inch-thick slices. Serves 6 to 8.

Skillet Potatoes Anna

½   **cup melted butter or margarine**
5   **or 6 large russet potatoes, peeled and sliced**
    Salt and pepper

Brush a 10-inch heavy frying pan (one that can be put in the oven) or shallow baking dish with part of the melted butter and overlap the potato slices in the pan, sprinkling each layer with salt and pepper to taste. Pour remaining melted butter over the potatoes. Bake uncovered in a 450° oven for 45 minutes, or until the top is crusty and the potatoes are tender when pierced. Serves 6.

Sautéed Red Bell Peppers and Onions

4   **large onions, peeled**
4   **large red bell peppers**
2   **cloves garlic, minced or pressed**
2   **tablespoons *each* salad oil and butter or margarine**
2   **tablespoons chopped fresh basil leaves (optional)**

Thinly slice onions and cut peppers into thin strips, discarding stems and seeds. In a 10- to 12-inch frying pan over medium heat, cook onions and garlic in the oil and butter, stirring often, until onions are limp and golden, about 30 minutes. Add pepper strips and cook, stirring, until peppers are just limp, about 10 minutes. Stir in basil. Use hot, or if made ahead, cover and chill as long as 3 days. Reheat to serve. Serves 6.

Sherried Cream
with Red Grapes

- ½ cup sugar
- 3 tablespoons cornstarch
- 3 cups milk
- 6 tablespoons cream sherry or apple juice
- 3 egg yolks, slightly beaten
- 3 tablespoons butter or margarine
- 1½ teaspoons vanilla
  About 2½ cups seedless red grapes

In a 2- to 3-quart pan, stir together sugar and cornstarch. Gradually add milk and sherry, stirring until well blended. Cook over medium heat, stirring constantly, until mixture comes to a rolling boil; boil 1 minute. Remove from heat.

Stir part of the hot sauce into beaten yolks; then return all to the pan, turn heat to low, and cook, stirring, for 3 minutes. Remove from heat and stir in the butter and vanilla until butter melts. Cool to room temperature.

Layer spoonfuls of pudding and grapes into 6 stemmed glasses. Chill until serving time. Serves 6.

Calamari-Kiwi Salad

- 3¾ pounds whole small squid, cleaned (directions follow) *or* 1½ pounds cleaned mantles
- 2¼ cups dry white wine
- ¾ cup regular-strength chicken broth
- 2 large cloves garlic, minced or pressed
- ¾ teaspoon sugar
- 1 medium-size red bell pepper, stemmed, seeded, and cut into thin strips
- ⅓ cup olive oil
- ½ teaspoon freshly ground pepper
- 2 or 3 kiwis, peeled and sliced
  Watercress sprigs

With a sharp knife, cut squid mantles crosswise into ½-inch-wide rings (leave tentacles of whole cleaned squid intact).

In a 10- to 12-inch frying pan, combine wine, broth, garlic, and sugar; bring to a boil over high heat. Add squid rings (and tentacles from whole squid), return to boil, and poach until opaque, about 20 seconds. Lift out with a slotted spoon; set aside. On high heat, boil liquid down to ¼ cup, uncovered. Cover; chill liquid and squid separately.

Blend liquid, squid, red bell pepper, olive oil, and pepper. Spoon onto 6 salad plates. Garnish with kiwi and watercress. Serves 6 as a first course, 3 or 4 as a light entrée.

CLEANING SQUID

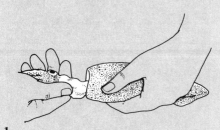

1.
Gently pull body to separate from mantle.

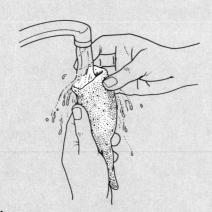

4.
Flush out mantle with water; drain briefly.

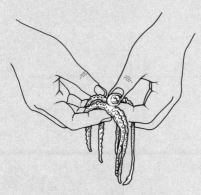

7.
Pop out and discard the round hard beak in the center of the tentacles. Leave purple skin on tentacles.

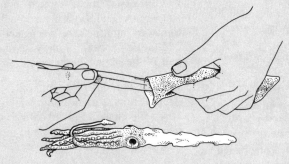

2.
Pull the long, clear quill from inside the mantle and discard.

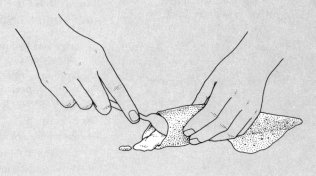

3.
Using your fingers or a small spoon, scoop out and discard interior of mantle.

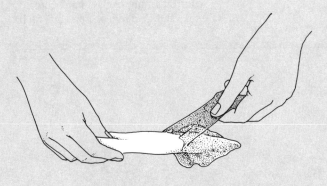

5.
With your fingers, pull off and discard thin, speckled skin from the mantle.

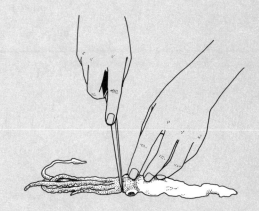

6.
With sharp knife, cut body between eyes and tentacles. Discard eyes and attached material.

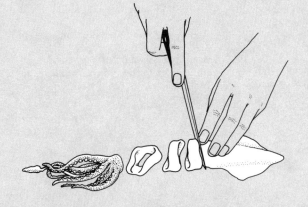

8.
Cut mantle crosswise into ½-inch-wide rings. Leave tentacles intact.

9.
Completed squid ready for cooking.

Roasted Red Pepper and Tomato Salad

6   **large red bell peppers, roasted (directions follow)**

5   **large firm-ripe tomatoes (about 2½ lbs.), peeled**

20   **whole pitted ripe olives**

¼   **cup olive oil**

½   **teaspoon *each* salt and pepper**

1   **teaspoon ground cumin**

4   **cloves garlic, minced or pressed**

1   **tablespoon finely chopped parsley**

6   **hard-cooked eggs, cut in halves or wedges**

1   **can (2 oz.) rolled anchovies (optional)**

Cut roasted peppers crosswise into strips ½-inch wide and place them in a bowl.

Cut tomatoes in half crosswise and squeeze out and discard seeds. Chop tomatoes into bite-size pieces and add to the peppers, along with about half of the olives, chopped.

In a jar, combine olive oil, salt, pepper, cumin, garlic, and parsley; cover and shake to blend. Stir into pepper mixture; taste, and add more salt, pepper, or garlic if desired.

Cover salad and let stand at room temperature up to 4 hours.

Pour into a serving dish and garnish with remaining olives, hard-cooked eggs, and anchovies. Serves 8 to 10.

ROASTING PEPPERS

Broil peppers, turning frequently with tongs, until well blistered and charred, about 30 minutes.

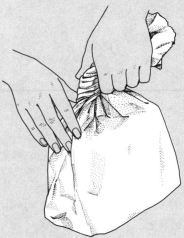

Place peppers in a paper bag, close tightly, and let sweat 15 to 20 minutes to loosen skin.

Strip off skins from cooled peppers.

Cut lengthwise, into quarters; remove stems and seeds. If made ahead, wrap and refrigerate 1 or 2 days. Freeze for longer storage.

Pine Nut Sticks

1 **package active dry yeast**
⅔ **cup warm water (about 110°)**
½ **teaspoon crushed anise seed**
2 **tablespoons *each* salad oil and olive oil**
¼ **teaspoon grated lemon peel**
1 **teaspoon salt**
1 **tablespoon sugar**
  About 2½ cups all-purpose flour
⅔ **cup pine nuts**
1 **egg, slightly beaten**
2 **tablespoons coarse salt**

Dissolve yeast in warm water; add crushed anise seed, salad oil, olive oil, lemon peel, salt, sugar, and 1 cup of the flour. Beat until smooth. Add the pine nuts and another 1¼ cups flour, or enough to make a stiff dough.

Turn out on a floured board and knead until smooth and elastic (about 5 minutes), using additional flour as required. Place dough in greased bowl, cover with plastic wrap, and let rise in a warm place until doubled, about 1 hour.

Punch down; divide dough in half. Cut each half into 20 equal pieces; roll each piece, using palms of hands, into a 7-inch rope. Place parallel on greased 12- by 14-inch baking pans about ½ inch apart. Cover and let rise until almost doubled, about 30 minutes; brush with slightly beaten egg, and sprinkle lightly with coarse salt. Bake in a 325° oven for 30 minutes, until lightly browned. Serve warm or at room temperature. (If made ahead, store in freezer. To crisp before serving, spread bread sticks in a single layer on baking sheets and reheat in a 325° oven for 5 to 10 minutes.) Makes 40 bread sticks.

Blueberry Meringue Torte with Rum Custard

4 **egg whites**
½ **teaspoon cream of tartar**
1 **cup sugar**
1 **teaspoon vanilla**
1½ **cups whipping cream**
1 **teaspoon grated lemon peel**
2 **cups blueberries**
  Thin strips of lemon peel (cut with a zester), optional
  Rum Custard (recipe follows)

In large bowl of an electric mixer, beat egg whites and cream of tartar at high speed until frothy. Gradually add sugar, beating until stiff, glossy peaks form. Then beat in vanilla until blended.

Trace an 8-inch circle on 2 greased and floured 9- by 14-inch (or larger) baking sheets. Using a pastry bag with a plain or fluted tip, or a spatula, pipe or spread half the meringue onto each pan in a solid 8-inch disk of even thickness. (For

PIPING MERINGUE DISKS

Trace circles with your finger around an inverted 8-inch pan on 2 greased and floured baking sheets.

Using a pastry bag, pipe half the meringue onto each pan in a solid disk.

individual tortes, make 16 to 20 meringue disks each about 3 inches in diameter.)

Bake meringues in a 250° oven for 1½ hours or until firm and dry. If you have only one oven, position the meringues just above and below the center; then switch positions halfway through baking. Turn off heat and leave meringues in the closed oven 3 to 4 hours to continue drying. Remove from oven; flex pans to pop meringues free, but leave in place to cool completely. Use, or store cooled disks airtight up to 5 days.

To assemble the large or individual tortes, place 1 large or 8 to 10 small meringue disks on flat plates. Whip the cream until stiff and fold in grated lemon peel. For the large torte, spread about half of the cream over the meringue to within about ½ inch of edge; for individual tortes, divide about half of the cream evenly among the 8 to 10 small disks. Sprinkle with the blueberries, reserving a few for garnish. Place remaining meringue(s) on top; spread with remaining cream. Garnish with thin lemon strips and remaining blueberries. Cover and chill at least 8 hours or overnight.

At the table cut large torte into wedges; pass Rum Custard to pour over each portion or individual torte. Serves 8 to 10.

Rum Custard

1½ **cups milk**
4 **egg yolks**
¼ **cup sugar**
2 **tablespoons rum *or* ½ teaspoon imitation rum extract**

In a 1- to 2-quart pan, warm milk over medium heat until steaming. In the top of a double boiler, stir together egg yolks and sugar. Gradually stir in hot milk. Place over simmering water; stir often until custard thickly coats a metal spoon, 15 to 20 minutes. Stir in rum. Cool; cover and chill until ready to use.

**A COOL LUNCH
FOR A
SUMMER DAY**

Just for 2
(Pictured on Pages 40–41)

Salmon Tartare

Fresh Chives   Toast Triangles

Grey Riesling

*Vanilla Fig Compote
with Ice Cream*

Salmon Tartare

¾ **pound salmon fillets**

2 **teaspoons fresh lime or lemon juice**

1½ **teaspoons *each* chopped capers
and minced shallots**

1 **teaspoon minced fresh marjoram
leaves or dill *or* ½ teaspoon of the
dry herb**

2 **pieces (½ by 3 inches) canned
roasted red pepper or pimento**

6 **whole chives**

4 to 6 **wedges lime or lemon**

2 **slices toast, crusts trimmed off**

If salmon is fresh, wrap and freeze
until firm, about 6 hours; thaw
slightly for easier slicing. (Freezing
kills any parasites that may exist,
although their incidence in raw
salmon is quite rare.)

With a sharp knife, cut off skin and
brown flesh from salmon, peeling
skin back with your fingers. Discard
skin, trimmings, and any bones; chop
pink flesh.

In a bowl, mix salmon, lime juice,
capers, shallots, and marjoram.
Mound equally on 2 salad plates.
Garnish with roasted pepper. Cut
toast diagonally in half. Serve
salmon with chives, lime wedges,
and toast. Serves 2.

Vanilla Fig Compote

⅓ **cup *each* dry red wine and water**

¼ **cup sugar**

2 **tablespoons fresh lemon juice**

⅓ **vanilla bean, split lengthwise *or* ½
teaspoon vanilla extract**

4 **small or 2 large figs (about ¼ lb.
figs), stems trimmed**

½ **cup fresh or frozen raspberries or
blackberries
Vanilla ice cream**

In a 1- to 1½-quart pan, combine
wine, water, sugar, lemon juice, and
vanilla bean (or omit vanilla bean
and substitute vanilla extract, as
directed below). Bring to a boil over
high heat, stirring until sugar is
dissolved; boil uncovered until
reduced to ⅓ cup.

Remove vanilla bean and scrape
seeds into syrup. (You can rinse
bean, let dry, and save to flavor
sugar and other foods.) Or, if using
vanilla extract, add at this point.
Continue with recipe; or cool, cover,
and chill syrup as long as overnight.
Reheat before using.

Cut small figs vertically into quarters;
large figs into sixths. Gently stir figs
and raspberries into hot syrup; cool
slightly.

For each serving, place 1 large scoop
ice cream in center of a dessert bowl
or rimmed plate. Spoon fruit and
juices around ice cream. Serves 2.

Garlic and onion relatives
team up in a buffet for 8
(Pictured on Pages 42–43)

Garlic-Jelly Cream Cheese

Unsalted Crisp Crackers

Garlic Soup

Garlic Tart

*Baked Garlic Sausages
with Mustard, Horseradish,
and Pickles*

Green Salad

Crusty Bread

Barbera   Cider

Apples

Sautéed Garlic and Onions

¼ cup (⅛ lb.) butter or margarine
5 pounds (10 to 12 medium-size) onions, thinly sliced
½ cup garlic cloves, finely chopped

Melt butter or margarine in a 4- to 5-quart kettle. Add onions and garlic and cook over medium-high heat, covered, for 25 to 30 minutes or until onions are limp. Stir frequently. Remove cover and continue cooking, stirring frequently, until onions and garlic begin to brown slightly; another 15 to 20 minutes. (Do not allow garlic to scorch; it will turn bitter.)

Measure the mixture, including any juice; divide in half. Set one portion aside for the tart; divide the remaining portion in half again—one portion for the soup and the other for the sausages. The cooked onions and garlic can be covered and chilled for as long as 2 days.

Garlic Tart

⅓ to ½ pound smoked pork chops or ham
1 to 2 teaspoons salad oil (optional)
¼ cup all-purpose flour
½ portion Sautéed Garlic and Onions (recipe precedes)
1 cup milk
1 teaspoon dry mustard
⅛ teaspoon ground nutmeg
3 eggs
1 cup sour cream
2 cups (about 8 oz.) shredded Swiss cheese
Salt
Pastry for a 2-crust 9-inch pie

Trim away bone and finely chop smoked pork chops (including fat). Place meat in a 10- to 12-inch frying pan and cook, stirring, over medium heat until meat is lightly browned. (Add salad oil if needed.) Add flour and Sautéed Garlic and Onions. Remove from heat and blend in milk.

Bring to a boil, stirring, and cook until thickened. Stir in dry mustard and nutmeg; set aside.

Beat eggs until blended; then mix in sour cream and cheese. Combine meat and sour cream mixtures; salt to taste. (This much can be done ahead; cover and chill as long as overnight.)

Roll dough out (using all of it) on a floured board to fit a 10-inch pie plate or pan with about a 1-inch overlap beyond rim. Fit dough into pan and fold excess under itself; crimp rim decoratively. Pour in filling. Bake on bottom rack of a 350° oven for 55 minutes or until crust is browned and filling is firm when dish is shaken gently.

Let stand at least 30 minutes to cool slightly before cutting into wedges to serve. (Or let tart cool completely, cover, and chill overnight. Freeze for longer storage, wrapped airtight; thaw, unwrapped. Place cool, unwrapped tart in a 350° oven for 30 minutes to reheat; then serve at once.) Serves 8.

Baked Garlic Sausages

8 garlic (knackwurst) sausages (about 2 lbs.), split lengthwise
¼ portion Sautéed Garlic and Onions (recipe precedes)
¼ teaspoon caraway seed

Lay out sausages side by side, cut side up, in a shallow, close-fitting baking dish. Mix Sautéed Garlic and Onions with caraway seed and spoon mixture down center of sausages.

Bake uncovered in a 350° oven for 25 to 30 minutes or until heated through. Serves 8.

Garlic Soup

¼ portion Sautéed Garlic and Onions (recipe precedes)

3 cans (14½ oz. *each*) regular-strength beef broth (or for a more subtle flavor, substitute 1 can regular-strength chicken broth for 1 can of the beef broth)

3 tablespoons port

Coarsely chop (or snip with scissors) the Sautéed Garlic and Onions. Combine with broth. Bring soup to boil, cover, and simmer about 5 minutes; then stir in port. Serve hot; or chill, covered, and reheat to serve. Makes 8 small servings.

Garlic-Jelly Cream Cheese

1 large package (8 oz.) cream cheese
Garlic Jelly (recipe follows)
Unsalted crackers

Place cream cheese on a small board or plate, generously spread Garlic Jelly on top, and accompany with crackers and a spreading knife. Serves 8.

Garlic Jelly

½ cup finely chopped garlic
About 3 cups white wine vinegar

2 cups water

6 cups sugar

2 pouches (3 oz. each) liquid pectin *or* 2 boxes (1¾ to 2 oz. *each*) dry pectin
Food coloring (optional)

In a 2- to 2½-quart pan, combine garlic and vinegar. Simmer gently, uncovered, over medium heat for 15 minutes. Remove from heat and pour into a 1-quart glass jar; cover and let stand at room temperature for 24 to 36 hours.

Pour flavored vinegar through a wire strainer into a bowl, pressing garlic

with the back of a spoon to squeeze out as much liquid as possible; discard residue. Measure liquid and add more vinegar if needed to make 2 cups.

To use liquid pectin: In a 5- to 6-quart kettle, combine flavored vinegar, water, and sugar. Bring to a full, rolling boil over medium-high heat. Stir in pectin and bring to a boil that cannot be stirred down. Boil, stirring constantly, for 1 minute.

To use dry pectin: In a 5- to 6-quart kettle, combine flavored vinegar, water, and pectin. Bring to a full, rolling boil over medium-high heat; then stir in the sugar. Stirring

constantly, bring to a boil that cannot be stirred down, and boil for 2 minutes.

If desired, stir in 2 drops red, yellow, or orange food coloring. Skim off and discard foam; then spoon hot jelly into hot, sterilized ½-pint canning jars to within ¼ inch of rim. Wipe rims clean with a damp cloth; top with scalded lids and bands.

Place jars on a rack in a canning kettle and cover with boiling water. Bring to simmering and simmer for 10 minutes. Lift jars from canner and set on folded towels to cool. Before storing, test for a good seal; refrigerate any jars that did not seal. Makes 3½ pints.

CANNING TECHNIQUE FOR GARLIC JELLY

Place filled jars on rack in canning kettle and cover with boiling water. Bring to a simmer, and simmer for 10 minutes.

Lift jars from canner and set on folded towels to cool.

Before storing, test seal by pressing lid with your finger; lid should stay down. Refrigerate any jars that did not seal.

SIMPLY DELICIOUS
DINNER

For 4
(Pictured on Pages 44–45)

*Harvest Chicken
with Vegetables
and Roasted Potatoes*

*Dry Chenin Blanc
or Gamay Beaujolais*

*Bartlett or Comice Pears
with Gorgonzola*

Coffee

Harvest Chicken with Vegetables and Roasted Potatoes

4 to 6 red thin-skinned potatoes, *each* 2 to 3 inches in diameter

3½ to 4-pound whole frying chicken

3 large carrots, cut into 1½-inch chunks

4 small pattypan squash

3 medium-size crookneck squash, cut into 1½-inch chunks

2 large red or green bell peppers, seeded and cut into eighths

2 cloves garlic, quartered

1 large onion, quartered

10 fresh rosemary sprigs (*each* about 6 inches long) or 1 teaspoon dry rosemary

6 to 8 cherry tomatoes, stemmed

Pierce potatoes in several places and set on rack in oven as it preheats to 375°.

Remove chicken neck and giblets; reserve for other uses, if desired. Discard lumps of fat. Rinse chicken inside and out, then pat dry. Place, breast down, in a shallow roasting pan (not on a rack). Arrange carrots, pattypan squash, crookneck squash, bell peppers, garlic, and onion around chicken. Lay 4 of the rosemary sprigs on vegetables (or sprinkle with all the dry rosemary).

Roast chicken and vegetables, uncovered, for 30 minutes; stir vegetables occasionally. Turn chicken over and continue to roast until a meat thermometer inserted in thickest portion of thigh (not touching bone) registers 185° or until meat near thighbone is no longer pink when slashed (30 to 45 more minutes). Add tomatoes during last 10 minutes of cooking.

Transfer chicken to a large platter; carefully lift vegetables from pan with a slotted spoon and mound alongside chicken. Arrange remaining 6 rosemary sprigs around chicken. Skim and discard fat from pan juices; spoon juices over vegetables. Makes 4 or 5 servings.

AN AUTUMN BRUNCH

Woodland brunch for 2
(Pictured on Pages 46–47)

Sweet Sausage Balls
Jack Cheese
Buttermilk and Currant Scone
Sweet Butter
Champagne or Sparkling Wine
Coffee or Tea

Ripe Persimmons

Buttermilk and Currant Scone

- 1 cup all-purpose flour
- 1½ tablespoons sugar
- 1 teaspoon baking powder
- ⅛ teaspoon baking soda
- ¼ cup (⅛ lb.) cold butter or margarine, cut into small pieces
- 3 tablespoons currants
- ¼ teaspoon grated orange peel
- ¼ cup buttermilk
- ⅛ teaspoon ground cinnamon mixed with ½ teaspoon sugar

In a bowl, combine flour, the 1½ tablespoons sugar, baking powder, and baking soda. Add butter; rub with your fingers to form fine crumbs. Stir in the currants and orange peel.

Make a well in the center and pour in the buttermilk. Stir with a fork until dough holds together.

Pat dough into a ball; knead on a lightly floured board for 5 or 6 turns.

Shape dough into a smooth ball and place in a greased 8- or 9-inch cake or pie pan. Sprinkle with the cinnamon-sugar mixture.

Bake in a 375° oven for 10 minutes. Then, with a sharp knife, quickly cut a cross ½ inch deep across top of scone. Bake until golden brown, about 20 minutes longer. Wrap in a towel and slip into an insulated bag to transport hot. Makes 1 scone, enough for 2 servings.

Sweet Sausage Balls

- About 1 pound mild Italian sausages
- ½ cup dry white wine

Remove sausage meat from casings and shape into 1½-inch-diameter balls. Place in an 8- to 10-inch frying pan over medium heat with wine and simmer, uncovered, until liquid boils away and meat browns; turn occasionally. With a slotted spoon, transfer sausages to a wide-mouth thermos to transport to the picnic spot. Serves 2.

MAKING A LARGE SCONE

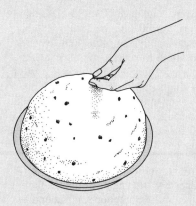

Shape dough into a smooth ball and place in a greased 8- or 9-inch pan. Sprinkle with cinnamon-sugar mixture.

Bake in a 375° oven for 10 minutes; then, with a sharp knife, quickly cut a cross ½ inch deep across the top of the scone. Continue baking until golden.

BIG BURGER BEFORE THE BIG GAME

Tailgate cookout for 8
(Pictured on Pages 48–49)

*Anaheim Chilies
with String Cheese*

*Platter Burger
with Mexican Seasonings
on Round French Bread Loaf*

Green Salad with Sunflower Seed

Ice Cold Beer or Iced Tea

Chocolate-Nut Squares

Anaheim Chilies with String Cheese

6 to 8 ounces Armenian string cheese
6 to 8 green or red Anaheim (California) chilies, cut in half lengthwise

Pull or tear cheese into strips. (If done ahead, cover, and chill up to several days.)

Cut off stems from chilies and scrape out seeds. Cut each piece in half crosswise. Arrange chilies, cut sides up, like spokes around outside of a platter. Pile string cheese in a mound in center. To eat, fill a chili section with strands of cheese. Makes 24 to 32 portions; allow 3 or 4 per person.

Chocolate-Nut Squares

1 cup coarsely chopped filberts or almonds
3 ounces semisweet chocolate
3 eggs, separated
¾ cup unsifted powdered sugar
¾ cup (⅜ lb.) butter or margarine
Chocolate Frosting (recipe follows)
Whole filberts or sliced almonds

Place chopped nuts in an 8- or 9-inch baking pan. Bake, uncovered, in a 350° oven until golden, 10 to 15 minutes; shake often to mix. Let nuts cool.

In a food processor or blender, whirl chopped nuts until finely ground. Set aside. In a food processor or by hand, finely chop or grate chocolate; set aside.

In the large bowl of an electric mixer, beat egg whites until foamy. Gradually add ½ cup of the sugar, beating until egg whites hold stiff, moist peaks. In small mixer bowl, beat together butter and remaining sugar until creamy. Beat in egg yolks until blended. Fold in beaten whites, ground nuts, and chocolate until blended.

Grease an 8- or 9-inch square baking pan. Line with waxed paper; grease paper; then spread batter in pan. Bake in a 350° oven until a thin wooden skewer inserted in center of cake comes out clean, about 35 minutes. Let cool in pan on a rack for 10 minutes. Turn out of pan and carefully remove paper. Cool thoroughly. Spread top with Chocolate Frosting. Cut into about 2-inch squares and garnish each piece with a whole filbert or an almond slice. Pack pieces side by side in a box; wrap airtight with foil or clear plastic wrap and refrigerate as long as overnight. Transport to picnic without refrigeration. Makes about 16 pieces.

Chocolate Frosting

⅔ cup unsifted powdered sugar
3 tablespoons cocoa
1½ tablespoons hot water

Smoothly mix powdered sugar, cocoa, and hot water.

Platter Burger with Mexican Seasonings

¼ cup taco sauce
3 tablespoons minced onion
2 cloves garlic, minced or pressed
2 teaspoons *each* dry oregano leaves and chili powder
1 teaspoon ground cumin
1 teaspoon salt
2½ pounds ground lean (not more than 23% fat) beef
2 medium-size ripe avocados
3 tablespoons fresh lemon juice
   Garlic salt
   Liquid hot pepper seasoning
2 cans (4 oz. *each*) whole green chilies, drained, split, and flattened
2 medium-size tomatoes, sliced
3 whole pitted ripe olives
8 ounces Cheddar cheese, sliced
½ cup soft butter or margarine
1 tablespoon chili powder
1 round loaf (24 oz.) French bread, cut in half horizontally

With your hands or a heavy spoon, mix taco sauce, onion, garlic, oregano, the 2 teaspoons chili powder, cumin, salt, and ground beef. Shape seasoned ground beef into a ball by pressing it firmly into the bottom of a large bowl. (Wrap ball of meat and chill as long as overnight; transport to the picnic in an ice chest.)

Mash avocados with a fork; stir in lemon juice, and garlic salt and liquid hot pepper seasoning to taste. Pack avocado mixture in a watertight container; pack chilies, tomatoes, and olives in another; pack the cheese in a third. (Transport to the picnic in an ice chest.)

Mix together soft butter and the 1 tablespoon chili powder; spread equal portions on each half of the cut bread. (Wrap in foil to transport to the picnic.)

At picnic, mound 25 to 30 charcoal briquets on fire grate in barbecue.

Ignite them and let burn until they're covered with gray ash, 30 to 45 minutes. Spread the coals so that they're sparsely distributed in a single layer 6 inches below the grill; then set grill in place.

Put ball of meat onto a 12- by 17-inch rimless baking sheet covered with waxed paper; pat into a round patty that measures 1 inch wider than your bread (about 12 inches). Holding both ends of the baking sheet, invert patty onto grill; peel off waxed paper. Cook about 7 minutes on each side for medium-rare (or until done to your liking). To turn, use 2 rimless baking sheets. Slide patty onto one sheet, using the second sheet to help push it on. Hold patty between the baking sheets and invert sheets to flip patty. Slide patty back onto grill, cooked side up. Overlap cheese slices on top while it continues cooking.

When meat is almost done, lightly toast bread, cut side down. Cut upper half into wedges and keep warm.

To assemble, slide burger onto the bottom half of bread, using baking sheet. Arrange chilies, tomatoes, avocado mixture, and olives on cheese. Cut into serving-size wedges and accompany with previously cut bread. Serves 8.

COOKING A GIANT BURGER

On waxed paper on a rimless baking sheet, pat meat mixture into a patty 12 inches in diameter (or 1 inch larger than your bread round).

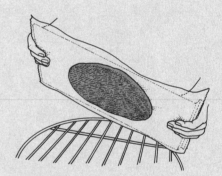

Holding both ends of the baking sheet, invert patty onto barbecue grill and pull off paper.

Turn the half-cooked patty over by sliding it onto a baking sheet, using a second sheet to help push it on.

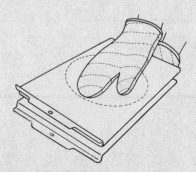

Sandwich burger between two sheets, hold together, invert patty, then slide back onto grill.

DINNER AT EIGHT

Formal dinner for 8
(Pictured on pages 50–53)

*Oysters on the Half Shell
with Ginger-Vinegar Sauce*

Cocktails or Chardonnay

Chilled Beet Soup

Chicken with a Pocketful of Leeks

Green Beans   Two-Tone Rice

Sauvignon Blanc

*Green salad
(optional)*

*Chocolate-Almond Torte
with Whipped Cream*

Coffee

Liqueurs

Oysters on the Half-shell with Ginger Vinegar Sauce

24 **to 40 small oysters in shells**
Crushed ice
4 **to 5 lemons, cut into wedges**
Ginger-Vinegar Sauce (recipe follows)
Pickled ginger for garnish (optional)

Keep oysters chilled until a few minutes before guests arrive. Designate someone to serve as oyster shucker. Insert an oyster knife or a sharp paring knife into the shell hinge and pry shell open. Discard the empty half-shell and run the knife underneath the oyster to loosen, being careful not to spill any of the oyster liquor. Place on top of a shallow tray of crushed ice.

Accompany with lemon wedges and the sauce in a bowl. Provide cocktail forks or wooden picks for dipping. Or add lemon or sauce and a bit of pickled ginger to oyster and sip from the shell.

Ginger-Vinegar Sauce

1 **cup rice wine vinegar or white wine vinegar**
2 **tablespoons water**
2 **teaspoons peeled, shredded fresh ginger**
½ **teaspoon salt**
4 **to 6 tablespoons mirin (sweet rice wine) or cream sherry**

Combine vinegar, water, ginger root, and salt. Stir in mirin or sherry to make sauce slightly sweet. Makes about 1⅓ cups.

CLEANING OYSTERS

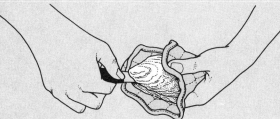

Holding oyster with a potholder to protect your hand, insert the point of an oyster knife into the pointed, hinged end of the oyster.

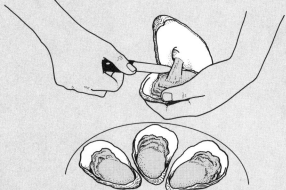

When oyster has been penetrated, cut muscle to release and pry shell apart. Cut oyster free. Discard flat half of shell and serve oyster from cupped half.

Chicken with a Pocketful of Leeks

4 **whole chicken breasts**
(about 1 lb. *each*)
Sautéed Leeks (recipe follows)
3 **to 4 tablespoons butter or**
margarine
½ **cup dry white wine**
¾ **cup regular-strength chicken broth**
1 **cup whipping cream**
¼ **teaspoon grated lemon peel**
1 **tablespoon fresh lemon juice**
Thin lemon slices (optional)

Remove and discard skin from chicken breasts. With a sharp knife, cut down both sides of each chicken breastbone and along ribs to free meat. Gently pull off the feather fillets (the slim fillets on the inside of each half-breast), which are distinguished by a small tendon. Then cut a pocket lengthwise through the thick portion of each half-breast. (Pocket should be about 3½ inches long and 2 inches deep.)

Tuck ⅛ of the Sautéed Leeks in each breast pocket. You can cover and chill breasts and fillets as long as overnight.

In a 12- to 14-inch frying pan, melt the butter over medium-high heat. Add chicken fillets and as many filled breasts as will fit in pan without crowding. Brown both sides, turning carefully. Remove from pan and brown remaining breasts; then add wine and broth. Return remaining filled breasts to pan. Simmer, covered, for 7 minutes.

Carefully turn filled breasts over and add fillet pieces to pan. Simmer, covered, until chicken is no longer pink in center, about 3 minutes. With a slotted spatula, transfer chicken to platter; keep warm.

Boil pan juices, uncovered, until reduced by half. Add cream and any juices that have drained from chicken and boil again until reduced to ⅔ cup. Stir in lemon peel and juice to make lemon cream sauce.

To serve, place a stuffed breast and a fillet on each plate. Pour lemon cream sauce over chicken. Garnish with lemon slices. Serves 8.

STUFFING CHICKEN BREAST POCKETS

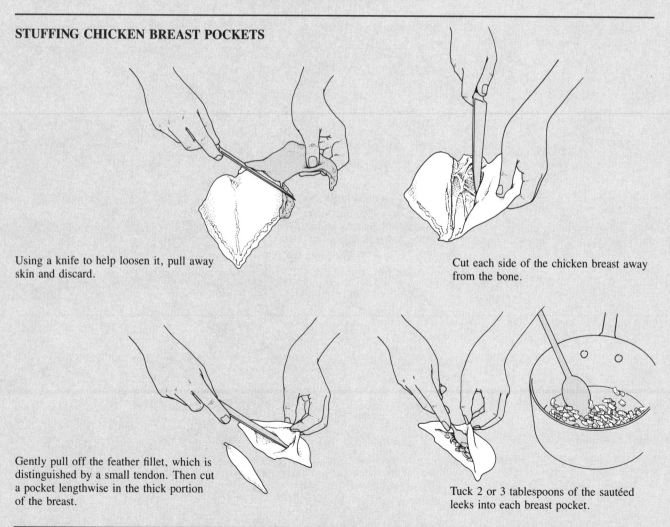

Using a knife to help loosen it, pull away skin and discard.

Cut each side of the chicken breast away from the bone.

Gently pull off the feather fillet, which is distinguished by a small tendon. Then cut a pocket lengthwise in the thick portion of the breast.

Tuck 2 or 3 tablespoons of the sautéed leeks into each breast pocket.

Sautéed Leeks

4 to 5 large leeks
¼ cup (⅛ lb.) butter or margarine
1 tablespoon fresh tarragon leaves *or* 1 teaspoon of the dry herb

Trim off root ends and green parts from leeks. Wash well. Thinly slice to make about 3½ cups. In a 10- to 12-inch frying pan, melt butter over medium heat. Add leeks and tarragon; stir until leeks are very soft. Use hot or cold.

Two-Tone Rice

¾ cup wild rice
4½ cups regular-strength chicken broth
¾ cup long grain white rice
¼ cup (⅛ lb.) butter or margarine

Pour the wild rice into a fine strainer and rinse thoroughly under hot running water; drain well. Add 3 cups chicken broth to a 1½- to 2-quart pan; bring to a boil and add wild rice. Cover and simmer until rice is tender, 30 to 45 minutes. (Wild rice can be kept warm over hot water for 2 to 3 hours.)

Cook white rice in butter until lightly parched. In a separate 2- to 3-quart pan, pour 1½ cups chicken broth; bring to a boil and add the parched white rice. Cover and simmer until liquid is absorbed or until rice is tender.

Drain off any liquid from wild rice and mix the wild rice with the white rice; season with salt and pepper. Serves 8.

Chilled Beet Soup

6 cups peeled, diced beets (about 7 medium-size)
2 cans (14½ oz. *each*) regular-strength chicken broth
2 cups buttermilk
1 tablespoon chopped fresh dill or 1 teaspoon of the dry herb
Salt and pepper
¾ cup thinly sliced green onion
1 large apple
2 teaspoons fresh lemon juice
Sour cream

Put beets in a 3- to 4-quart pan, add broth, and bring to a boil; reduce heat, cover, and simmer 25 minutes or until tender.

Whirl half of the mixture at a time in a blender until smooth. Stir in buttermilk, dill, salt and pepper to taste, and onion. Cover and chill as long as overnight.

To serve, pour into a tureen or individual bowls. Core and slice or dice apple and mix well with lemon juice. Offer apple and sour cream to add to soup. Makes 10 cups or 8 servings.

Chocolate-Almond Torte

5 ounces semisweet or bittersweet chocolate
¼ cup water
1 teaspoon instant coffee powder
5 eggs, separated
¼ teaspoon cream of tartar
1½ cups sugar
⅔ cup (⅓ lb.) butter or margarine, at room temperature
2 cups (8 to 10 oz.) ground blanched almonds
½ cup finely crushed zwieback crumbs (about 8 pieces)
Cocoa
1 tablespoon powdered sugar
Sweetened whipped cream (optional)

In a 1½- to 2-quart pan, combine chocolate, water, and coffee powder. Melt chocolate over low heat, stirring (takes about 6 minutes); set aside.

In large bowl of electric mixer, beat egg whites with cream of tartar at high speed until whites will hold stiff peaks; set aside.

In another large bowl, beat sugar, butter, and egg yolks on high speed with electric mixer until fluffy, about 1 minute. Beat in chocolate mixture, almonds, and zwieback crumbs. Gently but thoroughly fold in egg whites by hand.

Pour into a greased, cocoa-dusted 11-inch cheesecake or tart pan (at least 2 inches deep) with removable bottom. Bake in a 325° oven until torte feels firm and set in center when gently pressed, about 1¼ hours. (Because torte forms a crusty surface before center is set, pay attention to the test for doneness.)

Set torte in pan on rack to cool completely. Slip a knife between pan and cake to release. Remove rim from torte; put on plate, dust with powdered sugar, and garnish with whole unblanched or toasted almonds if desired. Cut into wedges and serve with whipped cream. Serves 8.

A BIG BUFFET THAT CAN GROW

Supper party for 25 to 125
(Pictured on Pages 54–57)

Cold Sliced Turkey, Ham, and Roast Beef

Cheese Tray

Condiments: Mayonnaise, Mustard, Whole Cranberry Sauce

Vegetable Tray Salad

Parsley-Potato Salad

Fresh Fruit Salad

Pasta and Pepper Salad

Pumpkin Bread *Double Cheese Bread*

French Bread *Butter*

White and Red Jug Wines

Sparkling Water *Apple Cider*

Spice Cake with Caramel Icing

Seed Cake *Pork Sausage Cake*

Coffee and Tea

Vegetable Tray Salad

2 cups salad oil
1 cup tarragon-flavored vinegar
1 tablespoon sugar
¼ cup chopped fresh or 2 tablespoons dry tarragon
4 large cucumbers
2 pounds *each* beets and carrots
6 large ripe avocados
Salt and pepper

Stir together oil, vinegar, sugar, and tarragon. Set aside.

To assemble salad, peel cucumbers and slice as thinly as possible with a sharp knife or the slicing blade of a food processor. Peel beets and carrots; coarsely shred each (separately) in a food processor or use the large holes of a hand grater. If made ahead, seal each vegetable in a plastic bag and chill as long as overnight.

On a large rimmed serving tray or platter, arrange the cucumbers, beets, and carrots in separate rows; leave room along one side of the tray for the avocados. If assembled ahead, cover and chill up to 6 hours.

To serve, peel, pit, and slice the avocados; arrange on tray with vegetables. Stir or shake dressing to blend; then pour evenly over all. Offer salt and pepper to season individual servings. Makes about 6 quarts (1½ gallons).

Parsley-Potato Salad

4 pounds thin-skinned potatoes, scrubbed
Boiling water
1 cup finely chopped parsley
Onion Cream Dressing (recipe follows)
Salt

In a covered 5- to 6-quart pan, cook potatoes in enough boiling water to cover until tender when pierced. Cool; then peel if desired. Cut into ¼-inch-thick slices into a salad bowl and add parsley and dressing. Stir gently to mix; add salt to taste. Cover and let stand for 2 to 3 hours or overnight; stir occasionally. Makes about 3 quarts (¾ gallon).

Onion Cream Dressing

1 cup *each* sour cream and mayonnaise
6 tablespoons white wine vinegar
1 large onion, finely chopped

Combine sour cream, mayonnaise, vinegar, and onion.

Pasta and Pepper Salad

1 pound small shell macaroni
Water
1 cup olive oil or salad oil
⅔ cup white wine vinegar
2 tablespoons dry basil
2 cloves garlic, pressed or minced
⅔ cup grated Parmesan cheese
¼ to ½ teaspoon pepper
Salt
¼ cup chopped parsley
2 large red or green bell peppers, diced

Cook the pasta in 4 quarts boiling water in a 5- to 6-quart pan just until tender to bite, about 10 minutes; drain. Rinse with cold water and drain well. In a large bowl, stir together olive oil, vinegar, basil, garlic, cheese, and pepper. Mix in macaroni; salt to taste. Cover and chill at least 4 hours or overnight. Shortly before serving, stir in parsley and red pepper. Makes about 3 quarts (¾ gallon).

Pumpkin Bread

⅔ cup (⅓ lb.) butter or margarine
2½ cups sugar
1 can (1 lb.) pumpkin
3⅓ cups all-purpose flour
1 teaspoon *each* baking powder, baking soda, and salt
4 teaspoons ground cinnamon
2 teaspoons ground allspice
1 cup *each* raisins and broken pieces walnuts or pecans

In the large bowl of an electric mixer, cream butter and sugar until fluffy; then blend in pumpkin.

Mix together flour, baking powder, baking soda, salt, cinnamon, and allspice. With mixer, thoroughly blend dry ingredients into pumpkin mixture; then stir in raisins and nuts. Pour batter equally into 2 greased and flour-dusted 5- by 9-inch loaf pans.

Bake in a 350° oven for about 1 hour or just until bread begins to pull away from pan sides and a wooden pick, inserted in center, comes out clean. Let cool 10 minutes; then turn out onto rack to cool thoroughly. If made ahead, wrap airtight and freeze. Thaw unwrapped; allow at least 3 hours. To serve, cut each loaf into 12 to 14 slices about ½ inch thick. Makes 2 loaves, enough for 25 servings.

Double Cheese Bread

⅔ cup (⅓ lb.) butter or margarine
1⅓ cups sugar
4 eggs
3 cups all-purpose flour
1 cup whole-wheat flour
4 teaspoons baking powder
½ teaspoon baking soda
1 teaspoon salt
1½ cups chopped walnuts
⅔ cup *each* milk and white wine (or use all milk)
1½ cups (6 oz.) shredded sharp Cheddar cheese
1 cup (4-oz. package) crumbled blue cheese
1 tablespoon *each* poppy seed and sesame seed

In the large bowl of an electric mixer, beat butter with sugar until fluffy. Add eggs one at a time, blending well after each addition.

Stir together flour, baking powder, baking soda, salt, and walnuts. To the butter mixture, add dry ingredients alternately with the milk and wine, mixing until blended.

Divide the batter in half; stir the Cheddar cheese into one portion, the blue cheese into the other.

Grease and flour-dust two 5- by 9-inch loaf pans. Spoon half of the Cheddar cheese batter into each pan, distributing down one long side; then spoon half the blue cheese batter alongside. Sprinkle poppy seed over the Cheddar cheese portions and sesame seed over the blue cheese sections.

Bake in a 350° oven for 1 hour or until a wooden pick, inserted, comes out clean. Let stand 10 minutes; then turn out onto a rack to cool completely. If made ahead, wrap airtight and store in the freezer. Thaw unwrapped; allow at least 3 hours. Carefully cut each loaf into 12 slices; it has a tendency to crumble. If you like, cut slices in half lengthwise. Makes 2 loaves, enough for 25 servings.

Note: If you prefer, you can make one Cheddar loaf and one blue cheese loaf; just put all the batter for one flavor in one pan, the other in another pan and bake as directed.

FORMING DOUBLE CHEESE BREAD

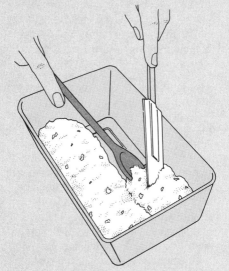

Distribute cheddar cheese batter down one long side of pan, then spoon blue cheese batter alongside.

Sprinkle poppy seed over the cheddar portion and sesame seed over the blue cheese side.

Spice Cake with Caramel Icing

1 cup (½ lb.) butter or margarine, at room temperature
2¼ cups sugar
5 eggs
3 cups all-purpose flour
1 tablespoon *each* ground cloves and ground cinnamon
1 teaspoon baking powder
½ teaspoon baking soda
1 cup sour cream
1 cup raisins
   Caramel Icing (recipe follows)
   Blanched almonds for decoration

In the large bowl of an electric mixer, beat butter and sugar until fluffy; add eggs, one at a time, blending well. Sift and measure flour; then sift again with cloves, cinnamon, baking powder, and baking soda.

Add flour mixture and sour cream alternately to butter mixture, blending with mixer in 2 or 3 additions. Stir in raisins.

Pour batter into a buttered and flour-dusted 10-inch tube pan. Bake in a 350° oven for about 1 hour or until cake just begins to pull from pan sides and a wooden pick, inserted in center, comes out clean. Let cool 10 minutes; then turn out of pan onto rack to cool completely. If made ahead, wrap airtight and freeze. Thaw unwrapped; allow at least 3 hours. Up to a day before serving, spread all the Caramel Icing very thickly over top of cake; some will flow irregularly down the sides. Decorate with almonds. Slice thinly to serve. Makes 12 to 16 slices.

Caramel Icing

½ cup (¼ lb.) butter or margarine
1 cup firmly packed brown sugar
⅓ cup half-and-half (light cream) or whipping cream
2 cups unsifted powdered sugar

Melt butter in a 2- to 3-quart pan. Add brown sugar and half-and-half. Quickly bring to a full boil and cook, stirring, for 1 minute. Remove from heat and let cool to lukewarm. Add powdered sugar and beat until blended and smooth. Use at once.

Seed Cake

¾ cup (⅜ lb.) butter or margarine, at room temperature
2 cups sugar
4 eggs
4 teaspoons grated lemon peel
3 cups all-purpose flour
2½ teaspoons baking powder
½ teaspoon ground nutmeg
1 cup milk
1 tablespoon *each* caraway seed, poppy seed, and anise seed
   Powdered sugar

In the large bowl of an electric mixer, beat butter and sugar until fluffy. Mix in eggs, one at a time, blending thoroughly; then add the lemon peel.

Mix flour with baking powder and nutmeg. Add dry ingredients to butter mixture alternately with milk; blend well.

Butter and flour-dust a 10-inch tube pan or a 12-cup fluted-tube cake pan. Spoon about ¼ of the batter into pan and scatter caraway seed on top. Cover with ⅓ of remaining batter and sprinkle with poppy seed. Top with ½ remaining batter and sprinkle with anise seed; spoon in the rest of the batter.

Bake in a 350° oven for about 1 hour or until a wooden pick, inserted in center, comes out clean. Let cool 10 minutes; then invert out onto a rack to cool completely. If made ahead, wrap airtight and freeze. Thaw unwrapped; allow at least 3 hours. To serve, dust with powdered sugar and cut in thin slices. Makes 20 to 25 slices.

Pork Sausage Cake

1 pound bulk pork sausage, uncooked
1 cup raisins
1 cup chopped walnuts or pecans
1½ cups firmly packed brown sugar
1½ cups granulated sugar
2 eggs
3 cups all-purpose flour
2 teaspoons pumpkin pie spice
1½ teaspoons ground ginger
1 teaspoon baking powder
1 cup water
2 teaspoons instant coffee
1 teaspoon baking soda
   Pecan halves, holly leaves, and candied (glacé) whole cherries for decoration (optional)

In a large bowl, mix together sausage, raisins, walnuts, sugars, and eggs. Mix flour with pumpkin pie spice, ginger, and baking powder. Stir together water, instant coffee, and baking soda. Add flour mixture and liquid alternately to sausage mixture. Pour into a buttered and flour-dusted 10-inch tube pan or a 12-cup fluted-tube cake pan.

Bake in a 350° oven for 1 hour 25 minutes or until a wooden pick, inserted in center, comes out clean. (Lightly cover cake with foil if it begins to brown excessively.) Let cool 10 minutes, then turn out onto a rack to cool completely. Wrap airtight to freeze; thaw unwrapped; allow at least 3 hours. To serve, decorate with pecans, holly, and cherries if desired. Cut in thin slices. Makes 20 to 25 slices.

WESTERN HARVEST THANKSGIVING

Holiday dinner for 10 to 12
(Pictured on Pages 58–61)

*Chilled Artichokes
with Herbed Goat Cheese*

*Roasted Squab or Quail
with Pears and Red Wine Sauce*

Wild Rice with Mushrooms

*Butter-steamed Brussels Sprouts
and Red Bell Peppers*

*Spaghetti Squash
with Orange-Filbert Butter*

Pueblo Bread

Chardonnay and/or Merlot

Fruit Salad Platter

*Nut Mosaic Tart
with Whipped Cream*

Custard Persimmon Pie

*Late-Harvest Riesling
or Sparkling Wine*

Coffee

Chilled Artichokes with Herbed Goat Cheese

5 or 6 artichokes (3-in. diameter)
4 quarts water
⅓ cup white wine vinegar
¼ cup olive oil or salad oil
2 bay leaves
½ teaspoon whole black peppers
**6 ounces unripened chèvre
    (goat cheese) with herb coating**
12 to 14 cherry tomatoes

Pull small base leaves (bracts) off artichokes and discard. With a knife, cut stems flush with bottoms. Trim off the thorns at the tip of each artichoke; then, with scissors, snip thorns off remaining leaves.

As each artichoke is trimmed, drop it into an 8-quart kettle that contains the water, vinegar, olive oil or salad oil, bay leaves, and peppers.

Bring to a boil over high heat, cover, and simmer until stem ends are tender when pierced, about 35 minutes. Lift artichokes from liquid and let drain, top sides down. Serve at room temperature, or cover and chill until next day.

Before serving, gently push apart leaves in the center of each artichoke. Reach in with a spoon and scrape out the fuzzy choke; discard. Place artichokes on a large platter and, if you like, push leaves on one artichoke back from the base onto the platter, making a wreath of leaves. (See illustration.) In the cupped bottom of this artichoke, mound the goat cheese, which has been blended in food processor or blender until creamy. Garnish with cherry tomatoes; serve with a knife to cut up artichoke bottoms and wooden picks to spear the pieces. Serves 10 to 12.

PREPARING ARTICHOKES

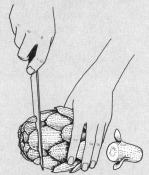

Cut off stem flush with bottom. Trim off thorns at tip.

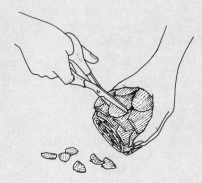

With scissors, cut off tips of remaining leaves.

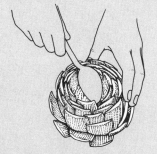

Gently push apart leaves in center of cooked artichoke. With a spoon, scrape out fuzzy choke and discard.

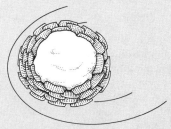

Place artichoke on serving platter and push leaves back to make a wreath. Mound filling in center.

Roasted Squab or Quail with Pears and Red Wine Sauce

    3 cups dry red wine
    ½ cup sugar
    1½ teaspoons whole black peppers
    6 medium-size firm-ripe Bosc or
       Comice pears, peeled, cut in half
       lengthwise, and cored *or* 12 whole
       Seckel or other miniature pears
    10 to 12 squab (*each* 12 to 16 oz.) *or* 20
       to 36 quail (*each* about 3½ oz.)
    1⅓ cups (⅔ lb.) butter or margarine
    ⅔ cup minced shallots or red onion
    1½ cups regular-strength beef broth

In a 4- to 5-quart pan, combine
wine, sugar, peppers, and pears.
Bring to boil, cover, and simmer,
turning pears several times until
tender when pierced, about 7
minutes. Set aside in a warm place.

Rinse birds inside and out and pat
dry; save necks and giblets for other
uses. Melt 4 to 6 tablespoons of the
butter in a 10- to 12-inch frying pan
over medium-high heat. Add birds
without crowding; turn to brown all
sides (takes 3 to 5 minutes per bird).

Arrange birds, breast up and slightly
apart, on racks in 2 roasting pans,
each 12 by 17 inches. Roast birds in
separate 400° ovens until breast meat
near bone is still moist but not
wet-looking (make a slash in breast
just above wing joint to test); the
meat should still be red. Allow 20 to
25 minutes for squab; 12 to 15
minutes for quail. If you don't have
2 ovens, roast each batch separately
in the same oven; cook the first batch
the shorter amount of time and keep
the birds warm while the second
batch cooks.

Drain juices from birds into pan;
arrange birds on a large platter; lift
pears from wine and put alongside;
keep warm.

Pour pan drippings into the frying
pan, add shallots, and stir over high
heat for 2 minutes. Add broth and
1½ cups of the pear poaching liquid.
Boil rapidly until sauce is reduced to
1⅓ cups. Turn heat to low and add
remaining butter all at once; stir
constantly until butter melts and
blends into sauce. Pour sauce
through a strainer into a small bowl.

Ladle sauce over individual portions.
Allow 1 squab or 2 or 3 quail per
serving. Serves 10 to 12.

Wild Rice with Mushrooms

    2½ pounds mushrooms
    ¼ cup (⅛ lb.) butter or margarine
    ¾ teaspoon dry thyme leaves
    2 cups wild rice
    6 cups regular-strength chicken broth
       Salt and pepper

Rinse mushrooms, pat dry, trim off
woody ends, and slice mushrooms.
Melt butter in a 12- to 14-inch frying
pan. Add mushrooms and thyme and
cook over medium heat, stirring
often, until liquid has evaporated and
mushrooms are slightly browned,
about 20 minutes. (At this point,
mushrooms can be set aside for 3 to
4 hours; reheat before using.)

Rinse rice. Add broth to a 4- to
5-quart pan; bring to a boil and add
rice. Cover and simmer until rice is
tender to bite, about 40 minutes. Set
aside, covered, for up to 2 hours if
desired; reheat.

To serve, drain off any liquid; season
rice with salt and pepper; reheat
mushrooms if necessary and mix
with rice. Serves 10 to 12.

Butter-steamed Brussels Sprouts and Red Bell Peppers

    2 pounds Brussels sprouts
    3 quarts water
    2 large red bell peppers
    6 tablespoons butter or margarine
    1 teaspoon *each* dry basil and
       prepared mustard
       Salt and pepper

Trim off and discard stem ends from
washed Brussels sprouts. Bring water
to a boil in a 4- to 5-quart kettle.
Add sprouts and cook, uncovered, at
a gentle boil until tender when
pierced, about 8 minutes. Drain,
immerse in ice water, and drain
again. Cover and chill overnight, if
desired.

Seed peppers and cut into ¾-inch
strips. Melt butter or margarine in a
4- to 5-quart pan on medium-high
heat; add peppers; cover and steam
until slightly limp, about 3 minutes.
Stir in basil, mustard, and Brussels
sprouts. Cook, uncovered, stirring
frequently, until sprouts are heated
through, about 5 minutes. Season
with salt and pepper to taste. Serves
10 to 12.

Spaghetti Squash with Orange-Filbert Butter

    2 spaghetti squash (about 3 lb. *each*)
    1 cup filberts (hazelnuts), chopped
    1 cup (½ lb.) butter or margarine, at
       room temperature
    1 tablespoon grated orange peel
    2 tablespoons fresh orange juice
    2 tablespoons firmly packed brown
       sugar
    ½ teaspoon ground nutmeg
       Salt

With a fork, pierce spaghetti squash
shells in 5 or 6 places; set on a
rimmed 10- by 15-inch baking sheet.
Bake in a 325° oven until shells give
when pressed, about 2 hours. Turn
squash over after 1 hour.

Place filberts in a rimmed pan in oven with squash until the nuts are golden under the skin, about 15 minutes.

Blend butter with orange peel, brown sugar, and nutmeg; set aside.

Cut the top third off each squash, or cut in half horizontally. Scoop out seeds and discard. Pull squash strands free with a fork; pile all the strands either in a ⅔ shell or in 2 shell halves. Add the nuts and orange butter and mix gently with a fork; season to taste with salt. Serves 10 to 12.

COOKING SPAGHETTI SQUASH

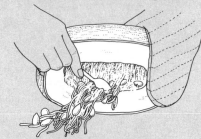

Cut spaghetti squash horizontally; scoop out seeds with a spoon.

Pull cooked squash strands free with a fork.

Pile strands into the squash bottoms.

Pueblo Bread

2 **tablespoons butter, margarine, or shortening**
1 **cup hot water**
2 **teaspoons** *each* **salt and sugar**
½ **cup warm water (about 100° F)**
1 **package yeast (active dry or compressed)**
   About 5 cups all-purpose flour

Measure butter into a bowl; add hot water, salt, and sugar; stir occasionally until fat melts. Meanwhile, blend warm water with yeast in another small bowl.

Measure 4 cups of the flour into a large bowl, making a well in the center. When water with fat is cooled to lukewarm, combine with yeast mixture and pour into flour well. Blend ingredients thoroughly.

Measure the remaining 1 cup flour onto a board, spreading part of it in a medium-heavy layer; turn dough out onto this area. Knead dough vigorously for 15 minutes, gradually working in a little of the flour at a time until all is absorbed by the dough. (If dough still feels a little sticky, add a little flour to board to prevent sticking.) At the end of 15

minutes, the dough should feel smooth and velvety with no flour on the surface.

Place dough in a deep bowl; cover with plastic wrap and set in a warm place; let rise until doubled. Knead again on a very lightly floured board to remove air bubbles.

Divide dough into 2 equal portions; shape each into a ball and flatten slightly. To shape each loaf, roll the ball of dough out on a lightly floured board to make a circle 8 inches in diameter. Fold circle almost in half; the top circular edge should set back about 1 inch from the center section of the bottom edge. (See illustration.)

Divide shaped dough into 3 equal sections by making 2 slashes about ⅔ of the way through loaf on the curved side. (See illustration.) Set each loaf in a greased 9-inch pie pan, spreading slashes apart and letting ends of loaf extend up rim of pan.

Cover shaped loaves lightly with plastic wrap and let rise in a warm place until about doubled. Bake in a 350° oven for 1 hour or until richly browned. Place a small pan of water in the oven with the loaves; do not put directly beneath baking pan. Serve loaves hot or cold, and tear or cut apart. Makes 2 loaves.

SHAPING PUEBLO BREAD

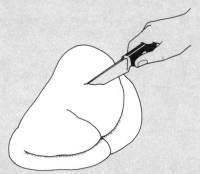

Roll out dough to 8-inch diameter circle. Fold almost in half, with top edge set back 1 inch from bottom edge. Divide into 3 sections by slashing ⅔ through curved side of dough.

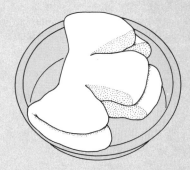

Set in a greased 9-inch pie plate, spreading slashes apart and letting ends of loaf extend up rim of pan.

Fruit Salad Platter

1 pineapple (about 3 lbs.)
½ teaspoon grated lime peel
2 tablespoons *each* fresh lime juice and chopped fresh (or dry) mint leaves
1½ tablespoons sugar
1 tablespoon *each* white wine vinegar and salad oil
   Dash of salt
2 ripe papayas
1 pound seedless red grapes
2 large avocados

Cut top off pineapple; discard. Put pineapple on a rimmed board or plate to collect juice; quarter fruit lengthwise; then slice off and discard core sections and cut meat from skin with a curved (grapefruit) knife. Discard skin and cut meat in 1-inch chunks; set aside.

Measure pineapple juice; you should have ⅓ cup. (If you don't, crush several pieces of fruit.) Combine juice, lime peel, lime juice, mint, sugar, vinegar, salad oil, and salt; stir to make dressing. Cover and chill.

Group pineapple in one corner of a large platter. Peel, seed, and slice papayas and arrange on platter. Rinse and drain grapes; then snip into small bunches. Arrange grapes on platter. At this point, you can cover and chill fruit as long as 4 hours.

Just before serving, peel, pit, and slice avocados and arrange on platter. Drizzle fruit with dressing and serve. Serves 10 to 12.

Nut Mosaic Tart

3 cups whole or half nuts (almonds, walnuts, filberts, macadamias, pistachios, or pecans; use one kind or equal parts of 3 varieties)
   Butter Pastry (recipe follows)
3 eggs
1 cup honey
½ teaspoon grated orange peel
1 teaspoon vanilla
¼ cup (⅛ lb.) butter or margarine, melted
   Sweetened whipped cream (optional)

Place nuts (if unroasted) in a shallow pan and put in a 350° oven until lightly toasted, about 10 minutes; let cool. Press Butter Pastry evenly over bottom and sides of an 11-inch tart pan with removable bottom.

In a bowl, combine eggs, honey, orange peel, vanilla, and melted butter; beat well until blended. Stir in toasted nuts. Pour into pastry-lined tart pan. Bake on the bottom rack of a 350° oven until top is golden brown all over, about 40 minutes. Let cool on a wire rack. Remove pan sides. Offer wedges with whipped cream. Serves 10 to 12.

Butter Pastry

1⅓ cups all-purpose flour
3 tablespoons sugar
½ cup (¼ lb.) butter or margarine, cut in pieces
1 egg yolk

Combine flour, sugar, and butter. Whirl in a food processor or rub between your fingers until coarse crumbs form. Add egg yolk; process or stir until dough sticks together.

Custard Persimmon Pie

   Pastry for a 9-inch single-crust pie
3 eggs
2 cups Persimmon Purée (recipe follows)
½ cup firmly packed brown sugar
1 teaspoon ground cinnamon
½ teaspoon *each* ground ginger and salt
¼ teaspoon ground cloves
1 large can (13 oz.) evaporated milk
   Sweetened whipped cream (optional)

Roll out pastry on a floured board and fit into 9-inch pie pan. Flute the edge.

With an electric mixer, beat eggs to blend. Add purée, sugar, cinnamon, ginger, salt, cloves, and milk; beat to blend thoroughly. Pour into pastry. If desired, cut leaves and stems from pastry scraps, bake on a separate pan along with pie until golden, and decorate top.

Bake on the lowest rack of a 425° oven for 15 minutes. Reduce temperature to 350° and continue baking until pie looks set but jiggles slightly in center when pan is gently shaken, about 45 minutes more. Cool to room temperature to serve. Offer whipped cream if desired. Serves 10 to 12.

Persimmon Purée

4 large, very ripe (should feel very soft), pointy-tipped 'Hachiya' persimmons

Cut tips off persimmons and scoop flesh from the shell with a spoon. Discard skin, stem, and any seeds. Whirl pulp in a blender until smooth; you need 2 cups.

BIG BREAKFAST BONANZA

Supersize pancake for 6
(Pictured on Pages 62–63)

Freshly Squeezed Orange Juice
Big Dutch Baby Pancakes
Powdered Sugar
Lemon or Lime Wedges
Warm Honey and Syrups
Sliced or Sautéed Fresh Fruits
Sliced Ham
Coffee or Tea

Big Dutch Baby Pancakes

½ cup (¼ lb.) butter or margarine
6 eggs
1½ cups *each* milk and all-purpose
   flour
   Ground nutmeg
   Toppings (suggestions follow)

To make 1 large pancake, you will need a shallow 4½- to 5-quart pan; to bake 2 smaller pancakes at once, you'll need 2 shallow pans each 2 to 3 quarts. Choose a paella pan; an iron frying pan; a ceramic, glass, or metal baking dish; or a foil roasting pan. Any shape will work, but the pan should be fairly shallow—not much more than 3 inches deep. Measure its volume by pouring in quart measures of water.

Put all the butter in the large pan, or half in each of the 2 small pans; set pan or pans in a 425° oven. Then mix batter quickly while butter melts.

In a blender on high speed or a food processor, whirl eggs for 1 minute. With motor running, pour in milk; then add flour, a spoonful at a time. When all is added, whirl 30 seconds more. (With a rotary mixer, beat eggs until light and lemon colored; gradually beat in milk, then flour.)

Remove pan or pans from oven. Quickly pour all the batter into the large pan, or half into each of the small pans. Return to oven and bake until puffy and well browned—20 to 25 minutes, depending on pan size. Dust with ground nutmeg. Offer a choice of toppings. Serves 6.

Toppings

The classic. Have a shaker or bowl of powdered sugar and thick wedges of lemon at the table. Sprinkle sugar on hot pancake; then squeeze lemon over it.

Syrups. Pass warm honey, maple syrup, or any favorite fruit syrup.

Fresh fruit. Serve a bowl of sliced strawberries, sweetened to taste; defrosted frozen peach slices; or any fruits in season, cut and sweetened. (You'll need about 4 cups.)

Hot fruit. Gently fry fresh apple or pear slices in a little butter (you'll need 3 to 4 large apples or pears and 2 to 3 tablespoons butter) until tender and translucent. Sweeten with sugar or honey to taste and offer with cinnamon-sugar and sour cream or yogurt. Or heat banana or papaya slices in melted butter over medium heat, turning until hot; serve with lime wedges.

WINTER WARM-UP

Cold-day lunch or dinner for 6
(Pictured on Pages 64–65)

Hot Buttered Cauliflower Soup

Crusty Bread

*Spinach-filled Pasta Roll
with Tomato-Cream Sauce*

Watercress and Apple Salad

Chianti Classico or Barbera

Chestnuts in Port

Espresso

Hot Buttered Cauliflower Soup

2 cans (14½ oz. *each*) regular-strength chicken broth

1 medium-size (about 1½ lbs.) cauliflower, thinly sliced

2 large leeks (green leaves trimmed off), split lengthwise, washed well, and thinly sliced

1 cup whipping cream

½ teaspoon ground nutmeg Salt

About 3 tablespoons butter or margarine

In a 3- to 4-quart pan, combine chicken broth, cauliflower, and leeks. Bring to a boil, cover, and simmer until cauliflower is tender enough to mash easily, about 15 minutes.

In a blender or food processor, whirl mixture, a portion at a time, until smooth (or force through a food mill). Return to pan, add whipping cream, ¼ teaspoon of the ground nutmeg, and salt to taste; heat to simmering (or chill, covered, up to 3 days; then heat to serve). Ladle into bowls and, if desired, add to each a small lump of butter; then sprinkle with more ground nutmeg. Makes about 1½ quarts or 6 first-course servings.

Spinach-filled Pasta Roll

⅓ cup pine nuts

About 1⅓ cups all-purpose flour

2 eggs

2 teaspoons olive oil or salad oil

Spinach Filling (recipe follows)

Tomato-Cream Sauce (recipe follows)

Freshly grated Parmesan cheese

Spread pine nuts in a single layer in a rimmed 8- or 9-inch pan. Shaking nuts occasionally, bake in a 350° oven until golden, about 8 minutes. Set aside.

Place 1 cup of the flour in a food processor or bowl. Beat together eggs and olive oil; process (or stir) into flour until dough sticks together. Gradually add enough of the remaining flour so that dough forms a nonsticky ball. (Or knead hand-mixed dough on a floured board until velvety, about 5 minutes.) Cover dough with plastic wrap; let rest at least 5 minutes.

Roll dough out on a floured board to form a 15- by 17-inch rectangle; lift edges of dough and add flour to board frequently to avoid sticking. Trim edges.

Spread Spinach Filling on dough to within 3 inches of long side near you, 1 inch of other sides. Starting from long side near you, roll dough over filling to form a smooth, compact cylinder. Dampen roll at ends and along seam with droplets of water; press together firmly with your fingers to seal. Wrap roll in 20-inch-long piece of cheesecloth; tie string around ends and at several places along roll (or wrap 2 half-rolls individually). To cook in a long pan, put roll on rack and lower into boiling water to cover. (Or set halves in kettle or Dutch oven at least 10 inches in diameter and add boiling water to cover.) Cook on high heat until boil resumes; then reduce to simmering. Cover pan and cook until pasta looks very crinkly (you can see it through the cheesecloth) and roll feels firm when pressed with back of a spoon, 25 to 30 minutes.

Drain most of the water from pan; then lift roll (on rack or with string) from pan and let cool 5 minutes. Snip strings. Gently turn onto a large platter, removing cheesecloth; if cooked in two pieces, join halves on platter. (If made ahead, put roll on ovenproof platter or on a rimmed baking sheet at least 18 inches long; cover and let stand at room temperature up to 3 hours. Then bake, covered, in a 350° oven until hot in the center, 25 to 30 minutes.)

Spoon the warm Tomato-Cream Sauce around the pasta roll; sprinkle roll with pine nuts. To serve, cut into 1½-inch slices, spooning sauce alongside or on top. Pour any remaining sauce into a bowl and offer along with Parmesan cheese. Serves 6.

Spinach Filling

2¼ **pounds spinach**
¼ **cup (⅛ lb.) butter or margarine**
1 **large onion, chopped**
2 **cups chopped mushrooms**
⅓ **cup (about 1 oz.) chopped prosciutto or cooked ham (optional)**
1 **pound ricotta cheese**
2 **eggs**
1 **cup freshly grated Parmesan cheese**
¼ **teaspoon *each* ground nutmeg and pepper**
   Salt

Discard stems and coarse leaves from spinach. Wash leaves; place half at a time in a 10- to 12-inch frying pan over medium heat. Cover and cook until spinach wilts, about 3 minutes; stir once. Drain well; chop coarsely.

Melt butter or margarine in the frying pan on medium-high heat. Add onion and mushrooms; cook, stirring, until onion is limp and juices evaporate. Remove from heat; beat in prosciutto, ricotta cheese, eggs, spinach, cheese, nutmeg, pepper, and salt to taste. (If made ahead, cover and chill as long as overnight.)

Tomato-Cream Sauce

½ **cup (¼ lb.) butter or margarine**
1 **small onion, chopped**
1 **large carrot, peeled and chopped**
1 **can (28 oz.) pear-shaped tomatoes**
½ **teaspoon sugar**
   Salt
½ **cup whipping cream**

Melt butter in a 10- to 12-inch frying pan on medium-high heat. Add onion and carrot; cook, stirring, until onion is limp. Add tomatoes and their liquid, and sugar. Simmer, uncovered, until reduced to 3 cups, about 30 minutes.

Purée in a blender or food processor. Add salt to taste. (If made ahead, cover and refrigerate as long as overnight.) To reheat, blend tomato sauce with whipping cream in a 1- to 2-quart pan; bring to a boil, stirring. Serve hot.

Chestnuts in Port

1 **pound fresh chestnuts**
½ **cup ruby or Tinta port**
¼ **cup sugar**

With a sharp pointed knife, cut a slit about ½ inch long through shell into meat of each chestnut (this keeps them from exploding in the oven); discard any with mold. Arrange nuts in a single layer on a 10- by 15-inch baking sheet; bake at 400° for 40 minutes; shake occasionally. Also, mix port and sugar in a deep bowl.

Remove chestnuts from oven. Using a thick potholder to protect your hand, squeeze each nut to pop the shell open so that it can absorb the port; drop nuts into port-sugar mixture, stirring with each addition. Let stand until cool enough to touch comfortably, stirring occasionally. Transfer the nuts to a serving bowl and serve.

To eat, peel nuts with your hands. Serves 6.

MAKING A PASTA ROLL

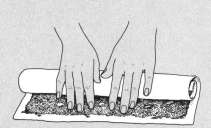

Starting from long side near you, roll pasta over filling to form a smooth, compact cylinder.

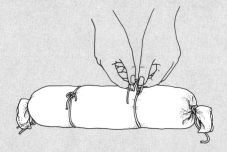

Wrap roll in cheesecloth, and tie string at ends and at several places along the roll.

Spirited Chocolate Fondue

1 **pound bittersweet, semisweet, or milk chocolate (or a mixture of all three)**
1 **cup whipping cream**
¼ **cup orange-flavored liqueur or brandy**

Combine the chocolate and cream in the top of a double boiler. Set over simmering water and stir just until chocolate melts, about 10 minutes. (Or use a chafing dish set over hot water.) Stir in the liqueur.

Serve from a chafing dish set over hot water. Serves 10.

Coffee Toppings and Seasonings

Grated semisweet chocolate. Allow about 1 tablespoon for each guest. Serve in bowl.

Whipped cream. Allow about 2 tablespoons of unwhipped cream for each guest (or about 1 quart for 50 to 60 cups). Whip just before party time, sweeten with powdered sugar, and flavor with vanilla if you wish. Pile into bowl and nest in a larger bowl filled with crushed ice. Refrigerate any extra whipped cream, covered; stir before using. Cream stays fresh for at least 3 hours, but you may need to replenish the ice.

Sugar. Provide a bowl or shaker of granulated sugar.

Lemon zest. Remove thin outer peel of lemon with a vegetable peeler. With a sharp knife, cut into strips. (Allow 1 lemon for every 10 guests.)

Cinnamon sticks. Provide 1 stick for each guest.

Cardamom. Fill a small bowl with whole cardamom pods.

Nutmeg. Place several whole nutmegs and a nutmeg grater on the coffee bar.

Liqueurs and spirits. Present a bottle or decanter of three or four different liqueurs, such as coffee-flavored Kahlua or Tia Maria, chocolate-flavored crème de cacao, almond-flavored amaretto, or orange-flavored Cointreau. Provide bottles of brandy or Cognac, light or dark rum, and a whiskey (Irish, Scotch, Canadian, American rye, or bourbon).

Coffee Recipes

Brazilian: crème de cacao, cinnamon stick, coffee, whipped cream, grated chocolate.

Caribbean: rum, coffee, whipped cream, grated nutmeg.

Irish: whiskey, coffee, whipped cream.

Italian: amaretto, coffee, whipped cream.

Mexican: Kahlua, cinnamon stick, coffee, whipped cream, grated chocolate.

Parisian: coffee, Cognac, whipped cream.

Viennese: coffee, Cognac, whipped cream, grated nutmeg.

HOLIDAY FIESTA

A Mexican-American party for 12
(Pictured on Pages 68–71)

Stuffed Cheese Appetizer

*Tomatillo, Jicama,
and Apple Salad*

Chile con Queso

Mexican Chili-Cheese Logs

*Turkey in Molé Sauce
with Warm Tortillas*

Guacamole

*White   Margarita
Sangria Punch   Wine Punch*

Tropical Fruits

Walnut Butter Cookies

Coffee

Stuffed Cheese Appetizer (*Queso Relleno*)

- 2 **tablespoons salad oil**
- 1 **medium-size onion, chopped**
- 4 **cloves garlic, minced or pressed**
- ½ **teaspoon ground cinnamon**
- ¼ **teaspoon** *each* **ground allspice and cloves**
- ⅛ **teaspoon** *each* **ground cumin and cayenne**
- 2 **cans (14½ oz.** *each***) pear-shaped tomatoes**
- 1 **can (7 oz.) chopped green chilies**
- 2 **teaspoons** *each* **sugar and wine vinegar**
- ¼ **cup raisins**
- 1 **pound ground lean pork**
  Salt
- 1½ **cups regular-strength beef broth**
- ½ **cup sliced Spanish-style pimiento-stuffed olives**
- 1 **tablespoon cornstarch mixed with 1 tablespoon water**
- 1¼ **to 1½ pounds jack or teleme cheese**
- 2 **hard-cooked eggs, chopped**
  Fried Tortillas (directions follow) *or* **1 bag (7½ oz.) purchased tortilla chips**

Heat oil in a 3- to 4-quart pan over medium-high heat; add onion and garlic and cook, stirring, until onion is limp. Stir in cinnamon, allspice, cloves, cumin, cayenne, tomatoes and their liquid (break up tomatoes with a spoon), chilies, sugar, vinegar, and raisins.

Cook, stirring frequently, until most of the liquid evaporates and a very thick tomato sauce forms, about 15 minutes. Crumble meat into an 8- to 10-inch frying pan set over medium heat and cook, stirring, until browned; drain excess fat. Stir in half the tomato mixture; remove from heat. Salt to taste. Cover and chill if made ahead of time.

To the remaining tomato mixture add broth, olives, and cornstarch mixture. Cook, stirring, over high heat until mixture boils and thickens. Salt to taste. Cover and refrigerate if made ahead of time.

To assemble, reheat meat and sauce mixtures separately to boiling; keep warm. Cut cheese into ½-inch-thick slices; place half the slices in the center of a large (about 10- by 15-inch) heatproof serving platter. Spread meat mixture over cheese; sprinkle with eggs.

Place remaining cheese on top; bake, uncovered, in a 400° oven for about 8 minutes. Or cook in a microwave oven at full power for 1½ to 2 minutes or until cheese melts. Pour hot sauce down center. Surround with Fried Tortillas. Serves 12.

Fried Tortillas

- 1 **dozen corn tortillas**
  Salad oil
  Salt (optional)

Cut tortillas into quarters. In a deep 1½- to 2-quart pan, heat about 2 inches of oil to 350° on a deep-fat thermometer. Add several tortilla pieces at a time and cook until crisp and light brown; lift out with slotted spoon and drain on paper towels; salt if desired. Serve, or store airtight at room temperature as long as overnight.

Tomatillo, Jicama, and Apple Salad

3 tart, green-skinned apples
About 3 tablespoons fresh lime juice
About 1½ pounds jicama (1 small or piece of larger root), scrubbed
12 tomatillos (1-in. diameter)
Fresh cilantro (coriander) leaves
Coarse salt

Core apples and cut each into 16 thin wedges. Dip into lime juice to coat.

Peel jicama. Cut in half; then cut into 48 thin slices. Husk and wash tomatillos; cut to make 48 slices.

On each slice of jicama, stack a piece of apple, a tomatillo slice, and a cilantro leaf. Arrange, overlapping, on a platter. Serve, or cover and chill up to 2 hours. Drizzle with remaining lime juice and sprinkle with coarse salt. Serves 12.

Chile con Queso

12 to 16 fresh California (Anaheim) green chilies or 2 cans (7 oz. each) chopped green chilies
2 medium-size onions, chopped
2 tablespoons salad oil
1 small can (5⅓ oz.) evaporated milk
2 cups (8 oz.) shredded jack or Longhorn Cheddar cheese
Salt
Crisp raw vegetables for dipping (allow 5 or 6 pieces per person)

To use fresh chilies, arrange them close together in a 10- by 15-inch pan. Broil 1 inch from heat until blistered and lightly browned all over; turn as needed. When all are charred, enclose chilies in a paper bag; close bag. When cool enough to handle, pull off blackened skin with a knife; leave any small pieces that refuse to come off easily. Cut chilies open and remove seeds. Chop enough chilies to make 2 cups.

In a 10- to 12-inch frying pan, cook onions in salad oil over medium-low heat, stirring occasionally, until onions are very limp. Add chilies and simmer, stirring, until juices have evaporated, about 5 minutes. Add evaporated milk and simmer gently, stirring, until slightly thickened, about 4 minutes. (At this point you can let mixture stand as long as overnight; reheat to continue.) Remove from heat; cool about 2 minutes; then add cheese. Cover until cheese melts; then stir, salt to taste, and serve hot.

If desired, keep warm over hot water and surround with vegetables for dipping. Makes about 4 cups. Serves 12.

Turkey in Molé Sauce

3 tablespoons butter or margarine
1 large onion, chopped
2 cloves garlic, minced or pressed
3 tablespoons chili powder
¾ teaspoon each ground cinnamon and ground cloves
¼ to ½ teaspoon cayenne
2¾ cups regular-strength chicken broth
1 day-old corn tortilla, torn into pieces
¼ cup each sesame seed and raisins
2 ounces semisweet chocolate
6 cups cooked turkey or chicken, boned and skinned and cut into ½- by 2-inch pieces
Salt
¼ cup chopped fresh cilantro (coriander)
2 dozen flour or corn tortillas
Guacamole (recipe follows)

Melt butter in a 10- to 12-inch frying pan over medium heat; add the onion and garlic and cook, stirring, until onion is limp. Stir in the chili powder, cinnamon, cloves, and cayenne to taste; cook until bubbly. Gradually stir in 1 cup of the broth until blended.

PREPARING VEGETABLES FOR SALAD

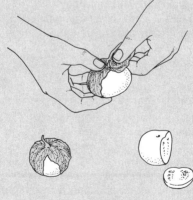

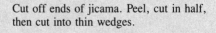

Cut off ends of jicama. Peel, cut in half, then cut into thin wedges.

Husk and wash 12 tomatillos. Cut each into 4 slices, to make 48 slices in all.

Transfer mixture to an electric blender or food processor; add the tortilla pieces, sesame seed, and raisins. Whirl on lowest speed, stopping and stirring as necessary, until smoothly puréed.

Return molé mixture to frying pan over medium heat; gradually stir in the remaining broth until well blended. Cook, stirring, until mixture comes to a simmer. Remove from heat; add the chocolate and stir until it melts. (If made ahead, cover and refrigerate as long as 1 week.)

Combine molé sauce and turkey in a 12- to 14-inch frying pan over medium heat; cook, uncovered, until sauce is hot and thick. Add salt to taste; then transfer to a serving dish; top with coriander.

Meanwhile, stack each dozen tortillas separately and seal each stack securely in foil. Bake in a 375° oven for 10 minutes or until hot.

To serve, let guests spoon chunks of the turkey molé mixture into warm tortillas and embellish with a spoonful of Guacamole. Allow 2 filled tortillas per person. Serves 12.

Mexican Chili-Cheese Logs

  2 **eggs**
  2 **slices firm-textured bread, torn into small cubes**
  1 **beef bouillon cube, dissolved in 1 tablespoon hot water**
  ½ **cup taco sauce**
     Meat Seasonings (recipe follows)
2½ **cups (10 oz.) shredded sharp Cheddar cheese**
  2 **cloves garlic, minced or pressed**
1¼ **pounds bulk pork sausage**
  1 **pound ground turkey**
  2 **cans (4 oz. *each*) whole green chilies**
  1 **can (4 oz.) sliced ripe olives, drained**
  ¾ **teaspoon cumin seed**

Beat eggs to blend in a large bowl. Add bread, bouillon, ¼ cup of the taco sauce, the Meat Seasonings, 1

cup of the cheese, garlic, sausage, and turkey. Use your hands or a heavy spoon to mix thoroughly.

To shape logs, scoop meat onto a 12-inch-wide, 20-inch-long piece of foil. Pat meat into a neat 10- by 18-inch rectangle. Cut meat through foil into 3 rectangles, each 6 by 10 inches.

Split chilies and pat dry. Lay chilies flat in centers of meat rectangles; use a third of the chilies for each. Top each with ⅓ of the remaining cheese, olives, and cumin seed. Starting from

long side, tightly roll each rectangle into a cylinder; pinch seam and ends of meat together to seal in cheese.

Peel off foil and place logs slightly apart, on a greased 10- by 15-inch rimmed baking sheet; brush tops with remaining taco sauce. Bake in a 350° oven for 45 minutes or until meat feels firm. Cool; wrap in foil and chill for at least 2 hours or up to 3 days. Or freeze up to 2 months.

To serve, slice logs into thin rounds. Makes 3 logs, 1⅓ pounds each. Each log makes about 36 pieces.

SHAPING CHILI-CHEESE LOGS

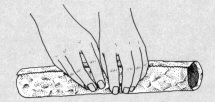

Pat meat on foil into a 12- by 20-inch rectangle. Cut through foil into 3 rectangles, each 6 by 10 inches.

Lay chilies flat in centers of meat rectangles. Top each with cheese, olives, and cumin. Starting from long side, roll each piece into a tight cylinder. Pinch seam and ends to seal in cheese.

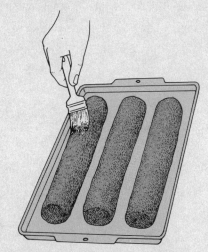

Peel off foil and place logs slightly apart on a greased baking sheet. Brush tops with taco sauce before cooking.

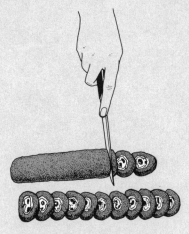

To serve, slice chilled logs into thin rounds.

Meat Seasonings

2 tablespoons instant minced onion
1½ teaspoons *each* dry oregano leaves and chili powder
¾ teaspoon salt
½ teaspoon ground cumin

Blend minced onion, oregano, chili powder, salt, and cumin.

Guacamole

2 medium-size ripe avocados, peeled and pitted
1 to 2 tablespoons fresh lemon juice
¼ cup chopped fresh cilantro (coriander)
¼ teaspoon garlic powder
1 large tomato, peeled, seeded, and chopped
  Salt and liquid hot pepper seasoning to taste

With a fork, thoroughly mash avocado with lemon juice to taste. Add cilantro, garlic powder, tomato, and liquid hot pepper seasoning and salt to taste; stir gently to blend. Serve, or cover and chill if made 6 to 8 hours ahead.

Walnut Butter Cookies

1 cup (½ lb.) butter or margarine
½ cup unsifted powdered sugar
2 tablespoons cold water
1 teaspoon vanilla
2 cups unsifted cake flour
1 cup finely chopped walnuts
  About ¾ cup sifted powdered sugar

With an electric mixer, beat butter until creamy. Beat in the ½ cup unsifted powdered sugar; then blend in cold water and vanilla. Gradually mix in flour, blending well. Stir in walnuts. Cover and chill the dough until firm.

Using about 2 teaspoons for each, shape dough into 2-inch logs. Place slightly apart on ungreased baking sheets and gently curve the ends in opposite directions to make an S shape. If dough becomes too soft, chill until firm again.

Bake in the middle of a 325° oven until bottoms are golden, about 20 to 25 minutes. Transfer cookies to wire racks to cool.

In a bag filled with the ¾ cup sifted powdered sugar, gently shake a few cookies at a time to coat evenly with the sugar. Serve, or package airtight and freeze up to 2 months. Thaw unwrapped. Makes about 4 dozen.

Margarita Wine Punch

  Ice ring or cubes
3 cans (6 oz. *each*) thawed frozen concentrate for limeade
1 can (12 oz.) thawed frozen concentrate for lemonade
1 jug (1.5 L) cold dry white wine (such as chablis or Chenin Blanc)
  Green food coloring (optional)
  Lemon or lime wedges
  Salt

If you want an ice ring, fill a 1-quart ring mold with boiled and cooled water; cover and freeze indefinitely.

In a punch bowl, stir together limeade and lemonade concentrates and wine. If desired, tint with green food coloring. Shortly before serving, add ice ring.

Set out a bowl of lemon or lime wedges and a bowl of salt. Guests can rub glass rims with citrus wedges and then dip rim in salt before ladling in the punch. Makes 3 quarts.

White Wine Sangría

  Ice ring or cubes
1 jug (1.5 L) cold dry wine (such as chablis or Chenin Blanc)
3 cans (6 oz. *each*) thawed concentrate for lemon-limeade
1 can (6 oz.) thawed orange juice concentrate
2 cups cold water

Prepare ice ring if desired.

In a large punch bowl, stir together wine, lemon-limeade and orange juice concentrates, and cold water. Shortly before serving, add ice ring. Makes about 3 quarts.

Tangerine-sauced Roasted Duckling with Baked Whole Onions and Yam Chunks

1 duckling (about 4½ to 5 lbs.), thawed if frozen
2 or 3 whole onions (*each* about 3-in. diameter), unpeeled
   About 1½ pounds yams, peeled and cut into 2-inch pieces
   Tangerine Sauce (recipe follows)

Remove giblets from body cavity of duckling and reserve for sauce. Pull out and discard lumps of fat. Rinse bird with cold water, drain, and pat dry. Fasten neck skin to back with a skewer.

Place duckling breast down on a folding meat rack set in a 12- by 15-inch roasting pan. Roast in a 375° oven for 1 hour. Using a bulb baster, siphon fat from pan (or spoon out). Turn duckling breast up; protect hands with potholders. Add onions and yam chunks to roasting pan, around or under the roasting rack; turn vegetables to coat with drippings. Continue roasting, turning vegetables several times, until yams are tender when pierced, onions give readily when gently squeezed, and duckling skin is brown and crisp and begins to pull from leg bone, about 1 hour longer. Lift duckling and vegetables from pan and keep warm. Skim fat from pan; reserve the drippings for sauce.

To serve, cut duckling into quarters with poultry shears; garnish with thin strips of tangerine peel. Cut onions in halves and serve to eat from skins, along with yams. Spoon Tangerine Sauce over individual servings. Serves 2 or 3.

Tangerine Sauce

1½ cups water
    Duck neck and giblets (reserve liver for another use)
1 small onion, quartered
1 bay leaf
   Duck drippings in roasting pan (see preceding recipe)
1½ teaspoons slivered tangerine zest (orange part of peel only)
¾ cup tangerine juice (about 2 large tangerines)
1½ tablespoons honey
2 teaspoons cornstarch mixed with 2 teaspoons water
   Salt and pepper

In a 1- to 1½-quart pan, combine water, duck neck and giblets, onion, and bay leaf. Cover and simmer 1 hour. Pour through wire strainer; discard seasonings and measure broth. Boil broth, if needed, to reduce to ¼ cup. (If made ahead, cover and chill as long as overnight.)

To duck drippings in roasting pan, add tangerine zest, broth, tangerine juice, honey, and cornstarch mixture. Boil over high heat, stirring, until sauce thickens, about 1 minute. Season to taste with salt and pepper.

Winter Melon Soup with Crab

Coriander Chicken Salad

Sweet and Sour Deep-fried Fish

Peking Beef with Chinese Pea Pods

Eight Immortal Jai

Steamed Rice

Gewürztraminer

*Almond Custard
with Loquats or Mandarins*

Almond Cookies

Tea

Winter Melon Soup with Crab

½ **cup dried lotus seeds (optional)**

6 **to 8 medium-size dry Oriental mushrooms** *or* ½ **cup thinly sliced fresh mushrooms**
   Hot water

2 **quarts regular-strength chicken broth**

2 **thin slices fresh ginger**

½ **pound boneless pork chops, cut into ½-inch cubes**

½ **pound winter melon or zucchini (omit if whole winter melon is used), cut into ½-inch cubes**

1 **can (about 7 oz.) bamboo shoots, drained and thinly sliced**

¼ **cup frozen peas**

¼ **pound crab meat**

2 **tablespoons minced cooked ham**
   Winter Melon Bowl (optional; directions follow)

Cover lotus seeds and dry mushrooms with hot water; let stand until soft, about 30 minutes. Cut soaked mushrooms into strips; discard tough stems.

In a 3- to 4-quart pan, combine chicken broth, ginger, and lotus seeds. Bring to a boil and add pork; cover and simmer until pork and seeds are tender when pierced, about 30 minutes. (If done ahead, set aside several hours; return to boil to continue.)

Add melon cubes to broth along with bamboo shoots and mushrooms; cover and simmer 10 minutes longer. Remove and discard ginger. Stir in peas, crab, and ham; heat through. Serve from Winter Melon Bowl or tureen. Serves 8 to 10.

Winter Melon Bowl

1 **well-shaped winter melon (about 10 lbs.)**

Wash and scrub melon. Find the more stable end of the melon and use it as the base. Cut 1½ to 2 inches off the opposite end and reserve this lid. Scoop out and discard seeds and stringy portions. If you like, carve a chrysanthemum design in the melon as shown.

Place melon in a shallow pan and set melon lid in place. Bake in a 350° oven until flesh feels soft when gently squeezed, 1½ to 2 hours. (Melon can be kept warm for about 1 hour in a 200° oven.) Remove from the oven.

Scoop any flesh from lid, cut into bite-size pieces, and reserve. With a ladle, carefully remove liquid from melon interior. Using hot pads, gently transfer melon to a wide bowl that will support its base; if desired, cut a zigzag design around top edge. Ladle enough hot soup into melon to almost fill it; then add reserved cut melon. Scrape free some of the melon wall to add to each serving, taking care not to break through melon skin. Refill melon with more hot soup as needed.

CARVING WINTER MELON BOWL

To enlarge our pattern: Cut tissue paper or newsprint to fit completely around melon. With ruler, divide paper into graph squares. Copy pattern square by square to fit onto paper.

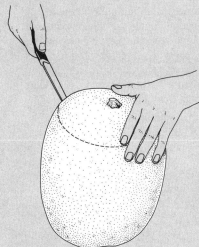

Cut off top of melon and scoop out the seeds.

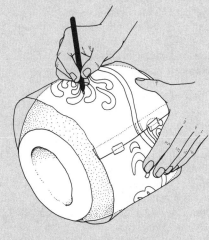

With a ballpoint pen, trace pattern around melon. Do not push pen point through paper, but push hard enough to make indentation in melon.

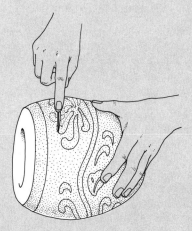

Using a small sharp paring knife, score melon around outlines.

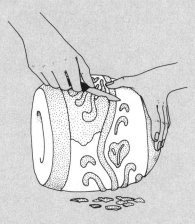

Pare away background, taking off thin green skin to expose white melon.

Using hot pads, gently transfer cooked melon to a wide, shallow serving bowl or tray. If desired, cut a zigzag pattern around top.

Ladle hot soup into melon, and add reserved cut melon pieces.

Coriander Chicken Salad

1 broiler-fryer chicken (3¼ to 3½ lbs.)
2 tablespoons soy sauce
1 tablespoon *each* dry mustard
and water
¼ cup *each* Oriental sesame oil
and salad oil
2 tablespoons fresh lemon juice
4 teaspoons *each* sugar and soy sauce
1 teaspoon five spice *or* ½ teaspoon
ground cinnamon
5 to 6 cups shredded iceberg lettuce
¼ cup *each* chopped fresh coriander
(Chinese parsley), sliced green
onion, and toasted sesame seed
(see page 84 for instructions)

Rinse chicken and pat dry. Place in a
deep bowl with the 2 tablespoons soy
sauce; turn chicken to coat. Cover
and chill at least 2 hours or
overnight; turn chicken several times.

Lift chicken from soy and place
breast up on a rack in a 12- by
15-inch roasting pan. Roast in a 425°
oven until skin is crisp and brown
and thigh gives easily when pressed,
about 45 minutes. Cool on rack.
Strip meat and skin from carcass and
cut into ¼-inch slivers; if made
ahead, chill, covered, as long as
overnight.

Smoothly blend dry mustard and
water; then stir in sesame oil, salad
oil, lemon juice, sugar, the 4
teaspoons soy sauce, and five spice;
dressing can stand at room
temperature, covered, as long as
overnight.

Shortly before serving, arrange
lettuce in a ½-inch-thick bed on a
large serving platter. Combine
chicken, coriander, green onion,
sesame seed, and dressing. Mix by
lifting with 2 forks until blended.
Mound chicken in center of lettuce.
Serves 8 to 10.

Sweet and Sour Deep-fried Fish

1 whole red snapper or rock cod
(2 to 2½ lbs.), cleaned and scaled
¼ cup dry sherry
About ½ cup cornstarch
Salad oil
Sweet and Sour Sauce (recipe
follows)
1 small green bell pepper, slivered
1 small tomato, cut into 6 wedges
Sprigs of fresh coriander (Chinese
parsley)

Rinse fish and pat dry. Make about 6
slashes, ½ inch deep, on each side of
fish. Rub all over with sherry; cover
and chill as long as overnight if
made ahead. Coat fish with
cornstarch, patting on liberally.

Pour enough salad oil into a wok or
a 12- to 14-inch frying pan to fill it
halfway. Place on highest heat. When
temperature reaches 380°, slowly slip
fish into oil. Oil temperature will
drop; adjust heat to stabilize oil at
360°. Cook fish until golden brown,
about 5 minutes; if fish is not
completely immersed, spoon hot oil
over it as it cooks.

With a large wire skimmer or two
slotted spatulas, carefully lift fish
from oil, draining it briefly. Place on
rimmed serving platter; you can keep
it warm in a 200° oven as long as 15
minutes.

Stir Sweet and Sour Sauce on high
heat until bubbling. Mix in pepper
and tomato. Pour sauce around, not
over, fish. Garnish with coriander.

To serve, lift portions of fish onto
plates; spoon on Sweet and Sour
Sauce. Serves 8 to 10.

Sweet and Sour Sauce

2 tablespoons salad oil
1 small onion, sliced and separated
into rings
½ cup *each* catsup, red wine vinegar,
and unsweetened pineapple juice
¾ cup sugar
½ teaspoon Worcestershire
⅛ teaspoon liquid hot pepper
seasoning
2 tablespoons cornstarch blended
with 2 tablespoons water

Pour oil into a 2- to 3-quart pan on
medium-high heat. Add onion; cook,
stirring, 1 minute. Add catsup,
vinegar, pineapple juice, sugar,
Worcestershire, liquid hot pepper
seasoning, and cornstarch blended
with water. Cook, stirring, until
mixture boils, thickens, and clears,
about 2 minutes. If made ahead,
cover and set aside several hours.

Peking Beef
with Chinese Pea Pods

1 pound lean beef steak, such as top round, sirloin, or flank steak

About 6 tablespoons salad oil

1 tablespoon *each* soy sauce, catsup, dry sherry, and cornstarch

1 tablespoon hoisin sauce *or* 1 tablespoon *each* sugar and vinegar

1 tablespoon Tientsin preserved vegetables (optional)

1 tablespoon Oriental sesame oil *or* crushed toasted sesame seed (see page 84 for instructions)

1 teaspoon Worcestershire

1 clove garlic, minced or pressed

¾ pound Chinese pea pods, ends and strings removed

1 tablespoon water

1 small onion, cut into thin slivers

1 tablespoon soy sauce mixed with 1 teaspoon sugar

Trim excess fat from meat and discard. Cut meat into 1-inch chunks and, with the flat side of a mallet, pound each piece ¼ inch thick. In a small bowl, mix together beef, 2 tablespoons of the salad oil, the 1 tablespoon soy sauce, the catsup, sherry, cornstarch, hoisin, preserved vegetables, sesame oil, Worcestershire, and garlic. Cover and chill at least 2 hours or as long as overnight.

Set wok or 12- to 14-inch frying pan on highest heat. When hot, add 2 tablespoons salad oil, pea pods, and water; cook, stirring constantly, until peas are tender-crisp, 2 to 3 minutes. Pour into serving dish. Return pan to heat and add another 2 tablespoons oil; when hot, add beef. Cook, stirring constantly, until meat is lightly browned, about 2 minutes. Add onion and soy-sugar mixture; cook about 1 minute more. Spoon over pea pods. Serves 8 to 10.

Eight Immortal Jai

1 tablespoon *each* cornstarch and water

1 cup regular-strength chicken broth

1 tablespoon soy sauce

2 tablespoons salad oil

½ teaspoon minced fresh ginger

1 small clove garlic, minced or pressed

1½ cups *each* broccoli flowerets and thinly sliced carrots

½ cup (¾ oz.) dry black fungus (also called cloud ears), soaked 15 minutes in hot water, drained, and cut into bite-size pieces

1 can (about 2¼ oz.) water chestnuts, drained and sliced

Blend cornstarch and water; then stir in broth and soy; set aside, covered, as long as several hours.

Pour salad oil into a wok or a 12- to 14-inch frying pan and set on highest heat. Add ginger, garlic, broccoli, carrots, and fungus. Cook, stirring constantly, for 1 minute. Stir broth mixture and add to vegetables along with water chestnuts. Cook, stirring, until sauce boils, thickens, and clears, about 1 minute. Pour into a serving dish. Serves 8 to 10.

Almond Custard
with Loquats

4 cups water

1½ sticks (about ⅜ oz.) white kanten (agar-agar) *or* 3 envelopes unflavored gelatin

½ cup sugar

1 can (5⅓ oz.) evaporated milk

1 teaspoon almond extract

1 can (16 oz.) chilled loquats *or* 2 cans (11 oz. *each*) chilled mandarin oranges

Measure water into a 2- to 3-quart pan. Break kanten into water and let stand about 30 minutes. (Or sprinkle gelatin over water; let stand 5 minutes.) Cook on medium heat, stirring, until kanten or gelatin dissolves. Add sugar and boil until sugar dissolves. Remove from heat and stir in evaporated milk and almond extract. Pour into an 8- or 9-inch square pan. Chill, covered, until firm or as long as overnight.

Cut into 1-inch squares and, with a spatula, transfer to serving dish or dishes. Spoon loquats and their syrup over custard squares; if made ahead, cover and chill several hours. Serves 8 to 10.

WINTER SALAD SUPPER

A buffet for 12
(Pictured on Pages 78–80)

Jicama with Oranges

*Beets and Pears
with Dandelion Greens*

Parsnips with Crackling Pork

*Soy-braised Onions
with Daikon and Carrot*

Turnips with Mustard Greens

Celery Root with Green Beans

Cold Sliced Roast Beef or Turkey

Baguettes and Butter

Assorted Cheeses

Sauvignon Blanc and Zinfandel

Mulled Cider

*Fresh Orange Baba-rin
(optional)*

Jicama with Oranges

2 **medium-size oranges, peeled with a knife to remove white membrane, then thinly sliced**
¾ **pound jicama (1 small root or a piece), peeled and cut into ¼-inch julienne sticks (about 4 cups)**
   Mustard greens or butter lettuce leaves
¼ **cup fresh orange juice**
2 **tablespoons fresh lime juice**
1 **to 2 tablespoons fresh coriander (cilantro) leaves**

Combine oranges and jicama. (At this point, you can cover and chill as long as overnight.)

Line a shallow serving dish with mustard greens and arrange oranges and jicama on the greens. Mix orange juice with lime juice and pour over the salad; then sprinkle with the coriander. Serves 12 if part of Winter Salad Supper, or 4 as a first course if served separately.

Beets and Pears with Dandelion Greens

2 **medium-size beets (about 3-in. diameter), with tops trimmed to about 1 inch, scrubbed**
   Water
1 **medium-size pear**
   Mustard Vinaigrette (recipe follows)
3 **cups slivered dandelion greens**
1 **to 2 tablespoons finely chopped walnuts**

In a 1½- to 2-quart pan cook beets in boiling water to cover, with lid, until beets are tender when pierced, about 35 minutes. Drain; let cool. Rub off skins; cut off ends and discard. Cut beets into ⅛-inch julienne sticks; set aside. (If made ahead, cover and chill up to 24 hours.)

Just before serving, peel and core pear; cut into ⅛-inch julienne sticks and mix at once with Mustard Vinaigrette to preserve color.

Arrange dandelion greens on one side of a shallow serving dish. Alongside, make 2 or 3 alternating layers of beets and pears; drizzle with pear marinade; then sprinkle with nuts. Serves 12 if part of Winter Salad Supper, or 4 as a first course if served separately.

Mustard Vinaigrette

2 **teaspoons *each* Dijon mustard and finely chopped red onion**
2 **tablespoons distilled white vinegar**
⅓ **cup salad oil**

Stir together mustard, onion, vinegar, and salad oil.

Parsnips with Crackling Pork

¾ pound tender parsnips (do not use if core is hard and woody), peeled and ends trimmed
1 cup *each* water and distilled white vinegar
   Butter lettuce leaves
1 small red-skinned apple, cored and cut into thin wedges
   Crackling Pork (recipe follows)

Cut parsnips lengthwise into ¼-inch julienne sticks. Bring water and vinegar to a boil on high heat in a 10- to 12-inch frying pan; add parsnips and boil gently, uncovered, just until tender-crisp to bite, about 5 minutes. Drain and set aside. (You can cover and chill parsnips as long as 24 hours.) Line a shallow serving dish with lettuce leaves and mound parsnips in center. Garnish with apple wedges and spoon Crackling Pork onto parsnips. Serves 12 if part of Winter Salad Supper, or 4 as a first course if served separately.

Crackling Pork

½ pound boneless pork shoulder (including fat), finely diced
3 tablespoons fresh lemon juice
2 tablespoons soy sauce
2 teaspoons honey
1 large clove garlic, minced

In a 10- to 12-inch frying pan, cook pork over low heat, stirring occasionally, until crisp, about 35 minutes. Add lemon juice, soy sauce, honey, and garlic. Continue to cook, stirring to free browned particles, until mixture boils. Use warm. If made ahead, cover and chill as long as 24 hours; stir over low heat to warm before adding to salad.

Soy-braised Onions with Daikon and Carrot

1 pound small white onions (¾- to 1½-in. diameter)
3 tablespoons salad oil
½ cup *each* soy sauce and sugar
⅔ cup distilled white vinegar
1 teaspoon minced fresh ginger
1 piece daikon (about 6 in. long and 1½ in. thick), peeled and ends trimmed
2 medium-size carrots, peeled and ends trimmed
   About 2 teaspoons finely chopped parsley

Peel onions and arrange in a single layer in a 10- to 12-inch frying pan. Add oil and cook on medium heat, uncovered, until lightly browned, about 10 minutes; shake pan to turn onions. Add soy, sugar, vinegar, and ginger, and bring to a boil. Reduce heat to simmer, cover, and cook small onions 10 minutes, larger onions 15 minutes. Remove lid and continue cooking until sauce is reduced by about a quarter and onions are tender but still slightly crisp when pierced, about 5 minutes. Set onions aside to cool. (They can stand, covered, as long as 24 hours.)

Using a knife or an Oriental shredder, cut daikon and carrot in long, very thin slivers (to use shredder, draw vegetables their full length across the fine shredding blade); vegetables can be covered and chilled as long as 24 hours.

To serve, make a wreath of the daikon and carrots on a shallow serving plate and spoon onions and soy dressing into the center. Sprinkle onions with parsley. Serves 12 if part of Winter Salad Supper, or 4 as a first course if served separately.

Turnips with Mustard Greens

2 medium-size turnips (*each* about 2½-in. diameter), peeled and cut into ⅛-inch julienne sticks
3 tablespoons *each* distilled white vinegar, water, and sugar
2 teaspoons toasted sesame seed (see page 84 for instructions)
3 tablespoons salad oil
4 cups lightly packed mustard greens
1 small red bell pepper, seeded and diced *or* 1 jar (2 oz.) diced pimento, drained

In a 12- to 14-inch frying pan, combine turnips, vinegar, water, and sugar. Cover and bring to a boil on high heat; boil about 3 minutes or just until turnips are tender-crisp to bite. (If made ahead, remove from heat, uncover, and let cool; then cover and chill as long as overnight. Reheat to continue.) Remove lid and quickly mix in sesame seed, salad oil, and mustard greens. Stir just until greens are slightly wilted. Pour into a shallow serving dish and sprinkle with red bell pepper. Serves 12 if part of Winter Salad Supper, or 4 as a first course if served separately.

Celery Root with Green Beans

1 celery root (1½ to 1¾ lbs.), scrubbed
1½ cups water
¼ cup distilled white vinegar
¼ pound green beans, ends and strings removed
    Anchovy Dressing (recipe follows)
12 thin slices dry salami (optional)

Peel celery root and cut into ½-inch cubes. At once, drop diced celery root into a 3- to 4-quart pan containing 1 cup of the water and the vinegar. Bring to a boil on high heat; then simmer, uncovered, just until root is tender when pierced, about 10 minutes. Drain. (If made ahead, celery root can be covered and chilled as long as 24 hours.)

With knife or French bean cutter, cut beans lengthwise into thin strands. Bring remaining ½ cup water to a boil in a 10- to 12-inch frying pan and add beans; boil, uncovered, until beans are bright green and just tender to bite, about 4 minutes. Drain and immerse at once in ice water to preserve color; drain again. (Beans can be covered and chilled as long as 24 hours.)

To serve, mix celery root, beans, and Anchovy Dressing; mound on a shallow serving dish. Fan salami slices out beside the salad if desired. Serves 12 if part of Winter Salad Supper, or 4 as a first course if served separately.

Anchovy Dressing

⅓ cup salad oil
1½ tablespoons white wine vinegar or distilled white vinegar
5 canned anchovy fillets, chopped
¾ teaspoon dry thyme leaves
⅛ teaspoon fresh ground pepper

Stir together salad oil, vinegar, anchovies, thyme, and pepper until well blended.

Fresh Orange Baba-rin

1 package yeast, active dry or compressed
¼ cup warm water (about 110°)
½ cup (¼ lb.) butter or margarine
¼ cup sugar
½ teaspoon salt
4 eggs
½ cup warm milk (about 110°)
2 cups all-purpose flour
    Fresh Orange Syrup (recipe follows)
3 or 4 large oranges
    Fresh Orange Custard Cream (recipe follows)

Blend yeast with warm water and let soften for about 5 minutes. With an electric mixer, cream butter with sugar and salt until blended; then beat in eggs, one at a time. Stir in yeast mixture and milk; then mix in flour and beat until smoothly blended; the dough is very soft.

Cover and set in a warm place to rise until about doubled, about 1 hour. Stir vigorously to remove air bubbles; then pour dough into a heavily buttered, flour-dusted 8- to 10-cup ring mold. Cover lightly and let rise for 30 to 45 minutes or until almost doubled.

Bake in a 400° oven for 30 minutes or until cake just begins to pull from pan sides and a wooden skewer, inserted in center, comes out clean. Let cool in pan for about 10 minutes; then invert on rack to release cake, but leave pan over it. When cake is cold, tip pan right-side-up again.

Pour hot Fresh Orange Syrup over cake, piercing with a fork or wooden skewer to aid penetration. Let cake stand in pan, covered, at room temperature as long as overnight.

At serving time, cut away peel and white membrane from oranges, and section or slice the fruit. Turn the cake out onto a serving plate and fill the center with the orange slices or sections. Pour Fresh Orange Custard Cream into a serving bowl.

To serve, slice cake, spoon custard and fruit over each portion, and garnish with thinly sliced orange peel. Serves 8.

Fresh Orange Syrup

1 cup sugar
½ cup water
1 teaspoon grated orange peel
½ teaspoon coriander seed
1 cup fresh orange juice

In a 1½- to 2-quart pan, combine sugar, water, orange peel, and coriander seed. Boil, stirring, until sugar dissolves. Remove from heat; add orange juice. Pour through a wire strainer. Save syrup; discard seeds. Use hot or reheated.

Fresh Orange Custard Cream

½ cup sugar
3 eggs
1 teaspoon grated orange peel
½ cup fresh orange juice
¼ cup (⅛ lb.) butter, melted
1 cup whipping cream

In the top of a double boiler, stir together sugar, eggs, orange peel, orange juice, and butter to blend well. Cook, stirring, over simmering water until thickened. Cover and chill thoroughly (as long as overnight). Whip cream until stiff, fold into the orange custard, and serve.

Planning
FOR EASY ENTERTAINING

PLANNING GUIDE

Successful entertaining doesn't have to be elaborate or showy. Many of life's happiest memories spring from the simple occasions when everything just naturally worked together: a comfortable group, great conversation, a pleasant setting, good seasonal foods, and perhaps most important, relaxed hosts. The sharing of your home and good food should be fun and relaxing for all, including the party giver.

Guest List

Ideally, invite guests who will be compatible, even though they may differ in many ways. Unless you're giving a party for a specific group, such as family members or business associates, design the guest list to bring together a good mix of people with shared or dissimilar interests—either approach can lead to lively conversation.

Match the number of guests to the kind of party you're having, and limit the group to a size you can accommodate comfortably. Both the setting and the season will influence the size of the gathering. Remember that you can serve many more people at a cocktail party with substantial appetizers or at a coffee and dessert tasting than you can at a sit-down dinner.

Invitations

Issue oral or written invitations early enough for people to accommodate their schedules to the party. Two weeks is a considerate lead for small, casual parties, but for large events, issue invitations as much as two months ahead. Handmade invitations via mail are always welcome—especially those that give some clue to the theme or mood of the party. Request an RSVP to help you make final plans.

Phone invitations are sufficient for small parties of people you know well, even though you may want to send out written reminders as well.

Menu

Whether you use the party menus in this book or create your own, keep the bounty of the season in mind. You'll be sure of having the freshest possible foods at the peak of flavor.

Encourage your guests to let you know ahead if they're dieting or have any food allergies or other special requirements. In cases where you aren't sure, you can select a menu that lets guests assemble their own entrée—such as a salad with a choice of toppings or a meat or fish dish to which they add the sauce.

Guests enjoy knowing what's coming next in a meal. A handwritten or printed menu at each place is a nice touch. For buffet dining you could place a menu at the beginning of the line, or hang it up behind the table.

The Setting

Dining settings can be as important as the food and drink. Choose a place to entertain that you enjoy: the kitchen, a corner of the patio, by the fireplace in the living room, under a backyard tree, the bank of a nearby stream. A survey of your home and garden may reveal entertaining areas that you've never thought of before: porches, cozy nooks, even cleared-out garages or attics. Be inventive; let your imagination show. Remember that entertaining and fun are synonymous.

Many of the events in this book can be held indoors or out, depending on the weather. But no matter where you stage the party, the setting should reflect your style and caring.

For a memorable party, make the room or outdoor space festive, as well as the tabletop. Flowers are always appropriate, of course; and each season brings obvious natural decorations: spring flowering

branches, flats of seedlings, or potted bulbs; tall summer grasses, sand and seashells, or baskets of garden-fresh produce; rich autumn leaves, straw, or pumpkins; and winter greens, cones, and berries.

Helium-filled balloons delight all ages and add fairly inexpensive splashes of color. Cluster them in tree branches, use them to mark the entrance, make a canopy over the table, tie them to chairs, fill up a room—indulge your sense of humor.

Ribbons and streamers are easy and festive. Outdoors, tie them to bamboo poles or tree branches to flutter in the breeze. Indoors, suspend them just about anywhere you want a party atmosphere. For gala events, purchase or make flags or colorful Japanese banners (see page 156); they'll give you years of entertaining pleasure.

Linens and Other Coverings

If you have a beautiful wood, marble, glass, or tile tabletop, you may choose to show it off—set the plates directly on it or use simple placemats only. At other times, you might want to create a mood or carry out a theme with some sort of table covering. The variety available today gives you plenty of options.

Tablecloths look best when they're sparkling clean and crisply ironed. Neutral colors adapt to almost any theme or season, but very bright hues and patterns can add sparkle or show off a special set of dishes.

Check the linen closet for throws, quilts, blankets, thin rugs, and interesting weavings to add texture as table coverings or as runners. Pieces of old lace or embroidery may be among your heirlooms or turn up at flea markets and garage sales. Use them as placemats or runners.

Painter's dropcloths made of muslin—cut to fit the table and pinked or hemmed—look good on their own. Or stencil, print, or paint them with special motifs. To cover large makeshift or odd-sized tables for big parties, cut and hem decorative bedsheets.

Straw matting can cover the whole tabletop, be used as a runner, or be cut for individual placemats. For autumn parties you could cover the top of the buffet with clean, fresh hay; a carpet of colorful leaves; or rough, weathered boards. Dried green moss, fresh green leaves, or fern fronds can be used in the same way for spring or summer entertaining. For sit-down dining, you may want to limit coverings of this sort to the center of the table.

Table Decorations

When fresh flowers are scarce or expensive, one or two perfect blossoms in a vase or floating in a dish can be all you need to create a pretty table. Or lay a single bloom across each plate or by each napkin—a slight fragrance is a bonus. Avoid overpowering fragrances that compete with the food. Dried flowers make attractive natural arrangements. Keep them in mind throughout the year.

Arrangement is a matter of personal preference: a mixed bouquet of many species in a basket, a mass of all one kind in a vase, a few blooms casually placed in a little bottle at each place. Choose containers that complement the dishes and other elements of the setting.

For decorations other than flowers, begin with a garden tour; look for attractive branches, small logs, mosses, berry clusters, grasses, weeds, and interesting vegetables that can be turned into festive arrangements.

Check the kitchen or produce markets for lemons, limes, oranges, cauliflower, artichokes, or any colorful fruit or vegetable. Sprouted onions can be beautiful. Eggs in pretty dishes or wire racks add interest. Move potted herbs from the kitchen window to the dining table.

Arrange family collections on the tabletop: bottles, vases, toys, shells, figurines. Group candlesticks or choose one dramatic candelabra. Float candles or fish in clear glass bowls or serving pieces.

You'll find numerous suggestions for flowers and other table decorations among the 28 parties pictured in this book—to get you started with creative table decorating.

Table-setting

Emphasis on informal and innovative entertaining has loosened the rules of table-setting, although the basic traditions still apply. Beyond these few accepted guidelines, the only limitation today is your imagination. You'll find these basic guidelines summarized in this section. For more ideas, study the photographs throughout this book.

Dishes

Whether you choose pottery or fine china, neutral colors and simple designs show off food well. If you like more color or pattern, add it with unusual saucers or bowls. Keep an open eye at flea markets or garage sales for interesting pieces to add zest to your table. For formal dining, you may want to have a service plate on the table on which to set the courses on smaller plates.

Generally, plates are set about one inch from the edge of the table. Bread-and-butter plates traditionally go to the left of the dinner plate, above the forks and parallel to the glasses (as shown). If salad accompanies the main course, as it often does in easy entertaining, the salad plate can replace the bread-and-butter plates—and also hold the bread.

In standard service, plates are placed from the left and removed from the right, the same way food is passed at the table. (The exception is bread-and-butter or salad plates, which are removed from the left since they're on that side.) When you serve soup from a tureen, salad from a bowl, or dessert at the table, bring a stack of dishes to your place, serve each, and then pass them to the right.

Cups and saucers intended for after-dinner coffee or tea may be on the table throughout the meal or added at serving time. They customarily go to the right of or behind the glasses.

Glasses

For easy entertaining, have all the glassware on the table when you seat your guests. Today most people opt for all-purpose wine glasses; if you wish to follow tradition, red wine glasses have wider bowls than those for white wine, so that the bouquet can be released when the wine is swirled. Champagne or sparkling wine is easiest to handle in a tall flute; it's apt to spill from saucer-type goblets, especially at large buffet or cocktail-party gatherings when everyone is standing. Glasses for water, iced tea, and other beverages can be goblets or tumblers—and so can those for wine.

Glasses are usually placed above the knife to the right of the plate. Start at the outside (away from the plate) and work toward it, placing glasses in the order in which beverages will be poured. Water usually goes closest to the plate and can be poured before guests are seated.

Flatware

Whether it's sterling silver, plated, or stainless, the knife is generally placed to the right of the plate (cutting edge facing in) with its bottom aligned with the bottom edge of the plate. If you use them, butter spreaders can be placed across the bread-and-butter or salad plate.

Spoons are usually placed to the right of the knife. If more than one is needed, start on the outside and place them in the order (toward the plate) in which they will be used during the meal. If you feel it's intimidating to have more than three pieces of silver on either side of the plate, even for formal dining, bring extra pieces as courses are served. Dessert or coffee spoons can be placed horizontally at the top of the plate or brought to the table at serving time.

Typically, forks go to the left of the plate with their handles lined up with the rim of the plate and the bottom of the knife. Again, start at the outside and work in according to the order in which they will be used. (If salad is served first, the salad fork goes on the outside; if salad follows the main course, its fork goes between the dinner fork and the plate.) One exception: seafood cocktail forks by tradition go on the far right of the spoons. Dessert forks can be placed (with or without a coffee spoon) horizontally at the top of the plate.

Extras

If you have enough, you can add salt and pepper servers at each place. Or put one or two sets on the table for passing. Cream and sugar containers can be brought out with the coffee. Old-fashioned fingerbowls—with a slice of lemon, fragrant blossom, or scented geranium leaf floating in the water—are nice touches after a meal that features finger foods. As an alternative, you might pass warm damp towels from a basket or covered dish.

Setting Up a Buffet

The easiest serving method yet invented is the buffet. For groups of 8 or 20 (or whatever your table or tables can accommodate), couple it with sit-down dining. Guests help themselves to food at the buffet before seating themselves at the table.

Bountiful is the key word when setting up the buffet. An opulent display of fresh fruit, a background of lush foliage or straw, textured fab-

SERVICE OR DINNER PLATE

APPETIZER

SOUP

MAIN COURSE

SALAD

DESSERT

rics, and banks of potted or cut flowers add depth to the food presentation and keep the table looking good even when the food runs low. The photographs in this book offer some ideas for creating a dramatic setting.

Stack plates on the buffet or on a side table near the beginning of the line. For a combination buffet-sit-down party, set tables and chairs with glasses, flatware, and napkins at each place. For a buffet without table seating, you'll need to arrange napkins and flatware for pickup as guests serve themselves. Place them at the beginning or end of the buffet. Napkins can be stacked, overlapped, or fanned out; rolled and tied around flatware; rolled and tucked into a basket; or arranged in any festive presentation that fits the mood. Flatware can be sorted by type or grouped into sets and placed flat on the buffet or in baskets, crocks, or other containers appropriate to the theme. For a buffet without table seating, you might consider providing lap trays.

Food should be beautifully displayed on complementary trays and serving dishes and placed on the table in the appropriate order—appetizers, cold salads, meats, warm vegetables or side dishes, cheeses, fruits, sweets. For fast service, put the entrée in the center of the table and arrange duplicate side dishes on either side of it. Guests can serve themselves from either end of the table. Arrange beverages at the end of the buffet or in a separate area. Remember, you don't have to present everything on the same table. Several small buffets often create more interest and scatter the guests for faster service. Another approach is to set up each course on a separate table.

Self-service also takes less time when you provide proper serving utensils for each dish and when meats, vegetables, breads, and desserts that need cutting are presliced and, if possible, reassembled to look whole.

Napkins

When you entertain large groups you'll want to select good-quality paper napkins. A wide range is available. Solid colors usually work best with foods, although you can create interesting effects with prints. Select an appropriate size: dinner-size for most meals, luncheon-size for lighter meals or appetizer buffets that include a number of finger foods, cocktail-size for drinks and light appetizers.

If you like cloth napkins for smaller gatherings, white ones are always appropriate, and colorful solids or prints give a festive air, especially for daytime or outdoor meals. Keep your eyes open at flea markets and garage sales for wonderful napkins from bygone days to dress up your table. Dish towels make great oversized napkins for barbecues and other messy outdoor meals.

You can place the napkin almost anywhere—to the left of the forks, on the dinner plate, or tucked into a glass. If you have an interesting collection of napkin rings, use them from time to time.

Napkin-folding

The standard way to fold a napkin is simply to fold it in half, making a rectangle with the fold at the top then fold it in half again to make a square with the open edges meeting on the left and at the bottom; and finally, fold it in half once again, placing the loose corners at the lower right of the napkin when you position it. Or you can take the quarter-folded napkin, and fold or roll it loosely in thirds and place it folded side down for a thin but elegant appearance.

For those times when you want to add drama or a touch of whimsy to the table, try one of the fancy folds explained here. You'll get the best results with starched napkins that are stored flat until you're ready to fold them.

The easiest way to learn the techniques is to follow the instructions step by step, using a practice napkin. Read the first step and then make that fold; read the next instruction and fold accordingly. You will produce a cone, fan, pyramid, or other shape quickly and without confusion. Restaurant waiters don't use a steam iron to press each fold, but it helps. You can prepare folded napkins hours or even days ahead.

CONE

1. Fold the napkin in half to make a rectangle with the fold at left.

2. Fold the top edge down to the bottom edge to make a square.

3. To form a cone, start rolling tightly from the lower left corner toward the upper right one; keep the point of the cone at the left and tightly rolled.

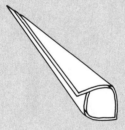

4. The upper left corner will become the point of the cone, and the open end will be at the right.

5. Turn up the wide end, forming a cuff on the outside to hold the cone together. Stand.

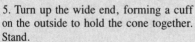

BISHOP'S HAT

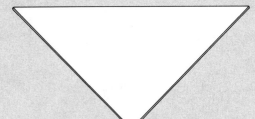

1. Fold the napkin in half to make a triangle with the point toward you.

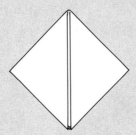

2. Bring upper left and right corners down to meet this point. (The folded edges should come together.)

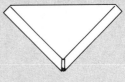

3. Fold the top corner down to within one inch of the point nearest you.

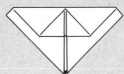

4. Now turn the same corner back up to meet the last fold.

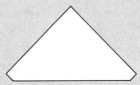

5. Turn the entire napkin over.

6. Bring right and left corners together, tucking the right corner inside the left to hold it in place.

7. Stand.

FAN

1. Fold the napkin in half to make a rectangle with the folded edge on the left and the open edges at the right.

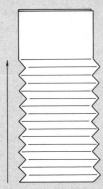

2. Starting with the short edge closest to you, crease in one-inch accordion pleats. Pleat to within about four inches of the top edge.

3. Fold in half by turning the left half of the rectangle underneath; pleats should be outside and at the bottom; the folded edge should be at the left. Turn down the upper right corner, and tuck it behind the pleat.

4. Holding the tucked-in corner in one hand, place it on the table, and spread the pleats into a Japanese-fan shape. The tucked-in corner acts as a stand at the back to hold the open fan upright.

CROWN

1. Fold the napkin in half to make a rectangle with the fold toward you.

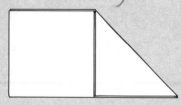

2. Bring the upper right corners down to meet the center of the fold, forming a triangle.

TRIANGLE

1. Fold the napkin in half away from you to make a rectangle with the fold toward you.

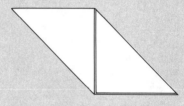

3. Bring the lower left corner up to the upper right corner to form a similar triangle.

4. Turn the napkin over, with one of the new, long folded edges parallel to you.

2. Fold the left side over the right one to make a square.

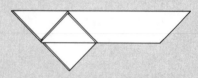

5. Fold the edge closest to you to the other edge, exposing a small triangle at the left, with its point at the bottom.

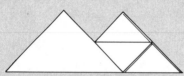

6. Turn over to expose two triangles whose points are at the top.

3. Bring the lower left corner to meet the upper right corner, forming a triangle.

7. Tuck the right end behind the large left triangle.

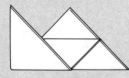

8. Turn the napkin over, and again tuck the right side behind the left side to complete the crown.

4. Fold in half and stand the napkin with the folded edge toward you.

9. Stand.

PYRAMID

1. Fold the napkin in half to make a rectangle with the fold toward you.

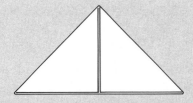

2. Bring the upper right and left corners down to meet the center of the fold.

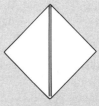

3. Fold the lower right and left corners up to meet at the top edge.

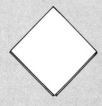

4. Turn over, end over end (by turning the point facing you forward).

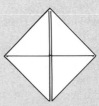

5. Lift the upper layer of the bottom corner closest to you to meet the top corner.

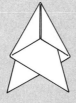

6. Lift the center of this triangle into a peak, and cross the bottom left corner over the right corner.

Seating

Thoughtful seating plans can contribute much to guests' enjoyment of any party. Whether you choose to follow conventional rules by separating couples and alternating sexes or create your own style of mixing, position people to encourage conversation. Intersperse extroverts throughout the group. It's your chance to play matchmaker in whatever sphere you please—perhaps pairing guests for romance, business ventures, or new friendships.

You may simply show guests where to sit as you invite them to the table, but placecards make assigned seating much easier on the host or hostess. Use your creativity to design placecards and holders that reflect the party theme or the season.

Entertainment

Music can fill conversation voids and establish a theme or mood. Select appropriate records or tapes ahead of time, or consider hiring a musician or group to entertain. Nearby colleges are excellent sources.

You may want to look into other types of entertainment as well—mimes, comedians, clowns, magicians, gymnasts, or whatever is available in your community. Check local theater groups for performers, or look in the Yellow Pages under "Entertainers."

Lighting

Create appropriate moods with candles, kerosene lanterns, torches, paper lanterns, plug-in spotlights, Christmas lights, or indirect lighting. Test night lighting ahead of time to be sure it is adequate to show off food and decoration. At the same time, you don't want to flood the space with bright light. Candles at each place or massed in the center of the table or clustered on the buffet can compensate for inadequate lighting.

When Guests Arrive

Complete your preparations early enough to greet your guests in a relaxed frame of mind. If you're comfortable with guests in the kitchen, invite the earliest arrivals to watch or help you with last-minute chores. Give a tour of the house or garden, show off the newest addition to your favorite collection, or bring out a game or puzzle that guests can enjoy on their own while waiting for the rest of the group.

For supereasy entertaining, let guests serve themselves to before-dinner drinks. This leaves you free to tend to last-minute details in the kitchen or just to visit with friends. Set up a self-service bar with crowd favorites, a selection of beer or wine (a sparkling wine is easy and festive), or whatever you feel goes with the party theme. Nonalcoholic beverages—mineral water, orange juice, a spicy tomato-based vegetable juice—should be available as well.

Cleanup

To avoid breaking the spell of the party, delay most cleanup tasks until the last guest departs. If you want to get a head start, you can rinse dishes as they're removed from the table so that they'll be easier to clean later. Or try a technique used by professional party givers: Station tubs of water in the kitchen and add dishes throughout the party. Extra garbage cans—or even bags hung, perhaps, on kitchen drawers—aid party cleanup.

Sometimes guests enjoy pitching in and helping with cleanup. If the offer seems sincere, accept graciously—or firmly decline if your energy is failing and you'd rather leave the cleanup for morning.

PLANNING LARGE PARTIES: WHEN YOU DO YOUR OWN CATERING

Successful large parties involve months of planning. The following guidelines should help you plot the logistics for groups of 50 or more when you act as your own caterer.

Choosing the Date

Before selecting a date, check for conflicts with other major events that might affect your guests. If it's a busy time of year, send out invitations six to eight weeks ahead.

Location

The size of the group determines the kind of space you'll need. If your home or garden is not adequate—or if you'd simply prefer to avoid the confusion at home—consider renting or borrowing a hall or some other private facility. Or hold the party in a park or at the beach. If you need reservations, make them as far in advance as possible.

When using a public place, check to determine whether the group will have sufficient privacy. Will you need a plan to deal with outsiders? What facilities (water, electricity, fire rings, tables, seating, rest rooms) are available? How far must you carry things?

If You Choose the Outdoors

In warm weather, you may need to protect both foods and guests from the sun. Cool days or evenings may require heat sources. Check the location for late-afternoon winds. Plan for bug control if necessary. You may need additional lighting for night events.

Plan for Rain

Always have an alternate plan in case of rain. Will umbrellas be enough protection? Can you move the crowd under eaves or overhangs? Can you set up in a garage or carport? If the party is indoors, where will you stash wet umbrellas and raincoats?

Parking and Transportation

If parking is limited, suggest that guests carpool. If space is totally inadequate, a parking shuttle is the solution. Direct everyone to use the parking lot of a school, shopping center, or another facility (arrange with the facility in advance if necessary); a vacant lot; or an area with generous roadside parking. Shuttle guests via bus, station wagons, carriages, or pickup trucks filled with hay or pillows. If security is a problem, hire a guard or someone to monitor the parking lot.

When Your Guests Help Out

When the guest list and the menu outpace the time of the host or hostess and the equipment of a single kitchen, think about involving your guests. For the Potluck Fisherman's Stew beach party on page 32, guests bring the fish, and can help you keep an eye on the pot as the meal cooks. Cooperatively prepared meals are another approach. Ask some of the guests to bring a certain type of food (a salad, an entrée, a bread), or plan the menu and split the recipes for the dishes among your helpers. Many foods can be prepared partially or completely ahead by individuals working together or independently at home; just put it all together on party day. Both the Salad-Sandwich Buffet (page 14) and Picnicking Made Easy (page 28) could be handled this way—and they're easy to expand for larger groups.

Remind guests to leave a fire lane when parking on a narrow road. In crowded residential areas or if parking is in a vacant lot, hire an off-duty policeman or other experienced person to direct the parking procedures. For safety, notify the fire department of your party.

Greeting Guests

If most of the guests are old friends, they will probably take care of themselves. If the crowd is mostly strangers, consider name tags or ice-breaking games for getting acquainted—they're easier on the host or hostess than countless introductions. If the group is large, it may be wise to screen arrivals, even at home.

Quantity of Food

Should you decide not to use one of the large-crowd menus in this book, the following per-person quantities are suggested for traditional meat, vegetable, and starch menus: ¼ pound boneless meat or fish or ¾ pound bone-in poultry, meat (such as ribs), or shellfish; about ¼ pound trimmed, ready-to-serve vegetable; and about ⅓ pound cooked starch.

The chart on page 57 offers further tips on estimating quantity for large groups.

When cooking for a large crowd, you'll have fewer complications if you prepare multiples of a dish, rather than tripling or quadrupling the recipe. (Some recipes don't multiply well, or don't perform as promised when cooked in utensils that are larger than those specified in the recipe.) It's also advisable to keep the variety of dishes to a minimum. But if you select several dishes of the same kind—such as several entrées, salads, or soups—add the number of servings each makes to determine how many people each kind of dish will serve. It never hurts to test a party meal to evaluate the recipes and estimate portion size. Testing also helps determine preparation steps, problems to avoid, equipment needed, storage requirements, and how to bring foods to serving temperature (thawing or heating). Make notes on the original recipes for your assistants (if you have them) to follow.

If You Do All the Preparation Yourself

An easy-to-handle menu is the way to go when you choose to tackle a large party alone. Select menus with dishes that can be made ahead (like Holiday Fiesta on page 68), incorporate some purchased foods into the meal (as in A Big Buffet That Can Grow on page 54), or plan a party where the guests bring something simple (such as An Afternoon of Cheese and Wine on page 30). Even easier, serve items that don't need to be cooked: Try the delectable Come for Chocolate and Coffee get-together on page 66.

Even Big Burger Before the Big Game (page 48) could be a cooperative party. To serve a group of 30, for example, you might supply the appetizer, salad, toppings, and bread. Then ask four individuals—or teams—to prepare four Big Burgers and supply the grills and utensils to cook them at the get-together.

Guest contributions—of energy, food and drink, or both—allow everyone to participate in the event and make large parties more manageable and affordable for the hosts.

Hiring Assistance

Teenage family members or friends are inexpensive kitchen or serving resources. Contact local high schools or nearby colleges for temporary helpers.

There are definitely times to use the services of a professional caterer. When you do, it helps to know what to expect, as described on page 152.

Supplemental Equipment

Portable electric appliances, such as microwave ovens and toaster ovens, may be the answer when you're cooking for a crowd. (Be sure to check your electrical capacity so as not to overload it.) Portable barbecues and camp stoves can provide additional cooking and heating sources.

A few portable ice chests can expand refrigerator space simply and inexpensively. Really big parties with many perishables may require a rented refrigerator truck.

Inventive hosts turn to inexpensive alternatives. Use a trick of many professional caterers: Mix and store in large heavy-duty plastic garbage bags. New plastic garbage cans also make great large-scale mixing bowls. Galvanized tubs or garbage cans are perfect for icing drinks. (Beverages cool in about 30 minutes when immersed in crushed ice combined with water.) Large baking pans camouflaged with leaves or ferns, big plastic garden pots or bowls, and hollowed watermelons or pumpkins all make dandy serving containers.

For annual events, consider purchasing a few large cooking or serving pieces to use through the years.

Serving Crowds

A self-service buffet is definitely the easiest way to handle large groups. See page 144 for hints on arrangement. For 50 or more guests, plan several access routes to the food and drink. Arrange buffets so that guests can reach in from all sides, allowing at least one buffet for every 100 guests. Dividing the food, or at least the desserts and beverages, among smaller scattered tables greatly reduces congestion.

Alternatives to Sit-down Dining for Crowds

The choice between a stand-up affair and chairs and tables for dining depends mainly on your facility, and to some extent on the theme of the party. Let guests know if they should come prepared to sit on the ground outdoors. At beach parties and picnics, provide mats or blankets. For less casual situations, large cloths and pillows offer inexpensive seating that's more comfortable than a bare or carpeted floor. Or borrow or rent chairs, tables, and coverings.

If you choose a stand-up party, serve foods that can be picked up to eat; don't expect guests to balance plate, utensils, and a glass while standing. Dishes for lap meals need to be sturdy. Good-quality disposable paper or plastic dishes are fine—particularly if they're supported by a wicker basket. If you want something stronger or fancier, check with local party rental suppliers. Or you might consider investing in a quantity of inexpensive plain dishes if you make a habit of entertaining large groups. For an informal event like Potluck Fisherman's Stew (page 32), you might even ask guests to bring their own bowls and spoons.

Garbage Disposal

Strategically locate plenty of containers for used paper plates and mark a place to deposit reusable glassware, dishes, and utensils. At the end of the party designate someone to collect all the garbage containers, fasten them securely, and transport them to the proper place for pickup.

Rest Rooms

If you feel that your own facilities are inadequate to handle the number of guests or in places where there's no other alternative, rent portable toilets from a sanitation service. Place them well away from the food preparation and serving areas. Assign someone to check rest room supplies.

Insurance

Check with your agent to be sure your household insurance covers accidents even when you're entertaining off the premises. If you're using a borrowed vehicle for shuttle service, ask about unowned vehicle coverage. Also discuss burglary and robbery coverage with your agent. If you hire a caterer, insist that he or she have adequate insurance to cover any liability.

Neighborhood Consideration

To minimize complaints be sure to notify your neighbors well ahead of time if your big party is at home. Better yet, invite them to the party.

WHEN IT'S TIME TO CALL A CATERER

There are times in life when professional catering is the best way to ensure easy entertaining. When your time is limited, when you want a party that is unique or beyond your own expertise, when you're celebrating a special occasion in your life, or if the size of the crowd makes you feel uncomfortable, secure the services of a caterer or a party planner (one who works with you to produce the total event).

This is one time you shouldn't rely on the Yellow Pages. Word of mouth is definitely the way to locate a professional party service that will suit your tastes and budget. If you've seen work you liked, ask the hostess for the party planner's or caterer's number. Collect caterers' cards at parties you enjoy. Unless the reputation of the caterer is exactly what you want, talk with several to compare services, styles, and costs. Weigh all of these points before choosing. Low cost alone is not the best basis for selection: in catering you do get what you pay for.

Some party planners or caterers take care of every detail from invitations to garbage pickup; hiring staff (cooks, waiters, bartenders); securing flowers, balloons, or other decorations; ordering rentals; providing live musicians or other entertainers; and countless other details in addition to the food and beverages. Others deal only in food and service. You can usually purchase whichever services you need. If you enjoy preparing a special dish or setting and decorating tables, then you can perform that task and leave the rest of the party to the pros. You can hire a caterer to deliver all the prepared foods or just part of the meal.

Realize what is involved in catering when you consider the price. You should expect the party to cost more than if you did it yourself when you purchase the services of profession-

als. For full service, expect to pay more per person for a dinner than if you took your guests to a restaurant. Realistically, the caterer is setting up a one-time restaurant in your home. In addition to food and beverage costs, you have to pay for the use and transport of all the equipment, as well as for the behind-scenes and service-staff time, including preparation and cleanup.

When you first talk with a professional party person, you'll want to ask about all of these areas:

☐ **What references can you check?** It's better to talk to people who have used the service than to rely on the pictures in the caterer's portfolio.

☐ **What specific services does the cost estimate cover?** Some caterers quote on a per-guest basis that includes everything; some itemize each category: decorations, rentals (tables, chairs, linens, dishes, and so forth), food, service. Be sure you are comparing the same services when you make a decision.

☐ **What is the payment schedule?** Usually you can expect to pay 50 percent in advance, with the balance due at the end of the party. Any last-minute changes you make are usually billed to you.

☐ **Are these services taxable in your state?**

☐ **What charges are made if the party runs longer than planned?** You are responsible for any extra time the catering staff must work.

☐ **What about insurance?** Either you assume the risks or you rely on the caterer to provide insurance (which can be purchased on a one-time basis for large parties).

☐ **What about a contract?** Insist on a detailed, written agreement to avoid any misunderstanding.

Once you've made a choice, worked out all the details, and signed a contract, relax and let the caterer have full freedom. Be sure the kitchen and party areas are cleared out before the professionals arrive. Give them plenty of room to work, but be available to answer any questions.

EASY OPENERS FOR ALL SEASONS

Many of the menus in this book do not include appetizers or first courses. Here are some simple ways to begin the meal, whether you wish to share a platter of appetizers in the living room, or arrange individual portions to serve at the table. Most of the foods on this list are readily available throughout the year. Those with fresh ingredients should be chosen when the produce is at the peak of its season. Make use of ready-to-eat appetizer foods available in delicatessens or take-out gourmet stores to save your cooking time for the main menu.

☐ Cold meats with fresh fruits: thinly sliced, allow about ⅛ pound per serving. Try coppa, prosciutto, baked ham, Westphalian ham, or dry salami with figs, melon (not watermelon), ripe pears, kiwi, papaya, peaches, mangoes, ripe plums, or apricots.

☐ Any of the mild chilies or bell peppers with rind-ripened or triple cream cheeses.

☐ Sweet butter and radishes.

☐ Red or yellow bell peppers or sliced tomatillos, dipped in lime juice and lightly sprinkled with salt.

☐ Golden Delicious apple slices with basil leaves and slices of sharp ripened chèvre.

☐ Hard-cooked quail eggs.

☐ Potato slices sautéed in butter and topped with sour cream and a bit of caviar.

☐ Lemon-brushed avocado slices with sour cream and a tricolor of caviars (black, golden, and red).

☐ Orange wedges on the peel, jicama wedges, sliced cucumber, Golden Delicious apples, and pineapple to dip in chili powder mixed with salt.

☐ Oysters or clams on the half-shell, plain or with lemon; hot sauce; or vinegar with minced shallots and lots of black pepper. For a fancy presentation, top them with bright orange salmon eggs.

☐ Caviar alone, or with lemon, sour cream, and chopped onion. Serve with black bread or thin white toast. One or two tablespoons makes a generous serving.

☐ Smoked salmon or lox with lemon, sour cream, fresh dill, and red onion.

☐ Small cooked shrimp with sour cream and red caviar.

☐ Herring salad from the delicatessen, plain, on lettuce, or on apple slices.

☐ Purchased pâtés (from chopped chicken liver to foie gras), or rillettes.

☐ Cheeses served with vegetables such as endive leaves, bell pepper pieces, or turnip slices instead of crackers.

☐ Assorted olives and salty cheese like feta or Mexican *queso fresca*.

☐ Breadsticks and butter.

☐ Canned anchovies rolled around capers, served on salt-free crackers spread with sweet butter.

☐ Marinated artichoke hearts or button mushrooms.

☐ Fresh whole strawberries to dip in aromatic aperitif wines.

☐ Raw peas with fruity white wine.

☐ Individual baskets of raw vegetables: peeled turnips, asparagus tips, green beans, Jerusalem artichokes, slices of daikon, tiny golden tomatoes, sprays of arugula. Serve the vegetables with plain or seasoned salt, or with an herb cheese like boursin or alouette.

MAKING THE MEAL LOOK SPECIAL

Visually pleasing, well-prepared foods tempt the palate all by themselves. Even so, garnishes add a festive touch, as long as they're compatible—not competitive—with food. They should enhance the food on the tray or plate without overwhelming it.

Ideas for Garnishing
Here are some of the many possibilities for garnishing food:

☐ Sprigs of fresh herbs, perhaps flowering—thyme, oregano, mint, basil, chervil, parsley, watercress, cilantro.

☐ Single leaves—grape, celery, chives, bay, flat Italian parsley, geranium (especially scented varieties), ti or other florist tropicals.

☐ Edible flowers (whole or petals)—pesticide-free borage, nasturtium, viola, geranium, squash, calendula, rose, violet, citrus, chrysanthemum.

☐ Citrus (paper-thin slices, wedges, or zest)—lemon, lime, orange, grapefruit, tangerine, tangelo, kumquat.

☐ Colorful vegetables (tiny whole, bunches, or sliced)—edible-pod peas, red bell peppers, chilies, tiny cooked artichokes, radishes with a few leaves, cooked beets, baby carrots, green onions.

☐ Fruits—small clusters of grapes; sliced kiwi; any berries; whole lady apples; apple slices (dipped in lemon juice); pomegranate or papaya seed; attractively cut pieces of fresh pineapple, melon, or other fruits.

☐ Nuts—toasted, slivered, chopped.

☐ Spices—whole peppercorns, stick cinnamon, star anise, whole cloves, sesame seed, poppy seed, fennel seed, sprinklings of paprika or turmeric.

☐ Eggs—slices, wedges, grated; whole quail (in shells, hard cooked, or pickled).

Beautiful Butter

One of those little touches that helps make entertaining special can be the way you serve the butter. Whether you prefer sweet (unsalted) butter, salted butter, or margarine, here are several ways to go. Serve your favorite spread at room temperature or chilled, whichever you prefer. But if it's cut or pressed into fancy shapes, present it on a bed of crushed ice to help retain the form.

Crocks. Soften butter or margarine at room temperature until it can be packed into shallow round crocks for passing or into small versions for each place setting. Smooth the top with the back of a spoon or your finger and wipe the edges clean with a paper towel.

Pats. Use a special cutter—it resembles a wire egg slicer—to cut a stick of butter into uniform squares. Take a firm stick directly from the refrigerator, position the cutter over the butter, and firmly press the cutter straight down. Place pats in ice water until just before you're ready to serve them. Arrange attractively on a dish for passing, or place a few on each bread-and-butter plate.

Curls. Pull a curler—a C-shaped metal band on a paddle—firmly across slightly softened butter; drop the finished curls into ice water. Dip the curler into hot water between curls. You can make several curls from each side of a stick of butter. Arrange curls on plates or atop crushed ice in a shallow dish.

Logs and Balls. Using two water-soaked paddles that are scored to give the butter a textured finish, you can make attractive logs or balls. Start with equal-sized chunks of slightly softened butter, and roll each into a ball between the paddles. Move paddles in tight circles, in opposite directions for a ball or back and forth for a log. Drop into ice water until just before serving time.

Molds. Fanciful wooden or plastic molds are available in gourmet cookware stores. Pre-soak wooden molds in water before adding butter. Fill the bottom half with softened butter, add the top, and press to spread butter evenly in the mold. Chill, remove the mold, and serve.

How to Make Sweet Butter. If you consider creamy sweet butter an extravagance or cannot find it to buy (usually in the freezer section), make your own from ordinary salted butter. Cut the butter into chunks and cover it generously with ice water; then mix with an electric mixer or in a blender. Pour off the water and add fresh at least twice, or until the salt is washed out of the butter. Drain, and knead or work with a spoon to remove surplus water; then pack in a jar and freeze until needed.

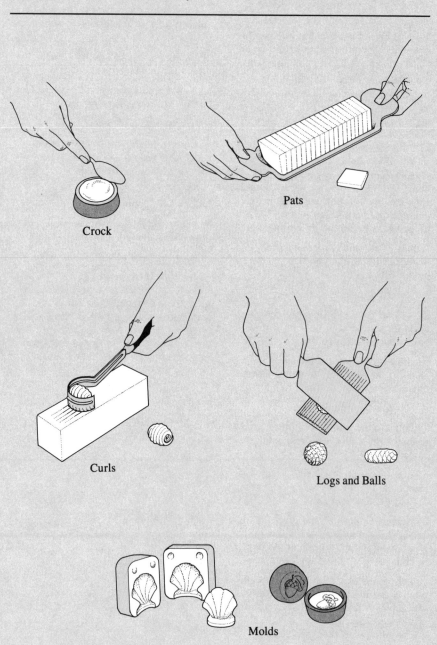

Crock

Pats

Curls

Logs and Balls

Molds

SPECIAL WOODS FOR FLAVORFUL BARBECUING

Barbecuing, or grilling, is a favorite and easy summertime entertainment. (See Dinner Under the Stars on page 34 and Big Burger Before the Big Game on page 48.) The most common fuel is pressed charcoal briquets, and mesquite charcoal has many advocates. But for aromatic smoke that flavors foods as they cook, burn fragrant woods.

Mesquite (or Mexican) charcoal is made by charring mesquite wood. It definitely burns hotter than pressed charcoal briquets, which are made from a variety of combustible substances. Although mesquite charcoal has a reputation for adding flavor to foods, in *Sunset* tests the flavor was barely perceptible—and only with beef and pork.

To ignite either type of charcoal, mound pieces on the barbecue fire grate, with dampers open. You can tuck kindling wood in the mound, stack the charcoal on an electric fire starter, or saturate it with a chemical starter.

Mesquite charcoal flames and sparks a bit as it catches. Pressed briquets or mesquite charcoal will be ready for cooking in 30 to 40 minutes, well spotted with gray ash and glowing red in the center of the mound. Spread out the hot coals for direct or indirect cooking, put the cooking grill in place, and arrange foods on the grill.

To maintain the heat, you'll need to replenish pressed briquets about every 30 minutes, mesquite charcoal after 45 minutes to an hour. Add about 25 percent more fuel. Lay the fresh charcoal against the rim of the fire until it ignites, then push it into the cooking area.

When you finish cooking in a barbecue with a lid, snuff the coals; when cool, sift ashes for chunks to use again.

To Add Smoke Flavor to Foods. Uncharred mesquite, alder, hickory, oak, grapevine, mountain mahogany, apple, and cherry woods are used to give foods a smoke flavor. These woods are sold in various forms: small logs, chunks or slices, and coarse or fine chips. Few stores carry all these woods, but well-stocked supermarkets, fancy food or cookware shops, feed and fuel stores, garden supply centers, hardware and department stores, and outdoor sport shops are likely sources.

To Smoke-Cook with Logs or Chunks. You can cook foods over burning wood logs or chunks or the coals they form, or you can soak wood pieces in water to place atop burning charcoal so that they'll smolder and give off smoke to flavor food.

Small chunks and sliced logs ignite quickly; pressed wood chunks or slices are more difficult to start. Loosely crumple several pieces of newspaper and lay in the center of the barbecue fire grate (dampers open); stack chunks laced with pieces of kindling and light with a match.

When most chunks are blazing, use long-handled tongs to spread them out in a single layer so that pieces just touch. Set the cooking grill in place about 4 inches above the surface of the wood. Place foods on the grill directly over the burning wood. Flames should just touch the grill (they'll die down shortly), but if they rise above it, raise the cooking grill, lower the fire grate, or partially close the dampers to slow burning.

About 2 pounds of wood (8 to 10 chunks or 4 to 6 small logs) is sufficient to cook about 4 pounds of beef to rare or medium, allowing 15 minutes for start-up and 20 minutes for cooking. A larger quantity of wood will form a bigger bed of hot coals, which will extend the effective cooking time. To maintain heat, add wood around the fire. As foods cook, turn them often.

To Smoke-Cook with Chips. When dropped onto hot coals, fragrant wood chips—either saturated with water or green from the tree—smolder with smoke that flavors food as it cooks.

You can use unsprayed garden cuttings, or buy peach, pear, apricot, orange, lemon, pecan, or walnut. Break clippings into small twigs and cut limbs into short pieces or chunks. If dry, soak in water. Do not use random clippings; some plants—oleander, for example—are poisonous. And don't use the wood of cedar, fir, pine, spruce, or eucalyptus; their smoke gives food a bitter, resinous taste.

COLORFUL PARTY FLAGS

Adapt Japanese message-bearing banners with loops, called *chitsuke-hata,* to serve as colorful outdoor party decorations that rustle in the breeze. Use them to designate food and beverage service areas for large parties, or just to add color and interest anytime.

Buy big bamboo poles (9 to 10 feet long and ¾ to 1 inch in diameter) and canes (about 3 feet long and ⅜ inch in diameter) from a garden supply or import store. If you can't find bamboo, use equivalent-size dowels from a builder's supply.

Wrap the tops of the long poles with tape (to keep them from splitting) and drill the tops to receive the small canes, as shown. If the small canes don't fit tightly in the holes, use rubber bands, string, or tape to lash the joints together.

Very lightweight ripstop nylon (also called spinnaker cloth) is the first choice for fabric. Its color won't fade in the sun, and light shines through it. The ripstop weave means that you don't have to finish raw edges. Check fabric stores, sailmaker shops, kite shops, and camping-gear stores. If you can't locate ripstop, choose another type of nylon, polyester, or taffeta from a fabric store, but plan to finish the raw edges. Precise measurements are not crucial; 2 yards of 42- to 45-inch-wide fabric will make two banners. Buy extra lengths of compatible or contrasting colors to make designs on the solid background.

To make the loops from which the banners hang, you'll need about 1 yard of 1-inch-wide white ripstop webbing or grosgrain ribbon, or ⅛ yard more ripstop fabric per banner. Cut 5-inch-long strips, fold in half, and stitch to top and one side of banner. Use the pattern shown as a guide. The top hem stiffens the edge so that the banner doesn't sag be-

tween loops. (A tack or tape on the end loop will help keep fabric taut.) With ripstop nylon, you can use straight stitching to make the hem and to attach loops; on other fabrics, use a zigzag stitch and also zigzag all raw edges.

To appliqué letters, numbers, or simple shapes, first draw them on the decorative fabric with chalk, cut them out, and pin or baste them to the background fabric. Using transparent nylon thread, topstitch them ⅛ inch from the edge. (Again, use zigzag stitch with any fabric other than ripstop.) Use small, sharp scissors to cut away the background fabric under the appliqué, cutting a safe ¼ inch

inside the stitching so that the appliqué will show equally well on both sides of the banner.

To anchor each banner in the ground, you'll need a ¼-inch-diameter metal rod, about 3 feet long, from a hardware store or builder's supply. First, insert the rod into the base of the pole and knock it firmly on a hard surface to drive about half of the rod through the knuckles inside the bamboo cane. Stick the metal rod into the ground to anchor the banner. To display banners on decks, tie the bamboo poles (you needn't reinforce them with metal rods) to the deck rails with nylon or sisal cord.

Precise measurements are not crucial. Here's a basic pattern. Two yards of fabric, 42 or 45 inches wide, will make two banners. To make loops, fold 5-inch-long strips in half and stitch on.

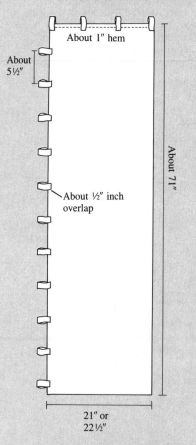

About 1″ hem

About 5½″

About 71″

About ½″ inch overlap

21″ or 22½″

Hole drilled through top of long pole holds small cane in place. Before drilling, put tape around pole to keep it from splintering.

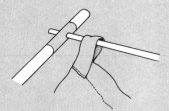

Metal rod anchors pole. First, insert rod into base of pole and knock firmly on hard surface to drive half of rod through knuckles inside bamboo cane.

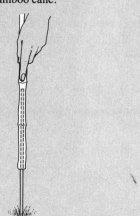

156

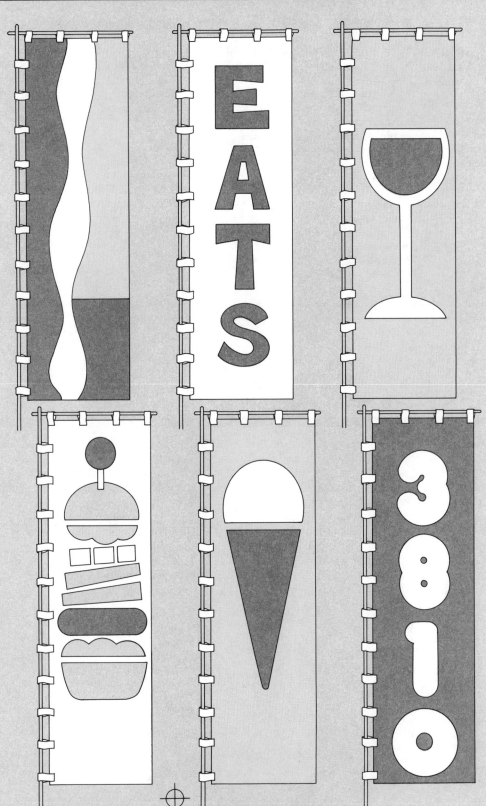

Colorful party flags are easy to sew. Bold banners at a garden party direct guests to food and beverage areas. Numbers sewn on a curbside banner make the party house easy to spot.

Varietals are wines that are named for the grapes from which they are made.

Generic wines are named—usually after a European wine district—to hint at the style or flavor of the wine.

Proprietaries are wines of a major type that are labeled with special names coined by the proprietors of wineries. These proprietary names frequently echo generic place names; the wines parallel generics in type and use.

WHITE WINES

White wines with light, fresh, fruity flavor are good with light chicken and turkey dishes that are seasoned with some sweetness, including curries and dishes served with sweet relishes. These wines are also complementary with such mildly sweet vegetables as carrots and peas. The following white wines are finished either dry or slightly sweet:

Varietals:
Chenin Blanc
French Colombard
Gewürztraminer
White Riesling
  (Johannisberg Riesling)

Generic:
Rhine

Dry white wines that do not have a flowery or fruity nose are easy to fit into most menus because their flavors do not dominate. They are good with shellfish, poultry, veal, and cheese dishes.

Varietals:
Emerald Riesling
Green Hungarian
Grey Riesling
Sylvaner

Generics:
Chablis
Dry Sauterne
Mountain White

ROSE WINES

Rosé wines are light, fresh, and fruity, sometimes dry but more often slightly sweet. They go well with dishes that contain a bit of sweetness, such as chicken salad with grapes in a creamy dressing; fruit salad; or ham with a sweet glaze. They also complement cold chicken, meat pâtés, grilled cheese sandwiches, and salty sliced meats like salami and prosciutto.

Varietals:
Rosé of Cabernet Sauvignon
Gamay Rosé
Grenache Rosé
Grignolino Rosé
Rosé of Pinot Noir
Zinfandel Rosé

Generics:
Rosé
Vin Rosé

RED WINES

Red wines that are light-bodied, dry or just off dry, fresh, and mildly fruity are good with all types of poultry—roast or grilled chicken, turkey thighs, quail, squab, duck, or goose; pork and veal; stews or braised dishes of those meats; beef; meats with rich dark or creamy sauces; richly seasoned tomato sauces and meat sauces for pasta; and dishes with lots of cheese.

Varietals:
Carnelian
Gamay
Gamay Beaujolais
Grignolino
Pinot St. George
Ruby Cabernet

Generics:
Burgundy
Chianti
Claret
Mountain Red

Full-bodied, oak-aged red wines with distinctive flavors have the ability to cut through rich flavors and refresh the palate. These wines complement red meats—beef, lamb, and pork; dark-fleshed birds like squab and quail; organ meats; sharp cheeses; dishes with rich sauces or lots of butter. They are also interesting with other intense flavors such as chocolate.

Varietals:
Barbera
Cabernet Sauvignon
Charbono
Merlot
Petite Sirah
Pinot Noir
Zinfandel

Generics:
Barberone
Vino Rosso

Wines with an intense oaky flavor, such as the Chardonnays, stand up well with mildly seasoned rich foods—those with butter and cream finishes. They also balance well with simply cooked (roasted, grilled, or poached) poultry, pork, veal, salmon, and swordfish. Other full-bodied wines in this group, such as dry Sauvignon Blancs, which are less forceful in character, go with these same foods, as well as with all kinds of fish. Try them also with hearty lentil soup; beans; grains and vegetables; and dishes with lots of cheese.

Varietals:
Chardonnay
    (Pinot Chardonnay)
Pinot Blanc
Dry Semillon
Sauvignon Blanc
    (Fumé Blanc)

Rich, fruity, sweet white wines are delicious in and with desserts of fruit, chocolate, or creamy mixtures. Try them also with nuts, or mildly sweet cookies and a triple cream or French process cheese. These wines are also interesting with sharp cheese like Roquefort, or liver pâté.

Varietals:
Malvasia Bianca
Muscat of Alexandria
Muscato Canelli
Sweet Semillon
Late-Harvest White Riesling

Generics:
Haut Sauterne
Sweet Sauterne
Light Muscat
Chateau _____
    (Often a winery or vineyard name)

White wines from black grapes vary in color from white to salmon. They may be crisp and dry or slightly sweet, and are generally more akin to rosé than to white wines. They are good with fish, poultry, and pork; stews of veal, pork, fish, or shellfish; cheese dishes; and lightly seasoned creamy mixtures.

Varietals:
Pinot Noir Blanc
Zinfandel Blanc
Cabernet Sauvignon Blanc
White Barbera

APPETIZER WINES

Appetizer wines have a higher alcohol content than table wine (17 to 20 percent, compared to 12 to 13 percent); they often have added fruit, herbal, or other natural flavors. Offer them as an aperitif with roasted nuts and other appetizers.

Sherry
    (Cocktail, Dry, Medium Dry)
Vermouth
    (Dry, Sweet)

DESSERT WINES

Like appetizer wines, dessert wines have a higher alcohol content than table wines, but they are markedly sweeter. Serve them with desserts of all types, nuts, fruit, and cheese.

Angelica
Cream Sherry
Madeira
Marsala
Muscatel
Port
    (Ruby, Tawny, White)
Tokay

SPARKLING WINES

Festive sparkling wines, in a variety of styles, with a range of colors, are a versatile accompaniment to appetizers, entrées, and desserts. Serve dry sparkling wines with the foods on lists 1, 2, and 5. Those with a sweeter taste, or a very fruity nose (typical of muscat-based wines), go well with the sweet foods suggested in lists 3 and 5. They are especially good with roasted nuts.

Champagne (white sparkling wine;
    labeled by degree of sweetness)
        Natural—very dry
        Brut—dry
        Extra Dry—hint of sweetness
        Sec—noticeably sweet
        Demi-Sec—very sweet
Blanc de Noir (White champagne from
    black grapes, usually styled as Brut)
Cremant (Fewer bubbles than regular
    champagne, usually sweet)
Sparkling Muscat, Sparkling Malvasia
    (From muscat grapes, usually sweet)
Pink Champagne (usually sweet)
Sparkling Burgundy, Champagne Rouge
    (Red sparkling wine, usually off-dry)

A

Add-on vichyssoise, 28, 29, 99
After the Egg Hunt party, 18–21, 89–92
Afternoon of Cheese and Wine, 30–31, 100–101, 151
Aioli sauce, 95
  fish, shrimp, eggs, and vegetables with, 24, 25, 94–95
Almond
  -chocolate torte, 50–53, 117
  cream, raspberries with, 26, 27, 98
  custard with loquats, 74–76, 137
Almonds
  in chocolate-nut squares, 49, 113
  in nut mosaic tart, 59, 60, 124
  on spice cake with caramel icing, 55, 57, 120
Alouette with raw vegetables, as appetizer, 153
Amaretto in coffee, 128
American golden caviar on pan-fried potato slices, 22, 23, 93
Anaheim chilies with string cheese, 48–49, 113
Anchovies with capers, as appetizer, 153
Anchovy dressing, 140
Appetizers
  anchovies with capers, 153
  avocado-shrimp cocktail, 28, 29, 99
  calamari-kiwi salad, 34–37, 104–5
  chilled artichokes with herbed goat cheese, 58–61, 121
  cold meats with fresh fruits, 153
  fresh tiny peas in the pod, 6, 7, 82
  steamed mussels provençal, 18–21, 89
  stuffed cheese, 68, 70–71, 129
  suggestions for, 153
  sushi, 9, 10–11, 83–84
Apple cider
  with Big Buffet That Can Grow, 54, 57, 118
  with Garlic Festival buffet, 42, 43, 109
  mulled, with Winter Salad Supper, 78–80, 138
Apple salad, with tomatillo and jicama, 68, 70–71, 130
Apples
  in appetizers, 153
  as dessert, 43
Apricots with cold meats, as appetizer, 153
Artichoke hearts, marinated, as appetizer, 153

Artichokes
  with aioli sauce, 25, 95, 96
  chilled, with herbed goat cheese, 58–61, 121
  Jerusalem, as appetizer, 153
  preparing, 121
  steamed, 96
  tiny cooked, 153
Arugula, raw, as appetizer, 153
Asparagus
  with aioli sauce, 95, 96
  pistachio-buttered, 18–21, 91
  raw, as appetizer, 153
  steamed, 96
  young, with shrimp and home-made mayonnaise, 22, 23, 93
  on young vegetable platter, 6, 7, 82
Autumn Brunch, 46–47, 112
Avocado-shrimp cocktail, 28, 29, 99
Avocados
  on fruit salad platter, 59, 60, 124
  guacamole, 71, 132
  sliced, with sour cream and caviar, 153
  in sushi selections, 9, 10, 11, 83
  in vegetable tray salad, 57, 118

B

Baked ham with fresh fruit, as appetizer, 153
Baked whole onions, tangerine-sauced roasted duckling with yam chunks and, 72–73, 133
Banana gelato, 14–15, 17, 88
Banners, making, 156–57
Barbecuing, special woods for, 155
Bartlett pears, Gorgonzola with, 44–45, 111
Basil
  apple slices with chèvre and, 153
  layered cheese torta with pine nuts and, 30, 31, 101
Beach party, 32–33, 102. See also Picnics
Beans, green
  with aioli sauce, 95, 96
  celery root with, 78–80, 140
  raw, as appetizer, 153
    with dipping sauce, 102
  steamed, 96
  in young vegetable platter, 6, 7, 82
Beef
  Peking, with Chinese pea pods, 74–77, 137
  platter burger with Mexican seasonings, 48–49, 114
  roast, aioli sauce for, 25, 95
  tenderloin, mesquite-grilled, in Cabernet Sauvignon marinade, 34–36, 103

Beehive bread, 12, 13, 85–86
Beer
  with Big Burger before the Big Game, 48–49, 113
  with Tabletop Sushi, 8–11, 83
Beet soup, chilled, 50–53, 117
Beets
  and pears, with dandelion greens, 78–80, 138
  in vegetable tray salad, 57, 118
Bell peppers. See Peppers
Berries, as garnish, 153. See also Specific berries
Beverages
  before-dinner, planning for, 150
  cooling, 151
  See also Apple cider; Beer; Coffee; Wine
Big Breakfast Bonanza, 62–63, 125
Big Buffet That Can Grow, 54–57, 118–20, 151
Big Burger Before the Big Game, 48–49, 113–114, 151
Big Dutch Baby Pancakes, 62–63, 125
Birdwatcher's Breakfast, 12–13, 85–86
Black fungus, in eight immortal jai, 76, 137
Blackberries, in vanilla fig compote, 108
Blue cheese
  spinach salad with shallots and, 18–21, 91
  with warm walnuts, 30, 31, 100
Blueberry meringue torte with rum custard, 38, 39, 107
Boursin with raw vegetables, as appetizer, 153
Brandy in coffee, 67, 128
Brazilian coffee, 128
Breads
  Beehive, 12, 13, 85–86
    wheat-flecked, 86
  buttermilk and currant scone, 46–47, 112
  double cheese, 54, 56–57, 119
  Golden Beehive, 85
  hot chèvre toast, 30, 31, 101
  pine nut sticks, 38, 39, 107
  pueblo, 58–61, 123
  pumpkin, 54, 56–57, 119
  seasoned bread rounds, 91
  toast rounds, 32, 33, 102
Breadsticks
  butter with, as appetizer, 153
  pine nut, 38, 39, 107
Breakfast parties. See also Brunch party
  Big Breakfast Bonanza, 62–63, 125
  Birdwatcher's Breakfast, 12–13, 85–86
Brie in wine aspic, 30, 31, 100
Broccoli, in eight immortal jai, 76, 137
Brunch party, 46–47, 112. See also Breakfast parties

Brussels sprouts, butter-steamed, with red bell peppers, 58–61, 122
Buffet parties
  Big Buffet That Can Grow, 54–57, 118–20
  catered, 152
  large, self-catered, 150–51
  Salad-Sandwich Buffet, 14–17, 87–88
  setting up, 144, 145–46
  Welcome Autumn with a Garlic Festival, 42–43, 109–10
  Winter Salad Supper, 78–80, 138–40
Butter
  breadsticks with, as appetizer, 153
  orange-filbert, spaghetti squash with, 58–61, 122–23
  pistachio, asparagus with, 18–21, 91
  radishes and, as appetizer, 153
  serving styles for, 154
  sweet, making, 154
Butter cookies, walnut, 68, 71, 132
Buttermilk and currant scone, 46–47, 112
Butter pastry, 124
Butter-steamed Brussels sprouts and red bell peppers, 58–61, 122

C

Cabbage, savoy, in young vegetable platter, 6, 7, 82
Cakes
  blueberry meringue torte with rum custard, 38, 39, 107
  chocolate-almond torte, 50–53, 117
  chocolate-nut squares, 48–49, 113
  fresh orange baba-rin, 78–80, 140
  pork sausage, 54, 56–57, 120
  seed, 54, 56–57, 120
  spice, with caramel icing, 54–55, 57, 120
Calamari
  -kiwi salad, 34–37, 104–5
  cleaning, 104–5
California caviar, 23
Candies, chocolate truffle, 22, 23, 93
Canning garlic jelly, 110
Capers, anchovies with, as appetizer, 153
Caramel icing, spice cake with, 54–55, 57, 120
Caribbean coffee, 128
Carrot
  and orange soup, 24, 25, 94
  soy-braised onions with daikon and, 78–80, 139

Carrots
  with aioli sauce, 95, 96
  in eight immortal jai, 76, 137
  with harvest chicken, 45, 111
  raw, with dipping sauce, 102
  steamed, 96
  in Tabletop Sushi, 10, 83
  in vegetable tray salad, 57, 118
Caterers, hiring, 151, 152
Catering, do-it-yourself, 150–52
Cauliflower
  with aioli sauce, 95, 96
  raw, with dipping sauce, 102
  soup, hot buttered, 64–65, 126
  steamed, 96
Caviar
  American golden, on pan-fried
    potato slices, 22, 23, 93
  as appetizer, 153
  avocado slices with sour cream
    and, 153
  California, 23
  lumpfish, 23
  salmon, in Sushi, 10, 11, 83
  sautéed potatoes with sour
    cream and, 22, 23, 93, 153
  small cooked shrimp with sour
    cream and, 153
Celery hearts, raw, with dipping
  sauce, 102
Celery root
  with green beans, 78–80, 140
  preparing, 88
  salad, 14, 16–17, 87–88
Charcoal, mesquite, 154
Cheddar cheese, on white cheese
  platter, 38, 106
Cheese
  Afternoon of Wine and,
    30–31, 100–101
  Alouette, with raw
    vegetables, 153
  Armenian string, Anaheim
    chilies with, 48–49, 113
  blue
    spinach salad with shallots
      and, 18–21, 91
    with warm walnuts, 30,
      31, 100
  Boursin, with raw
    vegetables, 153
  bread, 54, 56–57, 119
  Brie, in wine aspic, 30,
    31, 100
  cheddar, on white cheese
    platter, 38, 106
  -chili logs, Mexican, 68,
    70–71, 131–32
  with chilies or bell peppers, as
    appetizer, 153
  chile with, 68, 70–71, 130
  cream, garlic jelly, 42–43, 110
  decorated Brie in wine aspic,
    30, 31, 100
  feta
    olives with, 153
    on white cheese platter,
      38, 106

fruits with, 30, 31
Gorgonzola, Barlett or Comice
  pears with, 44–45, 111
herb, with raw vegetables, 153
herbed goat, chilled artichokes
  with, 58–61, 121
hot chèvre toast, 30, 31, 100
jack
  in stuffed cheese appetizer,
    71, 129
  on white cheese platter,
    38, 106
Jarlsberg, on white cheese
  platter, 38, 106
Mexican chili-cheese logs, 68,
  70–71, 131–32
Mexican queso fresca, 153
salty, olives with, 153
string, Anaheim chilies with,
  48–49, 113
stuffed, 68, 70–71, 129
teleme, in stuffed cheese
  appetizer, 71, 129
torta, layered with fresh basil
  and pine nuts, 30, 31, 101
tray with summer fruits, 30, 31
vegetables with, as
  appetizer, 153
white cheese platter, 38,
  39, 106
Cherry tomatoes
  with dipping sauce, 102
  with harvest chicken, 45, 111
Chestnuts
  in port, 64–65, 127
  water, in eight immortal jai,
    76, 137
Chèvre. See Goat cheese
Chicken
  and pea pod salad in pastry
    boat, 26, 27, 98
  breasts, boning and
    stuffing, 116
  harvest, with vegetables and
    roasted potatoes, 44–45, 111
  poached, aioli sauce for, 25, 95
  with a pocketful of leeks,
    50, 52–53, 116
  salad
    coriander, 74–77, 136
    curried, 14, 17, 87
  with vegetable platter and
    green sauce, 7
Chili
  -cheese logs, Mexican, 68,
    70–71, 131–32
  con queso, 68, 70–71, 130
Chili peppers
  Anaheim, with string cheese,
    48–49, 113
  with cheeses, as appetizer, 153
Chili powder, apple slices in salt
  and, 153
Chilled artichokes with herbed
  goat cheese, 58–61, 121
Chilled beet soup, 50–53, 117

Chinese New Year Celebration,
  74–77, 134–37
Chinese parsley. See Cilantro
Chinese pea pods. See Peas,
  edible-pod
Chocolate
  -almond torte, 50–53, 117
  fondue, spirited, 66–67, 128
  frosting, 113
  -nut squares, 48–49, 113
  tasting, 66–67, 128
  truffles, 22, 23, 93
Chocolate and coffee tasting
  party, 66–67, 128
Christmas party,
  Mexican-American, 68–71,
  129–32
Cider
  with Big Buffet That Can
    Grow, 54, 57, 118
  with Garlic Festival buffet, 42,
    43, 109
  mulled, with Winter Salad
    Supper, 78–80, 138
Cilantro (Chinese parsley)
  in chicken salad, 76, 136
Clams
  as appetizer, 153
  in potluck fisherman's stew,
    32–33, 102
Cleanup, 150, 152
Cloud ears, in eight immortal jai,
  76, 137
Coffee, liqueured, 67, 72–73,
  128, 133
Coffee spoons, 144
Cognac in coffee, 67, 128
Come for Chocolate and Coffee,
  66–67, 128, 151
Comice pears, Gorgonzola with,
  44–45, 111
Compote, vanilla fig, with ice
  cream, 40, 41, 108
Cookies
  chocolate-nut squares,
    48–49, 113
  walnut butter, 68, 71, 132
Cooky baskets, seasonal fruits in,
  18–21, 92
Cool Lunch for a Summer Day,
  40–41, 108
Coppa with fresh fruit, as
  appetizer, 153
Coriander chicken salad,
  74–77, 136
Crab
  in sushi, 8, 10, 83
  winter melon soup with,
    74–76, 134–35
Crackling pork, parsnips with,
  78–80, 138–39

Cream
  sherried, with grapes,
    34–37, 104
  sour. See Sour cream
  and tomato sauce, 65, 127
  whipped
    chocolate-almond torte with,
      50, 52–53, 117
    liqueured coffee with,
      72–73, 133
    nut mosaic tart with,
      58–60, 124
    with seasonal fruits in cooky
      baskets, 20, 21, 92
Cream cheese, garlic jelly,
  42–43, 110
Crème de cacao in coffee, 128
Croissants, with Spring Garden
  Supper, 6, 7
Crust, roast lamb in, 18–21,
  90–91
Cucumbers
  sliced, as appetizer, 153
  in sushi, 10, 83
  in vegetable tray salad, 57, 118
Currant and buttermilk scone,
  46–47, 112
Curried Chicken Salad, 14, 17, 87
Custard cream, fresh orange,
  80, 140
Custard persimmon pie,
  58–60, 124
Custards
  almond, with loquats,
    74–76, 137
  floating islands, 24, 25, 96–97
  rum, blueberry meringue torte
    with, 38, 39, 107

D
Daikon
  sliced, as appetizer, 153
  soy-braised onions with carrot
    and, 78–80, 139
  with sushi, 8–11
Dandelion greens, beets and pears
  with, 78–80, 138
Decorated Brie in wine aspic, 30,
  31, 100
Decorating, 142–43
  making party flags, 156–57
Dessert flatware, 144
Desserts
  almond custard with loquats,
    74–76, 137
  Bartlett or Comice pears with
    Gorgonzola, 44–45, 111
  blueberry meringue torte with
    rum custard, 38, 39, 107
  chocolate-almond torte,
    50–53, 117
  chocolate-nut squares,
    48–49, 113
  chocolate truffles, 22, 23, 93
  floating islands, 24, 25, 96–97
  fresh banana gelato, 14, 15,
    17, 88

fresh orange baba-rin, 78–80, 140
lemon ice, 6, 7, 82
nectarines in sweet white wine, 28, 29, 99
pears with Gorgonzola, 44–45, 111
raspberries with almond cream, 26, 27, 98
seasonal fruits in cooky baskets, 18–21, 92
sherried cream with red grapes, 34–37, 104
sliced kiwi and pineapple, 8–11, 83
vanilla fig compote, 40, 41, 108
See also Cakes; Pies
Dinner at Eight, 50–53, 115–117
Dinner Under the Stars, 34–37, 103–5
Dipping sauce, raw vegetables with, 31, 33, 102
Dishes, 143, 145, 152
Double cheese bread, 54, 56–57, 119
Drinks. *See* Beverages
Duckling, tangerine-sauced roasted, 72–73, 133
Dutch Baby pancakes, 62–63, 125

E

Easter dinner, 18–21, 89–92
Edible-pod peas. *See* Peas, edible-pod
Eggplant, in ratatouille salad, 14, 17, 88
Eggs, hard-cooked
with aioli sauce, 24, 25, 95
quail, 153
Eight immortal jai, 74–77, 137
Endive
with cheese, as appetizer, 153
salad, 72–73, 133
Entertaining with a French Flair, 24–25, 94–97
Entertainment, planning, 149

F

Feta cheese
olives with, as appetizer, 153
on white cheese platter, 38, 106
Fig compote, vanilla, 40, 41, 108
Figs, 41, 153
Filberts
in chocolate-nut squares, 49, 113
in nut mosaic tart, 59, 60, 124
orange-filbert butter, spaghetti squash with 58–61, 122–23
Fingerbowls, 144
Fireside Dinner, 72–73, 133
First courses. *See* Appetizers

Fish
deep-fried, sweet and sour, 74–77, 136
poached, with aioli sauce, 24, 25, 94–95
stew, potluck, 32–33, 102
in sushi, 8–11, 83
tuna salad, 14, 16, 17, 87
wrapping for poaching, 94–95
See also Shellfish
Fisherman's Stew, Potluck, 32–33, 102
Flatware, choosing, 143–44
for buffet dining, 145
Floating islands, 24, 25, 96–97
Fresh orange baba-rin, 78–80, 140
Fresh orange custard cream, 80, 140
Fried tortillas, 129
Frostings
caramel, 120
chocolate, 113
Fruits
cold meats with, as appetizer, 153
pancake toppings, 125
seasonal, in cooky baskets, 18–21, 92
with spirited chocolate fondue, 66–67, 128
tropical, with Holiday Fiesta, 68, 71, 129
See also specific fruits
Fruit salad platter, 58–61, 124

G

Garlic
aioli sauce, 24, 25, 95
jelly, 42–43, 110
canning, 110
cream cheese, 42–43, 110
mayonnaise, 32, 33, 102
and onions, sautéed, 42–43, 109
sausages, baked, 42–43, 109
soup, 42–43, 109, 110
tart, 42–43, 109
Garlic Festival buffet, 42–43, 109–10
Garnishes, ideas for, 153
Ginger
pickled, with sushi, 8–10, 83
-vinegar sauce, oysters on the half-shell with, 50–53, 115
Glassware, choosing, 143
Goat cheese
herbed, chilled artichokes with, 58–61, 121
hot chèvre toast, 30, 31, 100
Golden Beehive Bread, 85
Gorgonzola cheese, Bartlett or Comice pears with, 44–45, 111
Grapes
on fruit salad platter, 59, 60, 124
sherried cream with, 34–37, 104

Green beans. *See* Beans, green
Green onions, 102
Green peppers. *See* Peppers
Greens
dandelion, beets and pears with, 78–80, 138
mustard, turnips with, 78–80, 139
Green sauce, 6, 7, 82
Grilling, special woods for, 155. *See also* Outdoor parties
Guacamole, 68, 71, 132

H

Halibut, in sushi, 8, 10, 83
Ham
in add-on vichyssoise, 28, 29, 99
aioli sauce for, 25, 95
baked, as appetizer, 153
in garlic tart, 43, 109
Westphalian, as appetizer, 153
with young vegetables and green sauce, 6, 7, 82
Hamburger, platter sized, with Mexican seasonings, 48–49, 114
Hard-cooked eggs
with aioli sauce, 24, 25, 95
quail, 153
Harvest chicken with vegetables and roasted potatoes, 44–45, 111
Herbed goat cheese, chilled artichokes with, 58–61, 121
Herring salad, as appetizer, 153
Hiring party assistants, 151
Holiday Fiesta, 68–71, 129–32, 150
Homemade mayonnaise, young asparagus and shrimp with, 22, 23, 93
Hot buttered cauliflower soup, 64–65, 126
Hot chèvre toast, 30, 31, 100
Hot miso soup, 8–11, 83

I

Ice cream
fresh banana gelato, 14, 15, 17, 88
with seasonal fruits in cooky baskets, 19–21, 92
Ice, lemon, 6, 7, 82
Icings. *See* Frostings
Insurance, for large parties, 152
Invitations, 142
Irish coffee, 128
Italian coffee, 128
Italian sausage balls, 46–47, 112

J

Jack cheese
in stuffed cheese appetizer, 71, 129
on white cheese platter, 38, 106
Jarlsberg cheese, on white cheese platter, 38, 106
Jelly, garlic, 42–43, 110
canning, 110
Jerusalem artichokes, as appetizer, 153
Jicama
peeling, 130
salad, with tomatillo and apple, 68, 70–71, 130
sliced raw, with dipping sauce, 102
wedges of, as appetizer, 153
with oranges, 78–80, 138

K

Kahlua in coffee, 128
Kiwi
-calamari salad, 34–37, 104–5
with cold meats, as appetizer, 153
with pineapple, 8–11, 83
Knackwurst, baked, 43, 109
Kumquats, 153

L

Lamb roast, in crust, 18–21, 90–91
Late Night Romance, 22–23, 93
Layered cheese torta with fresh basil and pine nuts, 30, 31, 101
Leeks
in add-on vichyssoise, 28, 29, 99
chicken with a pocketful of, 50, 52–53, 116
sautéed, 116
in young vegetable platter, 6, 7, 82
Lemon ice, 6, 7, 82
Lemon juice and walnut oil dressing, 73
Lemons, 153
Lighting, party atmosphere with, 149
Limes, 153
Lingcod with aioli sauce, 94–95
Liqueurs
in coffee, 66, 67, 72–73, 128, 133
with Dinner at Eight, 50–53, 115
Lobster, in potluck fisherman's stew, 32–33, 102
Loquats, almond custard with, 74–76, 137
Lox, as appetizer, 153
Lumpfish caviar, 23

Luncheon parties
  Cool Lunch for a Summer Day,
    40–41, 108
  Entertaining with a French
    Flair, 24–25, 94–97
  Red, White, and Blue Lunch,
    38–39, 106–7
  Salad-Sandwich Buffet, 14–17,
    87–88

M

Macadamias, in nut mosaic tart,
  59, 60, 124
Macaroni, in pasta and pepper
  salad, 118
Mandarin oranges, almond custard
  with, 74–76, 137
Mangoes with cold meat, as
  appetizer, 153
Margarita wine punch, 68–69,
  71, 132
Marinated beef tenderloin,
  mesquite-grilled, 34–37, 103
Marinated mushroom salad, 14,
  17, 87
Mayonnaise
  garlic, 32, 33, 102
  homemade, young asparagus
    and shrimp with, 22, 23, 93
Meats
  aioli sauce for, 25, 95
  as appetizers, with fresh
    fruits, 153
  See also Beef; Lamb; Pork;
    Poultry
Meat seasonings, for chili-cheese
  logs, 132
Melon
  with cold meats, as
    appetizer, 153
  winter, 76, 134–35
Menu planning, 142
Meringue
  blueberry-meringue torte with
    rum custard, 38, 39, 107
  piping, 107
Mesquite charcoal, 155
Mesquite-grilled beef tenderloin
  in Cabernet Sauvignon
  marinade, 34–37, 103
Mexican chili-cheese logs, 68,
  70–71, 131–32
Mexican coffee, 128
Mexican queso fresca, olives
  with, 153
Mexican seasonings, platter
  burger with, 48–49, 114
Mexican-American holiday fiesta,
  68–71, 129–32
Mint sprigs, 153
Miso Soup, 8–11, 83
Molé sauce, turkey in, 68, 70–71,
  130–31
Monterey jack cheese
  in stuffed cheese appetizer,
    71, 129
  on white cheese platter, 38, 106

Mulled cider, with Winter Salad
  Supper, 78–80, 138
Mushrooms
  black fungus (cloud ears), in
    eight immortal jai, 76, 137
  marinated, as appetizer, 153
  marinated mushroom salad, 14,
    17, 87
  raw, with dipping sauce, 102
  in sushi, 10, 11, 83
  wild rice with, 58–60, 122
Mussels
  cleaning, 89
  in potluck fisherman's stew,
    32–33, 102
  steamed, provençal, 18–21, 89
Mustard, Dijon
  in green sauce, 7, 82
  in mustard vinaigrette, 138
Mustard greens, turnips with,
  78–80, 139

N

Napkins
  for buffet dining, 145
  choosing type of, 146
  folding, 146–49
Nectarines in sweet white wine,
  28, 29, 99
New potatoes rosemary,
  18–21, 91
Nori, seaweed wrappers, 8–11, 83
Nut-chocolate squares,
  48–49, 113
Nut mosaic tart with whipped
  cream, 58–60, 124
Nuts
  as garnish, 153
  with spirited chocolate fondue,
    66–67, 128

O

Olives with salty cheese, as
  appetizer, 153
Onion cream dressing, 118
Onions
  baked whole, with
    tangerine-sauced roasted
    duckling and yam chunks,
    72–73, 133
  and garlic, sautéed, 42–43, 109
  green, 102, 153
  red bell peppers and, sautéed,
    34–37, 103
  soy-braised, with daikon and
    carrot, 78–80, 139
Orange
  baba-rin, 78–80, 140
  and carrot soup, 24, 25, 94
  custard cream, 80, 140
  -filbert butter, spaghetti squash
    with, 58–61, 122–23
  syrup, 80, 140

Oranges
  as appetizer, 153
  jicama with, 78–80, 138
Outdoor parties
  Afternoon of Cheese and Wine,
    30–31, 100–101
  Big Burger before the Big
    Game, 48–49, 113–14
  Birdwatcher's Breakfast,
    12–13, 85–86
  decorating for, 142
  Dinner under the Stars, 34–37,
    103–5
  Entertaining with a French
    Flair, 24–25, 94–97
  lighting for, 149
  planning, 150
  Red, White, and Blue Lunch,
    38–39, 106–7
  Salad-Sandwich Buffet, 14–17,
    87–88
  self-catered, 150
  Showy Salad in an Edible
    Bowl, 26–27, 98
  Spring Garden Supper, 6–7, 82
  See also Picnics
Oysters
  as appetizer, 153
  on the half shell, with
    ginger-vinegar sauce,
    50–53, 115
  opening, 115
  in potluck fisherman's stew,
    32–33, 102

P

Pan-fried potato slices with sour
  cream and caviar, 22, 23, 93
Pancakes, Big Dutch Baby,
  62–63, 125
Papayas
  with cold meat, as
    appetizer, 153
  on fruit salad platter, 59,
    60, 124
Parisian coffee, 128
Parsley
  Chinese, in chicken salad,
    76, 136
  fresh sprigs of, 153
  -potato salad, 54, 57, 118
Parsnips with crackling pork,
  78–80, 138–39
Party flags, making, 156–57
Pasta and pepper salad, 54, 57,
  118–19
Pasta roll, spinach-filled, 64–65,
  126–27
Pastry, butter, 124
Pastry bowl, chicken and pea pod
  salad in, 26, 27, 98
Patés, purchased, as
  appetizer, 153
Pea pod and chicken salad, in
  pastry bowl, 26, 27, 98
Pea pods, Chinese. See Peas,
  edible-pod

Peaches
  with cold meat, as
    appetizer, 153
  in sweet white wine, 29, 99
Pears
  and beets, with dandelion
    greens, 78–80, 138
  Bartlett, with Gorgonzola,
    44–45, 111
  with cold meats, as
    appetizer, 153
  Comice, with Gorgonzola,
    44–45, 111
  roasted squab or quail with red
    wine sauce and, 58–60, 122
Peas
  edible pod
    chicken and pea pod salad in
      pastry bowl, 26, 27, 98
    Peking beef with,
      74–77, 137
    raw, with dipping sauce, 102
    on young vegetable platter,
      6, 7, 82
  fresh tiny peas in the pod, 6,
    7, 82
  raw, with fruity wine, as
    appetizer, 153
  Sugar Snap, in young vegetable
    platter, 6, 7, 82
Pecans
  in nut mosaic tart, 59, 60, 124
  in pork sausage cake, 57, 120
Peking beef with Chinese pea
  pods, 74–77, 137
Peppers, chili, 153
Peppers, green
  with cheeses, as appetizer, 153
  with harvest chicken, 45, 111
  in pasta and pepper salad, 54,
    57, 118–19
  raw, with dipping sauce, 102
Peppers, red
  butter-steamed, with Brussels
    sprouts, 58–61, 122
  with cheeses, as appetizer, 153
  with harvest chicken, 45, 111
  in lime juice, as appetizer, 153
  and onions, sautéed,
    34–37, 103
  in pasta and pepper salad, 54,
    57, 118–19
  raw, with dipping sauce, 102
  roasted, and tomato salad, 38,
    39, 106
  roasting, 106
Peppers, yellow in lime juice, as
  appetizer, 153
Persimmon
  custard pie, 58–60, 124
  purée, 124
Persimmons, with Autumn
  Brunch, 46–47, 112
Pesto filling, for layered cheese
  torta, 101
Pheasant, with vegetable platter
  and green sauce, 7
Pickled ginger, with sushi,
  8–10, 83

Pickled radish, with sushi, 8–10, 83
Picnicking Made Easy, 28–29, 99
Picnics
    Autumn Brunch, 46–47, 112
    Big Burger before the Big Game, 48–49, 113–14
    Birdwatcher's Breakfast, 12–13, 85–86
    Picnicking Made Easy, 28–29, 99
    Potluck Fisherman's Stew, 32–33, 102
    See also Outdoor parties
Pies
    custard persimmon, 58–60, 124
    garlic tart, 42–43, 109
    nut mosaic tart with whipped cream, 58–60, 124
Pineapple
    on fruit salad platter, 60, 124
    sliced kiwi and, 8–10, 83
Pine nuts, layered cheese torta with basil and, 30, 31, 101
Pine nut sticks, 38, 39, 107
Pistachio-buttered asparagus, 18–21, 91
Pistachios, in nut mosaic tart, 59, 60, 124
Place settings, 143–45
Planning a party, 142–52
    arrival of guests, 150
    buffet, 144–45
    dishes, 143
    entertainment, 149
    extra touches, 144
    flatware, 143–44
    glassware, 143
    guest list, 142
    invitations, 142
    large, 150–52
    lighting, 149
    making party flags, 156–57
    menu, 142
    napkins, 146–49
    seating, 149
    setting the scene, 142
    setting the table, 142–49
    table coverings, 142–43
    table decorations, 143
Plums with cold meats, as appetizer, 153
Poached chicken, aioli sauce for, 25, 95
Poached fish with aioli sauce, 25, 94–95
Pork
    chops, smoked, in garlic tart, 43, 109
    crackling, parsnips with, 78–80, 138–39
    ground, in stuffed cheese appetizer, 71, 129
    ham
        aioli sauce for, 25, 95
        baked, with fresh fruit, 153
        in garlic tart, 43, 109
        Westphalian, with fresh fruit, 153

knackwurst, baked, 43, 109
sausage cake, 54, 56–57, 120
sweet sausage balls, 46–47, 112
Port, chestnuts in, 64–65, 127
Potato
    -parsley salad, 54, 57, 118
    slices, pan-fried, with sour cream and American golden caviar, 22, 23, 93
Potatoes
    in add-on vichyssoise, 28, 29, 99
    with aioli sauce, 95, 96
    new, rosemary, 18–21, 91
    roasted, harvest chicken with vegetables and, 44–45, 111
    sautéed, with sour cream and caviar, as appetizer, 22, 23, 93, 153
    skillet, Anna, 34–37, 103
    steamed, 96
Potatoes, sweet, 72–73, 133
Potluck Fisherman's Stew, 32–33, 102, 150, 152
Potluck parties
    An Afternoon of Cheese and Wine, 30–31, 100–101
    planning, 150
    Potluck Fisherman's Stew, 32–33, 102
Poultry. See Chicken; Duckling; Pheasant; Quail; Squab; Turkey
Prawns, in sushi, 8, 10, 11, 83
Prosciutto with fresh fruit, as appetizer, 153
Puddings. See Desserts
Pueblo bread, 58–61, 123
Pumpkin bread, 54, 56–57, 119
Punches
    margarita wine, 68–69, 132
    white sangria, 68–69, 71, 132

Q
Quail, roasted, with pears and red wine sauce, 58–60, 122
Quail eggs, hard-cooked, 153
Queso fresca, olives with, 153
Queso relleno, 129

R
Radishes
    butter and, as appetizer, 153
    raw, with dipping sauce, 102
Raspberries
    with almond cream, 26, 27, 98
    in vanilla fig compote, 108
Ratatouille Salad, 14, 17, 88
Raw vegetables with dipping sauce, 32, 33, 102
Red grapes
    seedless, on fruit salad platter, 59, 60, 124
    sherried cream with, 34–37, 104

Red peppers. See Peppers, red
Red snapper
    deep-fried, sweet and sour, 74–77, 136
    in sushi, 10, 83
Red wine sauce, roasted squab or quail with pears and, 58–60, 122
Red, White, and Blue Lunch, 38–39, 106–7
Rice
    sushi, 9–11, 83
    two-tone, 50, 52–53, 117
    wild
        in two-tone rice, 52–53, 117
        with mushrooms, 58–60, 122
Rillettes, as appetizer, 153
Roast beef, aioli sauce for, 15, 95
Roasted duckling, tangerine-sauced, with baked whole onions and yam chunks, 72–73, 133
Roasted potatoes, harvest chicken with vegetables and, 44–45, 111
Roasted red pepper and tomato salad, 38, 39, 106
Roasted squab or quail with pears and red wine sauce, 58–60, 122
Roast lamb in crust, 18–21, 90–91
Rock cod, deep-fried, sweet and sour, 74–77, 136
Rockfish with aioli sauce, 94–95
Rosemary, new potatoes with, 18–21, 91
Rum, coffee with, 67, 128
Rum custard, blueberry meringue torte with, 38, 39, 107

S
Sake, with Tabletop Sushi, 8–11, 83
Salad dressings
    anchovy, 140
    mustard vinaigrette, 138
    onion cream, 118
    walnut oil and lemon juice, 73
Salads
    calamari-kiwi, 34–37, 104–5
    celery root, 14, 16, 17, 87–88
    chicken and pea pod, in pastry bowl, 26, 27, 98
    coriander chicken, 74–77, 136
    curried chicken, 14, 17, 87
    endive, 72–73, 133
    fruit salad platter, 58–61, 124
    jicama with oranges, 78–80, 138
    marinated mushroom, 14, 17, 87
    parsley-potato, 54, 57, 118
    pasta and pepper, 54, 57, 118–19
    ratatouille, 14, 17, 88
    roasted red pepper and tomato, 38, 39, 106

spinach, with shallots and crumbled cheese, 18–21, 91
tomatillo, jicama, and apple, 68, 70–71, 130
tuna, 14, 16, 17, 87
vegetable tray, 54–57, 118
Salad-Sandwich Buffet, 14–17, 87–88
Salami with fresh fruit, as appetizer, 153
Salmon
    caviar, in sushi, 10, 11, 83
    smoked
        as appetizer, 153
        in sushi, 8, 10, 11, 83
    tartare, 40, 41, 108
Sandwich fillings, 14, 16, 17, 87–88
    curried chicken salad, 14, 17, 87
    marinated mushroom salad, 14, 17, 87
    tuna salad, 14, 16, 17, 87
Sangria punch, white, 68–69, 71, 132
Sauces
    for Dutch Baby pancakes, 62–63, 125
    ginger-vinegar, with oysters on the half-shell, 50–53, 115
    green, 6, 7, 82
    molé, turkey in, 68, 70–71, 130–31
    red wine, roasted squab or quail with pears and, 68, 70–71, 130–31
    sesame, 8–11, 84
    sweet and sour, 76, 136
    tangerine, 72, 73, 133
    tomato-cream, 64–65, 127
    wasabi paste, 8–11, 84
Sausage balls, sweet, 46–47, 112
Sausage cake, 54, 56–57, 120
Sausages, garlic, baked, 42–43, 109
Sautéed garlic and onions, 42–43, 109
Sautéed leeks, 117
Sautéed red bell peppers and onions, 34–37, 103
Savoy cabbage, on young vegetable platter, 6, 7, 82
Scone, buttermilk and currant, 46–47, 112
Sea bass, in sushi, 10, 83
Seasoned bread rounds, 91
Seating plans, 149
    for a large party, 151–52
Seaweed wrappers, 8–11, 83
Seed cake, 54, 56–57, 120
Serving dishes, 145, 151
Serving sizes, 151
Sesame sauce, 8–11, 84
Sesame seed
    in coriander chicken salad, 76, 136
    toasted, 8–11, 84
Setting the scene, 142, 144–45
Setting the table, 143–49

Shallots, spinach salad with crumbled cheese and, 18–21, 91

Shellfish
stew, potluck, 32–33, 102
sushi selections, 8, 10, 11, 83
See also Clams; Crab; Mussels; Oysters; Prawns; Shrimp

Sherried cream with grapes, 34–37, 104

Showy Salad in an Edible Bowl, 26–27, 98

Shrimp
with aioli sauce, 24, 25, 95
-avocado cocktail, 28, 29, 99
deveining, 95
in potluck fisherman's stew, 32–33, 102
small cooked, with sour cream and caviar, 153
in sushi, 8, 10, 83
young asparagus and, with homemade mayonnaise, 22, 23, 93

Simply Delicious Dinner, 44–45, 111

Skillet potatoes Anna, 34–37, 103

Sliced kiwi and pineapple, 8–11, 83

Smoke-cooking, special woods for, 155

Smoked pork chops, in garlic tart, 43, 109

Smoked salmon
as appetizer, 153
in sushi, 8, 10, 11, 83

Smoked turkey, aioli sauce for, 25, 95

Snap peas, in young vegetable platter, 6, 7, 82

Snapper
deep-fried, sweet and sour, 74–77, 136
in sushi, 10, 83

Soups
add-on vichyssoise, 28, 29, 99
carrot and orange, 24, 25, 94
chilled beet, 50–53, 117
garlic, 42–43, 109, 110
hot buttered cauliflower, 64–65, 126
miso, 8–11, 83
winter melon, with crab, 74–76, 134–35

Sour cream and caviar
avocado slices with, 153
sautéed potatoes with, 153

Soy-braised onions with daikon and carrot, 78–80, 139

Spaghetti squash with orange-filbert butter, 58–61, 122–23

Spice cake with caramel icing, 54–55, 57, 120

Spinach
salad, with shallots and crumbled cheese, 18–21, 91
in sushi, 10, 83

Spinach-filled pasta roll, 64–65, 126–27

Spirited chocolate fondue, 66–67, 128

Spring Garden Supper, 6–7, 82

Squab, roasted, with pears and red wine sauce, 58–60, 122

Squash
crookneck, with harvest chicken, 45, 111
patty pan, with harvest chicken, 45, 111
sliced raw, with dipping sauce, 102
spaghetti, with orange- filbert butter, 58–61, 122–23

Squid. *See* Calamari

Stew, Potluck Fisherman's, 32–33, 102

Strawberries with aromatic wine dip, as appetizer, 153

String cheese, Anaheim chilies with, 48–49, 113

Stuffed cheese appetizer, 68, 70–71, 129

Supper parties
Entertaining with a French Flair, 24–25, 94–97
Late Night Romance, 22–23, 93
Showy Salad in an Edible Bowl, 26–27, 98
Winter Salad, 78–80, 138–40

Sushi, assembling, 84

Sushi selections, 9, 82–83

Sweet and sour deep-fried fish, 74–77, 136

Sweet and sour sauce, 76, 136

Sweet butter, making, 154

Sweet sausage balls, 46–47, 112

Syrups
fresh orange, 80, 140
vanilla, 41, 108

T

Table coverings, 142–43
Table decorations, 143
Table-setting, 143–49
Tabletop Sushi, 8–11, 83–84
Tangelos, 153
Tangerine sauce, 72, 73, 133
Tangerine-sauced roasted duckling with baked whole onions and yam chunks, 72–73, 133
Tangerines, 153
Tarragon, in green sauce, 7, 82
Tartare, salmon, 40, 41, 108
Tarts
garlic, 42–43, 109
nut mosaic, 58–60, 124
Teleme cheese, in stuffed cheese appetizer, 71, 129
Thanksgiving dinner, 58–61, 121–24
Toast
hot chévre, 30, 31, 100
rounds, 32, 33, 102
Tomatillo, jicama, and apple salad, 68, 70–71, 130

Tomatillos
in lime juice, as appetizer, 153
peeling, 130

Tomato
-cream sauce, spinach-filled pasta with, 64–65, 126–27
and roasted red pepper salad, 38, 39, 106

Tomatoes
cherry
with dipping sauce, 102
with harvest chicken, 45, 111
tiny golden, as appetizer, 153

Torta, layered cheese, with basil and pine nuts, 30, 31, 101

Tortes
blueberry-meringue, with rum custard, 38, 39, 107
chocolate-almond, 50–53, 117

Tortillas
fried, 129
in stuffed cheese appetizer, 71, 129

Truffles, chocolate, 22, 23, 93

Tuna
salad, 14, 16, 17, 87
in sushi, 10, 83

Turkey
in molé sauce with warm tortillas, 68, 70–71, 130–31
smoked, aioli sauce for, 25, 95
with young vegetables and green sauce, 7

Turnips
with mustard greens, 78–80, 139
raw, as appetizer, 153
with dipping sauce, 102
sliced, with cheese, as appetizer, 153

Two-tone rice, 50, 52–53, 117

V

Valentine party, 72–73, 133
Vegetable tray salad, 54–57, 118
Vegetables
with aioli sauce, 24, 25, 95, 96
eight immortal jai, 74–77, 137
fresh tiny peas in the pod, 6, 7, 82
harvest chicken with roasted potatoes and, 44–45, 111
raw, as appetizer, 153
with dipping sauce, 32, 33, 102
steamed, 96
young vegetable platter, 6, 7, 82
See also Specific vegetables
Vichyssoise, add-on, 28, 29, 99
Viennese coffee, 128
Vinaigrette, mustard, 138
Vinegar-ginger sauce, oysters on the half-shell with, 50–53, 115

W

Walnut butter cookies, 68, 71, 132
Walnut oil and lemon juice dressing, 73
Walnuts
in butter cookies, 68, 71, 132
in nut mosaic tart, 59, 60, 124
in pork sausage cake, 57, 120
warm, blue cheese with, 30, 31, 100
Wasabi paste, 8–11, 84
Water chestnuts, in eight immortal jai, 76, 137
Watercress
fresh sprigs of, 153
in green sauce, 7, 82
Welcome Autumn with a Garlic Festival, 42–43, 109–10
Western Harvest Thanksgiving, 58–61, 121–24
Westphalian ham with fresh fruit, as appetizer, 153
Wheat-flecked beehive bread, 86
Whipped cream
chocolate-almond torte with, 50, 52–53, 117
liqueured coffee with, 72–73, 133
nut mosaic tart with 58–60, 124
with seasonal fruits in cooky baskets, 20, 21, 92
Whiskey in coffee, 67, 128
White cheese platter, 38, 39, 106
White sangria punch, 68–69, 71, 132
White wine
nectarines in, 28, 29, 99
raw peas in, as appetizer, 153
Wild rice
with mushrooms, 58–60, 122
in two-tone rice, 52–53, 117
Wine
An Afternoon of Cheese and, 30–31, 100–101
aromatic, strawberries dipped in, 153
Barbera
with Welcome Autumn with a Garlic Festival, 42, 43, 109
with Winter Warm-Up, 64, 65, 126
Cabernet Sauvignon
with Chocolate and Coffee, 66, 67, 128
with Dinner under the Stars, 34, 36, 103
Chablis, with Salad- Sandwich Buffet, 14, 17, 87
champagne
with Autumn Brunch, 46, 47, 112
with Late Night Romance, 22, 23, 93

Chardonnay
    with Dinner at Eight, 50, 52, 115
    with Western Harvest Thanksgiving, 58, 59, 60, 121
Chenin Blanc
    with Showy Salad in an Edible Bowl, 26, 27, 98
    with Simply Delicious Dinner, 44, 45, 111
    with Spring Garden Supper, 6, 7, 82
Chianti Classico, with Winter Warm-Up, 64, 65, 126
choosing type of, 158–59
dry red, with Chocolate and Coffee, 66, 67, 128; see also Red
dry white
    with Potluck Fisherman's Stew, 32, 33, 102
    with Red, White, and Blue Lunch, 38, 39, 106
    see also White
Entre-Deux-Mers, with Entertaining with a French Flair, 24, 25, 94
fruity, raw peas with, as appetizer, 153
Gamay Beaujolais, with Simply Delicious Dinner, 44, 45, 111
Gamay Beaujolais Blanc, with After the Egg Hunt, 18, 20, 89
Gewürztraminer
    with Chinese New Year Celebration, 74, 76, 134
    with nectarines, 29
glassware for, 143
Grey Riesling, with Cool Lunch for a Summer Day, 40, 41, 108
Johannisberg Riesling, with nectarines, 29
with Late Night Romance, 22, 23, 93
Merlot, with Western Harvest Thanksgiving, 58–60, 121
Petite Sirah, with After the Egg Hunt, 18, 20, 89
Pinot Blanc, with Picnicking Made Easy, 28, 29, 99
Pinot Noir, with Chocolate and Coffee, 66, 67, 128
punches, with Holiday Fiesta, 68, 71, 129
red, with Big Buffet that Can Grow, 54, 118; see also Dry red
Riesling, with Western Harvest Thanksgiving, 58–60, 121
sake, with Tabletop Sushi, 8, 10, 83

Sauvignon Blanc
    with Dinner at Eight, 50, 52, 115
    with Dinner under the Stars, 34, 36, 103
    with Winter Salad Supper, 78, 80, 138
sparkling
    with Autumn Brunch, 46, 47, 112
    with Late Night Romance, 23, 93
    with Western Harvest Thanksgiving, 58–60, 121
sweet white, nectarines in, 28, 29, 99
white
    with Big Buffet that Can Grow, 54, 118
    raw peas in, 153
    see also Dry white
white burgundy, with Entertaining with a French Flair, 24, 25, 94
White Zinfandel
    with Picnicking Made Easy, 28, 29, 99
    with Showy Salad in an Edible Bowl, 26, 27, 98
    with Spring Garden Supper, 7
Zinfandel
    with Chocolate and Coffee, 66, 67, 128
    with Fireside Dinner, 72, 73, 133
    with Winter Salad Supper, 78, 80, 138
Zinfandel Rosé, with Spring Garden Supper, 6, 7, 82
See also Wine chart, 158–59
Wine margarita punch, 68–69, 71, 132
Wine tasting party, 30–31, 100–101
Winter melon
    carving, 135–36
    soup with crab, 74–76, 134–35
Winter Salad Supper, 78–80, 138–40
Winter Warm-Up, 64–65, 126–27
Woods, for barbecuing or smoke-cooking, 155

Y

Yam chunks, with tangerine-sauced roasted duckling, 72–73, 133

METRIC CONVERSIONS

Measuring Spoons

⅛ teaspoon = .625 ml
¼ teaspoon = 1.25 ml
½ teaspoon = 2.5 ml
¾ teaspoon = 3.75 ml
1 teaspoon = 5 ml
½ tablespoon = 7.5 ml
1 tablespoon = 15 ml

Liquid Measurements

1 tablespoon = 15 ml
1 fluid ounce = 30 ml
¼ cup = 59 ml
⅓ cup = 79 ml
½ cup = 118 ml
⅔ cup = 158 ml
¾ cup = 177 ml
1 cup = 237 ml
½ pint = 237 ml
1 pint = .47 l
1 quart = .95 l
1 gallon = 3.78 l

ml = milliliter ($\frac{1}{1,000}$ liter)
l = liter
cm = centimeter ($\frac{1}{100}$ meter)
g = gram
kg = kilogram (1,000 grams)

Oven Temperatures

Fahrenheit	Celsius
150° F	66° C
200° F	95° C
250° F	120° C
275° F	135° C
300° F	150° C
325° F	165° C
350° F	180° C
375° F	190° C
400° F	205° C
450° F	230° C
500° F	260° C
Water freezes	
32° F	0° C
Water boils	
212° F	100° C

Linear Measurements

¼ inch = .64 cm
½ inch = 1.27 cm
¾ inch = 1.9 cm
1 inch = 2.54 cm

Weight (Avoirdupois)

1 ounce = 28 g
¼ pound = 113 g
½ pound = 226 g
¾ pound = 340 g
1 pound = 454 g (.45 kg)